What People [SAY ABOUT]

Triumph Over Suffering . . .

Triumph Over Suffering is one of the most in-depth Biblical teachings on suffering that I have ever read. It's bathed in Biblical principles, yet so simply done and easy to read. I enjoyed it so much that I've marked it all up. You'll definitely want to devour this one!

Dr. John C. Maxwell, Founder of EQUIP
Best-Selling Author and International Leadership Expert

Triumph Over Suffering is God's gift to His people. Dr. Celeste Li finds in Scripture a framework that gives perspective and hope even when faced with the most crippling circumstances. These Biblical truths are practical, transformational and real. They reflect the very journey I traveled when grappling with suffering in our family. The powerful Biblical principles will bless the entire Body of Christ. I urge you to read, reflect, pray and open yourself to the redeeming of life's most painful experiences.

Pastor Don Bray, Executive Director of Ministries
Christ Fellowship Church

This book was birthed out of the need to see people gain a healthy perspective on suffering . . . *God's* perspective. As Celeste has taught this class over the years, she has truly refined the message God has entrusted to her. Our prayer is that many will be touched by this message that with God, you truly can triumph over suffering.

Pastor Tim Popadic, Christ Fellowship Church

This anointed book reminds us that suffering plays such an integral part in our daily life journeys of growing toward our Christlikeness. The Scriptures used in this book affirm us as triumphant victors and not victims through our sufferings. Everyone who reads this book will be so blessed with a much deeper insight of the Father's mercy and grace as He carries us through our adversities.

Rev. Dan Benham, Minister of Music and Senior Adults
First Baptist Lake Park

Triumph Over Suffering is truly anointed by God to touch hearts and souls. This God-directed study is saturated with Scripture, insightful, thought-provoking, and Spirit-filled. I highly recommend it for anyone!

Nancy Smith, Foiling Breast Cancer
Co-Founder of Cancer Support at Christ Fellowship

When I co-facilitated *Triumph Over Suffering* with Celeste, this course impacted me so greatly I felt called to give back. I wanted to run alongside others who were suffering and teach them the truth of God's purpose in suffering. The result of that calling is the Cancer Support Groups at my church, and the Men's Branch of *TOS*.

Richard Ekey, Demolishing Stage Four Throat Cancer
Founder of Men's Branch of Triumph
and Co-Founder of Cancer Support at Christ Fellowship

I did not understand suffering; but now I do. This course gave me the courage to allow God into some doors that I had shut hard in my heart. Now I am facing forward, I am learning contentment, I am rejoicing in suffering. I am no longer afraid of being weak, and no longer afraid of suffering, for He has a purpose in my adversity that only I can fulfill!

Kimberlymac, Triumph Servant Leader, Internet
and Author of thebridegroomscafe.com

I learned that suffering is a treasure, for in my weakness, I am made strong.

Anita Byrd, Prevailing Over AIDS

I came to accept my disease as God's master plan and I no longer fear my future. I now rely on God, allowing Him to use me to help those with suffering.

Betty Johnson, Victorious Over Multiple Sclerosis
Triumph Prayer Team

I realized that God planned my illness even before I was born, and has glorious plans for me now. I had wanted to die, but now I want to live.

Ann Maki, Thriving as She Multitasks Suffering

When I took this course, I wanted to believe I was at acceptance, but I discovered I was in anger and grief. *Triumph Over Suffering* has taken me to new spiritual levels. I no longer fear death, but have courage that Christ will be exalted in my body. God has given me a wonderful purpose in life, and I truly thank God for my disease.

Cindy Becker, Clobbering Breast Cancer

This course was an eye-opener. The testimonies of others, the work God is doing in their lives, and the results of their obedience to Him were most helpful.

Deloria Turner, Outwitting Multiple Physical Illnesses

I expected to learn coping skills to deal with my illnesses, but I got so much more than that! I learned to appreciate my illnesses and their purposes in my life.

Lynn Chimes, Trouncing Spinal Stenosis

Packed with many powerful Scriptures, this dynamite course challenged me to look to God's Word for answers, strength, and power to overcome. I learned that God will use every situation in our lives to draw us closer, and deeper, into Him.

Mary Jo Newton Ferguson, Defeating Trials With Faith

I was so surprised to learn how little I knew about God's work in and through our trials. I refer back to all I learned in *Triumph Over Suffering* as I continue to persevere in embracing every obstacle – not from the perspective of survival, but from the perspective of God's will.

Dr. Rhonda Cornell, Conquering Melanoma

TRIUMPH OVER SUFFERING

We are the clay; You are the Potter. ~ Isaiah 64:8

A Spiritual Guide
To Conquering Adversity
~ Third Edition ~

CELESTE LI, M.D.

With Illustrations by Jenna Julianna Li

PLUM
TREE
MINISTRIES

PLUM
TREE
MINISTRIES

Jupiter, Florida
plumtreeministries@gmail.com
"Take root downward and bear fruit upward." Isaiah 37:31 NASB

Triumph Over Suffering
A Spiritual Guide to Conquering Adversity
Copyright © 2009, 2010, 2013 by Celeste Li
Visit our website: triumphoversuffering.com

Plum Tree Ministries
210 Jupiter Lakes Blvd., #5105
Jupiter, FL 33458 USA

ISBN-13: 978-0-9841515-3-0

Library of Congress Control Number: 2009907338
Printed in the Unites States of America.

Cover photography and design by Alec Li. Book design and layout by Alec Li

If you find anything in this book to be valuable for your ministry – whether your ministry is a formal teaching or simply reaching out to your friend – you are welcome to teach it, reprint it, copy it, quote it, or repoduce it in any format, including written, visual, audio, or electronic, without my express permission. Please simply give acknowledgment according to industry standards.

This book is written for all who are suffering in this fallen world. Please understand that we do not belong here, for God has placed eternity in our hearts. In Jesus, our citizenship is in heaven.

This book is written for my precious patients, who live in physical, emotional, mental, and spiritual anguish every day. Thank you for opening your lives to me, and revealing the devastating effects of suffering on every corner of your hearts and lives. You have taught me what it means to overcome in the darkest of valleys.

This book is written for all the "graduates" of my classes *Why Me?* and *Triumph Over Suffering*, who have long asked me to put these teachings into writing. You have given me the privilege of watching you multitask trials and live out your lives in victory over adversity. By your examples, I have learned what it means to trust Him unconditionally and to walk daily in His strength and grace.

Lord Jesus Christ, I offer this book to You, for You are my Lord and my Savior, my Joy and my Song. Do with it as You please. I know that You do not need me, and You do not need this book. I also know that without You, this book is only ink on the pages. Yet because You can sympathize with our weaknesses, I come to Your throne of grace with confidence, to ask that You would use this book to draw people to Yourself, to transform hearts and lives, and above all else to bring glory to Your Name. With deep gratitude for Your perfect answer to my prayers, Amen.

TRIUMPH OVER SUFFERING

We are the clay; You are the Potter. ~ Isaiah 64:8

A Spiritual Guide to Conquering Adversity
~ 3rd Edition ~

Infinite Love + Absolute Sovereignty =
Intimacy With Christ

PART I: INFINITE LOVE

Experience the Love of God

PART II: ABSOLUTE SOVEREIGNTY

Understand Why We Suffer

PART III: INTIMACY WITH CHRIST

Seize Your Purpose Through Your Suffering

Contents

Part I: Infinite Love:
Experience the Love of God

Part II: Absolute Sovereignty:
Understand Why We Suffer

Part III: Intimacy With Christ
Seize Your Purpose
Through Your Suffering

Foreword

We must all face suffering in some form in some season of this life on earth. Jesus promised suffering when He said, "In this world you will have trouble. But take heart! I have overcome the world!" (Jn 16:33). So how do we "take heart"? How do we find peace in our trials and troubles? How do we triumph in our suffering?

I know that a sure heart of peace and joy is found in Christ alone. It is only as we draw close to Him that we are comforted and cared for through our pain. We must stand firm in Christ if we are to be overcomers. It is as we remain in Him that we are strengthened for the journey. But we must cling closely to His heart, to His Word, and to His people in order to stand victorious in our suffering.

There have been many books written about the traumas and tragedies of life, but very few authors have been able to address those who are suffering with the compassion and understanding that Dr. Celeste Li has in this book. I've never read anything as poignantly positioned to aid you in triumphing in your suffering. You are about to embark on a journey to more fully understand how God is intimately acquainted with your pain, that He loves you and suffered for you, and that He has a perfect plan for you. He will walk with you through your suffering, and He alone will help you to triumph over suffering.

Knowing Celeste personally, I have always been drawn to her strong pursuit of God as she humbly serves those who are facing trials at varying stages. Her undying devotion to bring hope and healing through Christ to the downcast and dying has prepared her to perfectly craft the words you will read here. And I believe, woven throughout this book, you will find evidence of her great faith cultivated in an intimate walk with Christ.

As I poured through her writings, I was reminded of Nancy Guthrie, who lost two infants in three years. She is quoted in USA Today (July 16, 2002) as saying, "The world tells us to run from suffering, to avoid it at all costs, to cry out to heaven to take it away. Few of us would choose to suffer. Yet when we know that God has allowed suffering into our lives for a purpose, we can embrace it instead of running from it, and we can seek God in the midst of suffering." Oh, that we would all gain a deeper, more thorough understanding of God's plan for our suffering; that we would become more like Christ because of that suffering; and that we would gain the gift of knowing Him intimately and perfectly through our pain!

I truly believe and pray that you will be encouraged by the many Biblical and contemporary examples Celeste shares of those who have blazed a trail of honor and healing for us all. May our great God refine you on the journey. May He grant you great peace and joy that far surpasses your understanding of your circumstances. May He draw near to you in intimate communion as you find rest in Him. And may our God, in all His majesty, bring you triumphantly through your suffering so you can boldly declare His great love to a lost and dying world that desperately needs to know Him.

Donna Mullins
Christ Fellowship Church

Introduction

We are the clay; you are the Potter.

Isaiah 64:8

Take a close look at the Potter on the cover of this book. Study His hands. This picture speaks of His infinite love plus absolute sovereignty. You are holding a very deep and daring book, and I am praying that the Potter will hold you gently in His nail-scarred hands and will heal you, shape you, and draw you into intimacy with Him through *Triumph Over Suffering*.

Triumph Over Suffering grew mostly out of my tender compassion for my dear patients, many who could not experience the love of God because of their intense sorrows. As I wrote, God drew from my own personal battles. While I do not believe my suffering comes anywhere close to what you may be enduring, God has taken me, and my family, through seasons of physical suffering as well as emotional and spiritual anguish. God developed in me an intensity of compassion for those who are suffering, and a depth of understanding of where He is in the midst of our pain.

In preparation for writing this book, I have studied a number of books on growing in Christ and on suffering, which are listed in the Endnotes and Resources. Some of the concepts and ideas laced throughout this book come from these writers, and two renowned authors in particular, Joni Eareckson Tada and Philip Yancey. Joni Eareckson Tada has been paralyzed from the shoulders down since she was a teen. Yet she has written over forty books and has founded an international ministry for disabled people; she is a shining testimony to living in triumph over suffering. Her award-winning *When God Weeps* has clearly influenced my writings. Philip Yancey lost his father when he was a child, and he wrestles with the questions of God and suffering in his numerous bestsellers. *Where Is God When It Hurts?* has also had great impact on my manuscript. I highly recommend both these books to delve deeper into questions about God and suffering.

However, although my reading and my experiences are part of my equipping, *Triumph Over Suffering* is not written based on these things; it is written based on *His Word*. Most of my preparation entailed combing the Scriptures to learn *God's perspective* on suffering. Together, we are going to study what God has to say in His Word about adversity. Together, we are going to immerse ourselves in Scripture, discovering that God has much to say about suffering, for He knew that none of us would pass through this life unscathed.

Throughout this book I have interlaced many real life accounts to illustrate the major points of each chapter. These are all true testimonies, given to me by men and women I know and cherish. Almost all of these contributions are published with real names; a few have names and other details changed to protect privacy. My family and friends have contributed some stories. My patients in HIV/AIDS Clinic have contributed some stories. And some stories of my own are also here, for I too am living in triumph over suffering.

For those who want to explore more intensely, don't miss the accompanying *Triumph Over Suffering Workbook* and the *DVD Series*. The full-color *Workbook* complements this book by providing thought-provoking questions and additional Scripture studies that parallel each chapter. The *DVD Series* is not designed to be a stand-alone series, but to provied deeper teachings for each chapter.

Discussing the Biblical principles taught here with a Bible study group or with a friend can increase the impact of God's message and the depth of your understanding. I recommend that you separate your classes by gender to provide a safe place for people to come to transparency before the Lord and others.

Living in triumph over suffering does not necessarily mean that the trial will come to an end. When we conquer adversity, I believe that suffering will have no hold on us, no power over us; suffering will have lost its sting. Through this book, you can embark on a journey of triumph over suffering. This book may help you to understand why you are facing this agony, it may inspire you to grow closer to God and to face forward, and it can guide you to understand and seize God's purpose for you through your suffering. Not despite your suffering, but *through* your suffering, *because* of your suffering. Trust Him. It is in your darkest times that He may be doing His most awesome work.

I will be praying for you as you triumph over suffering.

PART I: INFINITE LOVE

Experience the Love of God

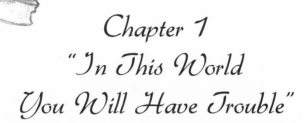

Chapter 1
"In This World
You Will Have Trouble"

ain. Suffering. Physical diseases, mental illness, emotional anguish. Loss of loved ones, loss of health, loss of financial security, loss of career. Fractured families, suffering children, abuse. Calamities, natural disasters, poverty, war. Persecution, rape, murder. God sees your pain. He knows. He tells us,

"In this world you will have trouble."

John 16:33

We will have trouble. I think we can all attest to that truth. The word **trouble** encompasses a broad spectrum; the Amplified Bible translates it **tribulation, trials, distress, and frustration.** "In this world you will suffer." No one passes through this life untouched by pain.

Did you ever notice how some people avoid you when you're suffering? How they pretend that you don't exist? They seem to think that what is going on in your life may be contagious and they had better stay away.

Those who do venture to come near can have some interesting comments. Here are some that I have heard:

"You must have done something to rouse the wrath of God. God uses these things to punish us. What is God punishing you for? What is God trying to tell you?"

"God never wants anyone to suffer. Just believe it, and claim the victory over your suffering!"

"The Bible says to be joyful in everything and to give thanks in everything. Are you thanking God for this situation?"

"You are suffering because your faith is just not strong enough."

"Cheer up. It could be a whole lot worse."

Although these comments may be well-meaning, they are probably not very helpful when we are in need of encouragement and comfort. You may also be wondering if there is any *truth* to these comments. Let's seek an answer to that together as we explore what God has to say in His Word about suffering.

In the meantime, I would like to offer a different response to you who are in adversity. If you are suffering, you have lost something. Perhaps you have been robbed of your health, your job, or your possessions. Perhaps you have been deprived of a relationship, or have had a loved one snatched away from you. Perhaps your dreams and plans for your life have been stolen from you. The *normal* response to loss, any kind of loss, is sorrow. I want to give you permission to *grieve* over your loss, to feel angry and depressed and hopeless and afraid, to experience deep spiritual pain, to feel abandoned by God. Grief is the *normal, healthy, natural* response to suffering. No one can tell you how grief should look, because it will be different for each person. Grief is simply reaction to loss.

Admit it. We don't want to be in any of those painful emotional states. We live in an instantaneous age – we want instantaneous healing. However, our relationship with God cannot be defined or experienced in instantaneous terms. It will require much time and much diligence.

Let's take a look at the stages of grief, described by Elisabeth Kubler-Ross in her well-known book *On Death and Dying*.[1] Although these stages originally described her observations of people who were dying, at this time we recognize that the stages are applicable to any who are experiencing loss. Understand that these five stages are neither wrong nor right, but are simply the natural human responses that most people travel through when they have experienced a loss. These stages are normal, expected, and part of the healing process.

1st **Stage**: Denial. Refusing to accept your situation. Thinking that if you ignore it, it will somehow go away. Passing through this stage involves honesty, not only about your pain, but also about the emotions that come with it.

2nd **Stage**: Anger. The stage many of us want to pretend we successfully skipped over. Yet we would not be human if we were not angry about our hardships. We will discuss anger in depth in Chapter 2.

3rd **Stage**: Bargaining. Trying to cut a deal with the Lord. "If You heal me, I will sell all I have and become a missionary." "If You cure my cancer, I will quit smoking."

4th **Stage**: Grief. Mourning your loss, mourning that life will never be the same again.

5th **Stage**: Acceptance. Peace. Trusting that the Lord has a plan, a specific plan, for you.

Replacing Lies With Truth

Now don't think that this is a process that can be rushed through in an afternoon now that we know the "proper" order. The key to spiritual healing, reaching peace and acceptance, rests in learning God's truths that are in His Word. For most of us, this will take much time, patience, and perseverance. When we believe lies instead of God's truth, we may be unable to triumph over suffering, we may be unable to pass through these stages and reach peace and acceptance. "Lies about what?" you ask. Lies about pain and sorrows, lies about God, lies about ourselves, lies about the world.

Grasping the connection between our beliefs and our behaviors is critical.

For as he thinks in his heart, so is he.
                                    Proverbs 23:7 NKJV

What we hold deep in our hearts to be true will determine our thoughts, our feelings, our words, our actions. Beliefs based on God's truth lead to righteousness and peace (Rom 8:6). Beliefs based on lies can lead to sinful words and behaviors, detrimental thoughts, painful emotions; we may become mired in grief.

Where do these beliefs come from? Most of our belief system is unconscious, learned gradually over many years: through our upbringing, through our life experiences, and through our education. Some of our beliefs may be true, and some may be false.

These false beliefs are the *weapon* of the enemy. Jesus says of Satan,

"When he lies, he speaks his native language, for he is a liar and the father of lies."

John 8:44

Satan works hard to build a root system that is a lie, lies seared into our conscience as with a branding iron (1Tim 4:2), because he knows that connection between the lies we believe and the sins we commit.

Let's go to Genesis, when we first meet Satan, to grasp a better understanding of Satan's deception. In Genesis Chapter 2, God placed Adam in the Garden of Eden, and commanded him,

"You are free to eat from any tree in the garden; but you must not eat from the tree of the knowledge of good and evil, for when you eat of it you will certainly die."

Genesis 2:16-17

God then created Eve, and in Chapter 3 of Genesis, Satan arrived on the scene.

Now the serpent was more crafty than any of the wild animals the LORD God had made. He said to the woman, "Did God really say, 'You must not eat from any tree in the garden'?"

Genesis 3:1

"Did God really say . . .?" Look where Satan is headed. Right to Eve's beliefs, causing her to question what she believes, sowing the doubt, leading her into uncertainty.

The woman said to the serpent, "We may eat fruit from the trees in the garden, but God did say, 'You must not eat fruit from the tree that is in the middle of the garden, and you must not touch it, or you will die.'"

Genesis 3:2-3

Stop right there. Did God say not to *touch* that particular tree? No, He said not to *eat* from it. Eve did not know the truth of God's word. Watch how Satan capitalized on the fact that she did not know the truth.

"You surely will not die," the serpent said to the woman. "For God knows that when you eat from it your eyes will be opened, and you will be like God, knowing good and evil."

Genesis 3:4-5

Listen to the truth intertwined with the lie. Truth: their eyes will be opened. Lie: they will not die. Yet anything that is not fully true is a lie, so Satan's half-truth is in reality a lie.

What happened next? Eve believed Satan's lie, and that false belief led her to sin, to eat the fruit and give it to Adam to eat. At that moment, as Satan had said they would, Adam and Eve did come to know good and evil (Gen 3:22), but they also died, both spiritually and physically. Their spiritual death was immediate, for they were separated from God in their sin, and they were driven out of the Garden of Eden. Physical death was also a result of their sin, but this consequence would be delayed.

Look at the connection, from the lie Eve believed to the sin she committed. It's the same with us. *If our deep heart beliefs are not truth, we can be led into sin.*

Eve did not seek out the truth. If she had forgotten God's command, or did not understand it, she could have simply asked God when He walked with Adam and Eve in the garden in the cool of the day (Gen 3:8). Or, she could have gone to Adam for clarification; the Bible tells us he knew the truth (1Tim 2:14, Gen 2:17). Imagine how different that scene in the Garden would have looked if she had sought out the truth.

Imagine how different our lives will look when we seek out the truth. If we desire healing in our suffering, a good place to start may be to invite God to examine our hearts and to reveal our false beliefs, and then to uproot those lies and replace them with God's truth. Come meet Kimberlymac, of my *Triumph* Servant Leadership Team, as she shares her story of replacing lies with truth.

I never thought I would hear Him through my sufferings, but I do hear Him through my sufferings now, because I have replaced a lie with the truth.

The lie I believed was that God could not use me when I am suffering because I am too weak and therefore useless.

The truth I have learned is that God will use my fully committed heart, no matter what state of physical or emotional suffering I am in. Even in the midst of my own suffering I can bring comfort to others because God has comforted me; I can encourage others because people have encouraged me; and I can give wisdom to others because it is through my suffering that I have learned wisdom.

Kimberlymac
Triumph Servant Leader, Internet
and Author of thebridegroomscafe.com
Charleston, South Carolina

Kimberlymac is so open to Christ, her relationship with Christ blossomed as she learned new truths each time she *taught* a class. Notice that as she replaced lies with truth, she received spiritual healing, but not complete physical or emotional healing at that time. She did, however, begin to hear God more clearly, and received peace, wisdom, and beautiful ministry work through her suffering.

Our false beliefs are seared into our conscience – *seared in* – they may be very hard to uproot. Some of these false beliefs we may have had since childhood, and it may take years to replace the lies with God's truth. How are we going to expose these lies and find these truths? One critical way is by studying God's Word under the power of the Holy Spirit. When we do our part, we invite God into our hearts to do His part. To be Christian means to be forever in the process of growing.

Not that I have already obtained all this, or have already arrived at my goal, but I press on to take hold of that for which Christ Jesus took hold of me.
Philippians 3:12

My prayer for us is that we will grow spiritually as we journey together through this book, opening our hearts to God's transforming power and replacing Satan's lies with God's truth. We desperately need God's truth, His Holy Spirit, and His transforming power as we overcome our trials.

Overcoming Suffering

"I have told you these things, so that in me you may have peace. In this world you will have trouble. But take heart! I have overcome the world."
John 16:33

What does Jesus mean that He has **"overcome the world?"** The world certainly does not look very overcome to me!

Jesus triumphed over Satan, sin, and death by His *own* death and resurrection (Rev 3:21). Right now there is still a spiritual war being waged in the heavens and on earth; a battle for each soul to be brought into the Kingdom of Light. A battle for each heart in the Kingdom of Light to surrender more fully to Jesus. The Victor of the war has already been determined – but He will not make His victory fully manifest until the end of time. Even so, the Victor gives us His Spirit right now – who gives *us* the necessary strength to overcome the world (Rev ch 2,3).

To overcome means "to subdue, to conquer, to overcome, to prevail, to get the victory."[2] I like how the Amplified Bible explains Jesus overcoming the world: **"I have deprived it of power to harm you and have conquered it for you."**

I want you to understand that when we overcome the world, when we conquer evil, when we are victorious over sin, when we triumph over suffering – the evil, sin, and tribulations here on earth will not necessarily be eradicated. However, when we overcome, these sorrows will no longer have *power* over us, because **"in me you may have peace."**

I want to draw your attention to a little word here, "may." This word "may" indicates the responsibility that we have. Jesus' work is certain and completed: **"I have overcome the world."** But whether *we* overcome, whether *we* receive the peace He offers us, is up to us. We will talk much about *our* responsibility as we journey through this book together. Realize that the more intently our eyes are fixed on Jesus, the less our hardships may control us. The more our focus is on developing our relationship with Jesus, the less we may be caught up in our own pain. The more we live our lives in trust of Him, the deeper may be our walk of peace. And the world loses its power to harm us, when, no matter the circumstances, we are secure in Jesus' peace.

Paul echoes Jesus' words, describing how we will live in these groaning and sighing bodies in this fallen creation, in agony physically and emotionally, for the rest of our earthly lives.

For we know that when this earthly tent we live in is taken down (that is, when we die and leave this earthly body), we will have a house in heaven, an eternal body made for us by God himself and not by human hands. We grow weary in our present bodies, and we long to put on our heavenly bodies like new clothing. For we will put on heavenly bodies; we will not be spirits without bodies. While we live in these earthly bodies, we groan and sigh, but it's not that we want to die and get rid of these bodies that clothe us. Rather, we want to put on our new bodies so that these dying bodies will be swallowed up by life. God himself has prepared us for this, and as a guarantee he has given us his Holy Spirit.

2 Corinthians 5:1-5 NLT

Suffering expert Philip Yancey sums it up succinctly, "We now live on a groaning planet."[3]   At times we may think that because we belong to the Lord Jesus Christ we should live in physical and emotional bliss. Not so! Pain and misery are part of this world simply because we live in these groaning bodies in this fallen world.

If we think *this* is a perfect world, if we think *these bodies* are the best God can do, if we think *this* is where we belong, we are not going to triumph over suffering. Root out these lies right now and replace them with God's truth:

God saw all the he had made, and it was very good.

Genesis 1:31

God *did* create a perfect world, but that perfection was shattered by sin.

- We were not built for this fallen world – we were built for eternity, for God **has set eternity in the human heart.**

Ecclesiastes 3:11

- We do not belong here – we are **foreigners and strangers on earth.**

Hebrews 11:13

- We are not citizens here – **our citizenship is in heaven.**

Philippians 3:20

Suffering makes us long for our heavenly bodies. Suffering makes us crave our true home. Suffering ensures we don't settle for citizenship here.

To overcome means to keep Jesus' deeds to the end, to do God's will to the end (Rev 2:26, 1 Jn 5:4-5). Living in triumph over suffering means that no matter how painful our trial is, we do not abandon our faith. We continue to live trusting God, obeying Him completely and loving Him unconditionally. Our faith can emerge from the tribulations of life strengthened in a way that would probably not have been possible without the suffering.

Triumphantly overcoming suffering means we have trounced evil by refusing to allow afflictions to drive us away from God. We may have explored the path of bitterness, resentment, anger, or unfaithfulness, but we have not chosen it. Through this book, God can empower you to overcome. Your suffering may still be present, but Jesus can deprive it of its power over you. Through your hardships you can grow closer to God and allow Him to use those trials for His eternal plan. And after you have lived out your life in triumph over suffering, you will join those who have also overcome. Jesus tells us,

"To him who overcomes, I will grant to sit with Me on My throne, as I also overcame and sat down with My Father on His throne."

Revelation 3:21 NKJV

The Physical, Mental, and Spiritual Disciplines

Speaking from experience, Philip Yancey writes, "For nearly everyone, doubt follows pain quickly and surely, like a reflex action. Suffering calls our most basic beliefs about God into question."[4] Suffering often causes us to doubt, to question our beliefs, to wrestle with everything we ever thought we knew about God: about who He is, about what He is up to, about the very nature of His heart. All these doubts and questions can be fertile ground for spiritual growth. Go ahead and doubt, question, wrestle – just be sure to use this time of doubt to seek to know Him desperately. Keep your heart open to God so that you can hear the answers to those questions.

How do we keep our hearts open? How do we grow closer to God in our trials, instead of crashing down into bitterness and despair? That is where the physical, mental, and spiritual disciplines come in.

The Physical Disciplines

Taking Care of Our Bodies

Do you not know that your bodies are temples of the Holy Spirit, who is in you, whom you have received from God? You are not your own; you were

bought at a price. Therefore honor God with your bodies.

1 Corinthians 6:19-20

When we surrender ourselves to God, when we are living in deep personal relationship with Him, *God Himself lives inside of us.* That is almost unfathomable! If we could just grasp the concept of this! We must take care of our bodies. We may not be strong enough to do God's Kingdom work if we do not take care of the basics of our health: plenty of exercise, a healthy diet, proper sleep.

It is useless for you to work so hard from early morning until late at night, anxiously working for food to eat; for God gives rest to his loved ones.

Psalm 127:2 NLT

I believe God wants you to get your proper rest.

Partnering with your doctor, taking charge of your own illness, and becoming knowledgeable about your diagnosis are critical parts of taking care of your health. I believe it is essential that you follow your doctor's instructions, take your medication as prescribed, and change your lifestyle and habits as recommended. All healing comes from God, but remember also that God can guide your doctors and other health professionals to help you, even if they are not Christians.

I believe that God wants us to do everything we can do, and then let Him take care of the rest. I want you to see this principle in action, so I am going to take you to Exodus, at the time Moses was born. Watch how his mother exemplifies this principle. As the Book of Exodus opens, Pharaoh, alarmed at the rate at which the Hebrew slaves were multiplying, has commanded all the Hebrew baby boys to be drowned in the Nile:

Then Pharaoh gave this order to all his people: "Throw every newborn Hebrew boy into the Nile River. But you may let the girls live." About this time, a man and woman from the tribe of Levi got married. The woman became pregnant and gave birth to a son. She saw that he was a special baby and kept him hidden for three months. But when she could no longer hide him, she got a basket made of papyrus reeds and waterproofed it with tar and pitch. She put the baby in the basket and laid it among the reeds along the bank of the Nile River. The baby's sister then stood at a distance, watching to see what would happen to him.

Exodus 1:22-2:4 NLT

You know the rest of the story. How Pharaoh's daughter found Moses, and his cries touched the princess' heart. How Moses' sister offered to run and find a Hebrew woman to nurse him, and brought back Moses' mother. How Pharaoh's daughter eventually adopted him and raised him in the palace.

Go back and take a look at what Moses' mother did. She didn't just throw her baby into the Nile; she made a papyrus basket for him and coated it with tar to make it waterproof. She didn't place her baby in the sun to die of dehydration; she placed him in the shade of the reeds. She didn't randomly deposit that basket in the Nile; she placed it at Pharaoh's daughter's bathing spot. And she didn't abandon her baby; she posted his older sister as guard. Moses' mother did everything *she* could do. She left the rest up to *God*.

Do Not Test God

"Do not put the Lord your God to the test."

Luke 4:12

We may be testing God when we do not do everything we can do. Unless we have heard specifically from God otherwise, we may be testing God when we refuse to take recommended treatment (treatment that we have access to, or can afford, or our insurance covers) – and just *expect* God to heal us. To me, this seems like throwing yourself off the highest point of the temple (Lk 4:9).

Remember Luke was a physician. God gave doctors their knowledge and skills to help His suffering people. I am not saying to put your faith in doctors and medications. Put your faith in God, pray to God for healing; and you do your part by taking responsibility for your work in the healing process. You do everything you can do; *then* let God take care of the rest (Phil 2:12-13).

The Mental Disciplines

Change Our Response To Suffering

. . . set your hearts on things above, where Christ is seated at the right hand of God. Set your minds on things above, not on earthly things.

Colossians 3:1-2

Those who live according to the flesh have their minds set on what the flesh desires; but those who live in accordance with the Spirit have their minds set on what the Spirit desires. The mind governed

by the flesh is death, but the mind governed by the Spirit is life and peace.

Romans 8:5-6

We may not be able to change our agony or tribulation or loss; however, what we *can* change is our *response* to this suffering. We can choose to set our minds on what our sinful nature desires, or we can set our minds on things above, on what the Holy Spirit desires. We can set our minds and hearts on the world, on ourselves, and on our woes and relief of the pain, or we can focus on Jesus and His Kingdom. **For the mind set on the flesh is death, but the mind set on the Spirit is life and peace** (Rom 8:6 NASB).

Are you obsessed with your misery and your desire for relief from suffering? Is your mind running off with crazy thoughts and worry? Is it **true,** is it **noble,** is it **pure** (Phil 4:8)? Are you thinking about Jesus? If not, **take captive every thought to make it obedient to Christ** (2Cor 10:5)!

It may be time to replace selfish thoughts with thoughts of things above. You may have tried this already and found it is not so simple. Me too. I now realize why: our thoughts come from our hearts. If we are simply trying to change our thoughts, we may be successful for a time, but unless our hearts are transformed, the mind change will probably not last. If we want to change our thoughts, we must ask the Spirit to examine the core of our beings, our beliefs, our hearts. Immersing in His Word can facilitate uprooting Satan's lies and replacing them with God's truths.

Connect With Christian Friends

A second key to mental wholeness can be connecting with friends, *same-gender* Christian friends. Strong believers who have a deep and growing relationship with Jesus – a *growing* relationship, not a stagnant one. The friendship between David and Jonathan is a good example. In First Samuel, David is on the run from Saul, hiding out in the caves, running for his life, and Jonathan came to him and . . . rescued him? Led him to a new hiding place? Brought him fresh provisions? No. Jonathan **helped him find strength in God** (1Sam 23:16).

We need friends who listen and love and comfort and empathize, but do not try to solve the problems that only Jesus can solve. We need friends who pray with us and point us to God for answers to our problems. My friend Linda Bloom, one of my loyal and tenacious *Triumph* Servant Leaders, found she really did have these kinds of friends. She discovered the depths of her friendships when her husband became ill:

My husband of twenty years was dying from cancer. We were overwhelmed with this struggle, both the deep spiritual pain of our impending separation, and the practical issues of medical care and financial disaster. I know that our suffering would have been unbearable through my husband's final months without the support of Christian men and women. Our friends simply gathered around us and poured their love into us – provided for us financially, lifted us up emotionally, and ushered us into the throne room of God in prayer. The wisdom, knowledge, and peace that we gained through that time was invaluable, and very beautiful.

During the weeks after my husband's death, I often wished there was a way to just transplant those things into the spirits of others. Then I realized that God provides constant opportunities to do just that – to transplant His

*love, care, and peace into the lives of everyone we meet,
everywhere, all of the time – and it has become my purpose
in living. Thank You, Father, for allowing that suffering
into my life!*

Linda Bloom
Triumph Servant Leader
New Life Assembly
Castlegar, Canada

I like Linda's idea of "pay it forward." It was not possible
for her to repay her friends, but she could pour comfort
and encouragement into others in the same way that she
had been comforted and encouraged. God has developed in
Linda a depth of compassion and understanding for those
in pain, and she lavishes that compassion not only onto her
Triumph students, but also upon every hurting soul in any
battlefield God takes her. She is the embodiment of one of
my favorite verses:

**He comforts us in all our troubles so that we can
comfort others. When they are troubled, we will be
able to give them the same comfort God has given us.**
2 Corinthians 1:4 NLT

Help Others

**He who refreshes others will himself be
refreshed.**
Proverbs 11:25

Helping others can get our focus off our own troubles,
off ourselves, and on to others. It can be one of the keys
to spiritual and emotional healing. I would like you to
meet my friend, Dr. Michael Chimes. He lost his practice

when he became blind. I have asked him to describe how helping others has been instrumental in his own mental and emotional healing.

Becoming blind has taught me not to concentrate on myself. When my focus is on my condition, it sets me into a tailspin of depression. <u>When my focus is on serving the Lord, I lose myself in the problems and needs of others. Serving helps me cope by distracting me from my own problems.</u>
Dr. Michael Chimes, Chiropractor
Palm Beach Gardens, Florida

Journal

Many find that another key to mental soundness is keeping a journal. There are several benefits to journaling that no other discipline seems to match:

- Transferring thoughts to paper as we write what God is teaching us in His Word may help us to process what we are learning and absorb it deeply into our hearts.

- Journaling right after we have encountered God can capture the fire of the experience. Later, when we are thwarted or discouraged when pursuing His call, our journal can provide us with a source of encouragement and confirmation of that call.

- Journaling can document our spiritual growth and give us an accurate account to refer to later if our memory of events has become hazy.

The Spiritual Disciplines

How do we come to know God more? I have heard this described as the legs of a spiritual three-legged stool:

- **Bible Study**
- **Prayer**
- **Your Church Family**

Imagine yourself on top of this tripod. If one of these legs is broken, your entire relationship with God may topple. I believe that God wants us to commit to these three spiritual disciplines and to make them a lifelong habit. God has so much to teach us about pain and adversity during this difficult time, and these three can be key to keeping our hearts open to His transforming power.

First Leg: Bible Study

In order to effectively communicate with God, we will want to know His language: the Bible. There are lots of different ways to study the Bible: alone or with others; King James or a version that is easier to read; covering lengthy sections daily or slowly meditating on a few verses. It seems to me that immersion is key – it doesn't matter the method. My husband John and I are going to contrast the different ways we engage with the Word.

Whether a formal Bible class in Women's Ministry, or informally with a friend or two, I love Bible study with other Christians, since iron sharpens iron. I am delighted when a friend calls me to share what God showed her in the Word today. I especially love when my husband comes to breakfast after reading his Bible and teaches me what he has just learned. Yet what I treasure the most is studying the Word alone with the Holy Spirit.

I find Scripture reading to be most effective when I immerse in it daily, prayerfully, and systematically. If I read it haphazardly, flipping open my Bible and reading wherever it falls open, it's too easy for me to read the encouragement on one side of the page instead of the conviction of my sin on the other side.

I've also discovered the importance of reading with an open heart. When I read out of obligation, with my heart closed off to the convicting words in the Bible, I really don't grow at all. To facilitate openness, before I even open my Bible, I pray for the Holy Spirit to teach me.

Sometimes, I like active reading. I take notes, I look up words I don't understand, and I journal. I journal what I have learned about God or about myself, or the Spirit's conviction of a sin, or when the Spirit has given me my next action step. Other times, I like to be more still, reading a bit at a time and then listening. Sometimes I read a number of chapters at one sitting, but other times I immerse in a shorter passage deeply, meditating on it and just listening to the Lord.

Often, I write down a verse that speaks to me. I carry it around for the day in order to memorize it. I work to memorize it when I'm stopped at a traffic light, or folding laundry, or chopping food for dinner, or out for a walk.

Celeste Li
Jupiter, Florida

I have asked my husband John to share his perspective.

I used to compare Bible study to a trip to the dentist. It was painful! I knew I had to change my thinking. I mean, if God loves me, and I supposedly love Him, why wouldn't I be overjoyed to study His Word? No matter how busy I am, isn't He important enough to devote five minutes, ten minutes, thirty minutes a day doing what He called me to do? Could I not at least honor Him by reading a few passages a day?

I realized I wanted to view Bible reading not as an obligatory chore, but rather as a privilege. Now I have to be honest here. The mental shift from "chore" to "privilege" was just too big a jump, so I settled for "commitment."

If you are having trouble "getting into the Bible," I want you to know that you are not alone. Not everyone can just open up a Bible and turn it into a spiritual habit. Although I made the decision to put my money where my mouth was, and to commit to the discipline of daily Bible reading, I still could not focus on what I was reading.

A few things changed that made it easier and more interesting.

- *I changed versions. King James felt like I was reading Shakespeare. The NIV or NLT seemed to flow so much more smoothly.*
- *I started a daily Bible plan. I read the assigned passage each day and the accompanying commentary. The commentary brought up perspectives that I never saw before!*
- *I found a like-minded friend and we read the same Bible plan together. Discussion bred interest, and I was drawn to the daily reading. Additionally, since I knew he was going to pepper me with questions, I cross-referenced and did additional research in order to be prepared.*
- *I tuned in to Christian radio, and I read Christian books such as* Case for Christ *and* Share Jesus

Without Fear. *When Christian radio and books referenced the Bible and quoted Scripture verses, it somehow heightened my interest in reading the Bible myself. It seemed that the more I heard about the Bible from outside sources, the more interesting the Bible became.*

My next hurdle was coming to terms with things that did not make scientific sense – like seas parting, donkeys talking, people rising from the dead. Hey, I went to medical school . . . I've done CPR . . . dead bodies don't suddenly jump up . . . or do they?

I had to readjust my worldly sensibilities. I read The Case for Christ *by Lee Strobel, and I concluded that if I truly believe that God exists and Jesus died for my sins, then the Book that supposedly is His manual needs to be true. If it is not, then God and Jesus do not exist. And if this Book is true, then I need to read it through in its entirety and context several times before I can make a judgment for myself.*

I brought some of my questions and concerns to my pastors and to apologists for direction, but I chose not to focus on scientific "inconsistencies" and "impossibilities." I came to realize that if God could create the world, life, and man, He can do anything.

I also chose not to focus on "incomplete justice." I realized that I was trying to understand nuclear physics with the mind of a baby. We cannot fully understand the ways of God, but one day we will grow up and understand. I came to understand that when Judgment Day comes, we will all be able to see clearly and will recognize that everything is fair after all.

I have been through the Bible many times now, and each time I learn more and more!

John Li, M.D.
Jupiter, Florida

All Scripture is God-breathed and is useful for teaching, rebuking, correcting, and training in righteousness, so that the servant of God may be thoroughly equipped for every good work.

2 Timothy 3:16-17

I am intrigued by the word **God-breathed**. The ESV translates it **breathed out by God.**[5] This word in the Greek is actually made of a combination of two words: Theos (God) and pneo, which means "to breathe or blow."[6]

God-breathed means that every word in the Bible is the complete truth, words "prompted by God, divinely inspired."[7] Satan, the father of lies, has deceived the world, saying that the Bible is not completely true. We may hear this lie as, "Nothing in the Bible is true." Or, we may hear this lie as, "*Some* of the Bible stories are true, but surely not the Old Testament passages such as Adam and Eve and Noah's ark." This lie declares these passages to be just a collection of "stories" and "parables" to teach us lessons. Yet God's truth is that *every word* in the Bible is true, *every word* is breathed out by God.

I have to admit that I had a little trouble uprooting this lie and replacing it with God's truth. But when I did successfully eradicate that lie from my belief system, my understanding of the Bible – and my relationship with God – exploded.

Second Leg: Prayer

Although we often think of prayer as asking God for something, prayer actually encompasses much more than just requests. I recall it was from Pastor Todd Mullins at my home church, Christ Fellowship,* that I first learned

---

*Christ Fellowship Church, Multiple Campuses in Florida, gochristfellowship.com

that prayer means "to move closer to God." Let's look at some ways we can do just that.

Certainly coming to God with requests for ourselves or interceding for others is part of prayer. And I believe this type of prayer really touches God's heart, for in praying this way we acknowledge His greatness, sovereignty, and power, as well as our dependence on and trust in Him. We are going to go into answered prayer further in Chapter 10, but let's look at a few hindrances to prayer right now.

If I had cherished sin in my heart, the Lord would not have listened.

Psalm 66:18

Wow. If we are sinning and not repentant, if we are cherishing sin in our hearts, we cannot expect God to listen.

When you ask, you do not receive, because you ask with wrong motives, that you may spend what you get on your pleasures.

James 4:3

James is teaching us that wrong motives hinder answered prayer. That drives me to ask myself, am I praying *His* will be done, or *my* will be done? Are my motives *His* glory, or *my* glory? Do I desire the advancement of *His* Kingdom, or the advancement of *my* dreams and earthly comforts?

God commands us to pray, and He reminds us that it is His job – not ours – to determine the answer. Remember how God answered Jesus' prayers in the Garden of Gethsemane. The night before He died, Jesus prayed for the cup to pass Him by. God answered by giving Jesus the strength to endure.

We may miss God's answer when it is not the answer we expected or desired. I think that there are many times when we think God did not answer, because we are so sure what the "proper" answer is, that if God's answer doesn't match up, we may miss it entirely! We may think that He didn't answer. We may jump to the conclusion that He is silent and that He has abandoned us. Yet, if we come to Him completely submitted to His will, praying sincerely to know what *His* plan is, we are not likely to miss that answer.

I have asked my friend Carlos to share a time when he initially thought that God had ignored his prayer.

I was accused of a robbery I did not commit. I prayed that I would be acquitted and set free, but I was not. I thought God had refused to answer my prayers, that He had abandoned me. I believed God existed; I had been taught how to pray; but when my request was not granted, I turned my back on God.

I was then imprisoned for four months – and that was the best thing that ever happened to me. You see, I was living a life so far from God, drinking, drugging, you name it – and when I was thrown into jail for a crime I did not commit, I learned what it felt like to be clean for the first time in my life.

When I was let out of jail, the first thing I did was drink for ten days straight. I felt so awful – physically and emotionally. I remembered how I felt when I was in jail and clean, and I realized I simply did not want to live this way any more. I knelt down and gave my life completely to God; I told Him I wanted to live His way, not mine, for the rest of my life.

God has completely changed my life. Now, I spend my time reaching back to my friends who are still drinking and drugging, telling them there is a better way of life, and the only way to find it is to give your life to Christ.

Carlos
Riviera Beach, Florida

Since God didn't respond as he wanted, Carlos had at first missed the answer! It was only later that Carlos recognized that God *had* listened and indeed had answered. He also realized that God's answer had his very best interests at heart.

Let's take it up a notch. Thessalonians instructs us,

✈**Pray without ceasing**.

1 Thessalonians 5:17 NASB

How do we pray *that* continually? I think that God desires us to be constantly connected with Him, continually talking to Him, checking in with Him moment by moment to be certain that we are on His path. He loves when we depend upon Him for guidance and wisdom, when we ask for His direction and pause for His answer before moving forward. He longs for us to wait patiently, open to His call. We can pray and remain open to Him no matter what we are doing, whether it is driving, cutting the lawn, doing dishes, going for a walk. We can even pray in the midst of a crowd, in the middle of work, or even while we are speaking to someone.

Let's talk now about a type of deeper praying that is beyond a simple list of requests, and that cannot be accomplished while multitasking. This kind of deeper prayer entails more listening than talking. To reach this kind of deeper prayer, it may be helpful to set aside time to be completely alone with God. We can then start by clearing out of our minds all the busyness of the world. Next, we can prepare our hearts to hear from Him by Scripture reading, journaling, thanking Him, praising Him, or listening to worship music. As we come quietly before Him, as we step into His presence, we can open our hearts to listen to what God has to say. For me, daily time focused on Him alone is imperative if I desire to draw closer to Him.

Third Leg: Your Church Family

I call this leg "your church family" instead of just "church," because I don't want you to simply envision a big building with stained glass windows and a full choir. "Church" is much more than that. "Church" is your church family, the body of Christ (1Cor 12:12), anyone who is a believer. *We* are the church.

Why is our church family so important? There are many parts of our lives that Scripture commands us to do *together*. We are instructed to encourage, love, admonish, pray for, and care for each other. Additionally, when we are connected with other believers, God can use our gifts in a complementary fashion and enable us to serve more effectively.

Corporate worship together with other believers is another important part of our church family. As we join our praise together with our brothers and sisters, the Holy Spirit may descend on us in a powerful way, for He is *enthroned* on our praises, He *inhabits* our praises (Ps 22:3, Mt 18:20). The pastors at Christ Fellowship explain that this is the difference between God's omnipresence and His manifest presence. God's *omnipresence* is God everywhere at all times, not bound by time or space. God's *manifest presence* is God making His presence known in a special way. Of course He may manifest His presence in many places other than church. And of course church does not guarantee His manifest presence. Yet it seems to me that God considers it a special invitation to manifest His presence when we worship together as believers.

Connection with other believers is also an essential ingredient for spiritual growth. In the body of Christ, we can find friends who help us find our strength in God.

When we are in a time of trial, we need other Christians the most. My friend Kim B. expresses it this way.

I entered a Bible study at my church at a time when I was ready for it the most. I had been intermittently bedridden for several years, and my condition had just improved enough to allow me to attend the study. I found that I had become very introverted; fear was gripping my life and I realized that my pain was greatly affecting my relationship with my husband.

I felt so connected in this Bible study class! The people understood me and my frustrations and fears, and they did not judge me. Week after week, God used this class and the participants in it to bring understanding and healing to my broken soul. I learned to understand and work through the fear, anger, and disappointment I had come to know.

Kim B.
West Palm Beach, Florida

Though one may be overpowered, two can defend themselves. A cord of three strands is not quickly broken.

Ecclesiastes 4:12

We can grow more Christlike together with Christian friends, and they can encourage us on our walk with the Lord and keep us accountable. They may be able to see in areas where we are blinded. We can forge unbreakable bonds with them as we support them and they support us, especially in times of suffering.

When trials hit, many of us may struggle with fear, doubt, worry, and anger. Satan prowls around like a

roaring lion, ready to devour (1Pet 5:8).   If afflictions
overwhelm us and drive us to question the very nature of
God, we can become easy prey for that lion.   Implementing
these physical, mental, and spiritual disciplines can help
us to resist him instead of becoming his next meal.

*Are you looking for more? Do you really want to go deep?
You may be most successful in your triumph over suffering
if you complete the accompanying* Triumph Over Suffering
Workbook. *After you read each chapter of this book, open
the* Workbook *and dive into the week of assignments,
answering the probing questions and delving deeper into
Scripture.*

*You can also check out our website
triumphoversuffering.com to learn more about this topic.*

Chapter 2
Experiencing and Expressing Emotions

he earth trembled and quaked,
the foundations of the heavens shook;
they trembled because he was angry.
Smoke rose from his nostrils;
consuming fire came from his mouth,
burning coals blazed out of it.

2 Samuel 22:8-9

Whom do you think these verses are describing? This is *God*, His reaction to the enemy attack on David. Smoke rising from His nostrils, consuming fire from His mouth. Astounding.

Our God is a God of intense emotions. Since we are made in God's image, we can also have powerful emotions. I do not believe that God created us to stuff difficult emotions inside ourselves and pretend they did not exist. Stifling unpleasant emotions somehow freezes up the pleasant ones. God created us to live abundantly (Jn 10:10); I believe abundant living includes experiencing both pleasant and unpleasant emotions to the fullest.

Emotions are not right or wrong; they just are. However, what we *do* with our emotions can be sinful or sinless. Understand that God expresses His emotions completely righteously and without sin. We strive for the same.

As we begin to unmask our emotions in this chapter, remember that God already knows them. He examines the depths of our hearts (1Th 2:4). We may be able to hide our emotions from others or from ourselves, but we cannot hide them from God.

Anger

I believe that God gives us all permission to feel angry, for this is a completely *normal* response to suffering. Now before you say, "Not me! I'm not angry!" let's look at the faces of anger, for anger can have some subtle looks.

- An impenetrable armor worn to block out pain: The more effective this armor is in blocking out pain, the more effectively it may suppress our emotions, both the unpleasant *and* the pleasant ones. The more it may hinder God's love and others' love from reaching us. The more it may thwart our love for God and our love for others from flowing out.

- Physical ailments on top of physical ailments: The person with a heart attack can next develop an ulcer from the stress.

- Anger turned inward: It can reveal itself in guilt, depression, worthlessness, or loss of self-respect.

- Passive-aggressiveness: Has your child ever grudgingly cleaned up his mess, making an even bigger mess than what was there originally? That can be anger, manifested as passive-aggressiveness.

Submissive on the outside, but on the inside possibly seething with anger, hatred, vengeance, and the desire to control.

One Christian author gives a shocking list of "anger's camouflage."[1]   Read through it slowly with your heart open to the Spirit's conviction:

- Criticism, petty complaints, gossip, sarcasm
- Silence, sulking, stubbornness
- Intimidation
- Hypochondria, depression
- Procrastination, forgetfulness, laziness, numbness
- Compulsive behaviors (excessive eating, shopping, working)

Anger and frustration and despair are natural responses to suffering and pain. Anger itself is not wrong. However, how we *handle* anger can be right or wrong.

How Does Anger Become Sinful?

In your anger do not sin.

Psalm 4:4

Note that David writes **in your anger**. He does not write, "Maybe possibly if you happen to have anger." There is no question that we will have anger. It seems God knows that we will have anger in these groaning bodies in this fallen world. So He cautions us, **In your anger, do not sin.** How can we sin in anger?

It's natural to feel a spark of anger when we are suffering, or when we have been hurt, or when we feel that life is unfair. Now if we choose to feed that spark, to cause it to grow and consume our hearts and souls, we can cross the line from normal healthy anger to sinful anger. Anger can become a sin when

- It becomes an obsession
- It leads to bitterness, hatred, or unforgiveness
- It develops into behavior that is aggressive, passive-aggressive, hateful, or revengeful

So exactly how long can we be angry before it becomes a sin? God knew we would ask that question, so He clarifies it for us in Ephesians,

"In your anger do not sin": Do not let the sun go down while you are still angry, and do not give the devil a foothold.

Ephesians 4:26-27

Do not let the sun go down on your anger. Do not carry it on for days and days. Do not give the devil even the smallest foothold. Satan can be so subtle . . . he is seeking a foothold to jump into our lives full-force. Sinful anger can be exactly that foothold he is searching for.

Realize that many great men of the Bible were angry with God, such as Job, Jonah, and Jeremiah. Jeremiah challenged God,

"Why then does my suffering continue? Why is my wound so incurable? Your help seems as uncertain as a seasonal brook, like a spring that has gone dry."

Jeremiah 15:18 NLT

Shocking! Those are pretty strong words.

You know, there is something interesting going on here between Jeremiah and God. Jeremiah was not afraid to come to God in complete honesty, his anger bursting forth, saying things I suspect he is probably going to regret later, calling God **uncertain** and accusing God of failing him. Yet there is something else to learn here. I think

Jeremiah's anger unleashed against God reveals three things about their relationship:[2] *A Key*

- It reveals that Jeremiah truly <u>believes that God is in control</u>, sovereign over the whole world, including every aspect of his life.
- It reveals <u>Jeremiah's dependence upon God,</u> admitting that he cannot handle things on his own.
- It speaks of Jeremiah's <u>complete trust in God</u>; it shows that he knows God wants to meet with him even when his emotions are raging out of control. It shows that he trusts God not to abandon him even when he is overcome by anger.

When my son Alec was fifteen, he had been experiencing some spiritual struggles. As we were talking about his struggles, a torrent of angry words suddenly burst forth from him, the vehemence of which I had not seen from him in a long time. I said to him, "You need to talk to God about all this." He got this defiant look in his eye and said, "Yeah, I'm going to tell Him this right now, just like I'm talking to you." It sounded like he was going to let God have it.

He ran off to his room and did not come out for a while. When he did come out, he was simply living, breathing this astonishing peace. Something got settled between him and God right then and there. The intensity of his anger and his willingness to go to God with it in complete honesty led to an amazing encounter with God, an encounter that would probably not have happened without that fiery anger coupled with the willingness to go to God and pour it out. Alec will probably never disclose that conversation to me, but God has granted me the privilege of watching what the fruit of that encounter has been.

Are you, like Jeremiah and Alec, angry with God? Admit it, rail against God! <u>Don't worry</u> – He can <u>handle</u> your anger. He already knows this about you anyway! He will not run from your anger but will meet it head-on. Use the intensity of your anger as a way to engage God, to seek out His comfort, to grow to know Him more and to learn His will for your life.

My friend Angela learned these truths about meeting God through her emotions, and then shared them with a friend. Let's listen in.

One day the mother of my daughter's best friend began talking about her co-workers and their affiliation with my church. I had not shared with her that I had recently given my life to Christ. She said her daughter had been wanting to go to church ever since she went to church with her Grandmother, but that she herself was not comfortable with going because she was angry with God. I told her that I was recently saved and was attending the church she mentioned. I told her that she should tell God she is angry. She looked at me in shock. I told her God already knew she was angry with Him, and that many Godly men of the Bible were angry with God. Men such as Job, Jonah, and Jeremiah let their anger loose against Him. I invited her and her family to go to church with our family that weekend. As the service ended that day she was in tears, tears of joy; she felt the Pastor was speaking directly to her heart. She has been coming to church ever since that weekend, and she is even bringing another family with her!

Angela
Baltimore, Maryland

What a difference a new perspective made in this woman's life.

Righteous vs. Unrighteous Anger

I want to take a moment to differentiate between these two. Joni Eareckson Tada gives a definition of unrighteous anger that really hits home: "anger that leads us away from God."[3] If you are wondering if your anger is righteous or unrighteous, test it by asking yourself this question: Is it drawing me towards God, or pushing me away from Him?

Anger can be very selfish: anger because *we* have been hurt, because *we* have been taken advantage of, or because life has been unfair to *us*. Anger because *we* cannot find God, because it seems He has abandoned *us*. If we bottle up this anger, or inappropriately vent it on others, it can drive us away from God. However, if we pour it out to God, then we can use it to encounter Him, to begin to move away from that selfish unrighteous anger. Realize that He already *knows* that we have been steaming with anger; admitting it and pouring it out to Him can be essential first steps in healing. Yet righteous anger has an even greater function: we can use it not only to encounter God, but also to hear His call on our lives. (More about this in upcoming chapters.)

Now hold on tight, because we're going up a level. God's anger – and how He expresses His anger – is pure, sinless, and righteous. God does not exhibit unrighteous anger. We do see His *wrath* associated with His judgment (Rev Ch 6-19) – wrath is reserved for our Just and Sovereign God. And we do see His *righteous anger,* anger that drives Him to set things right when someone He loves has been hurt. (Check out the passage from Second Samuel at the beginning of this chapter. And check out the time Jesus cleared the merchants out of the temple (Jn 2) because they were cheating the poor and desecrating His Father's house). But we do not see *selfish anger*, anger because someone has scorned, rejected, or tried to hurt Him. Yes, it is true that anger can be a natural *human* response to pain and loss, however,

. . . **the anger of man does not achieve the righteousness of God.**

James 1:20 NASB

If we are striving to become Christlike, will our response to suffering be to remain in anger, or to move to acceptance?

Hmmm . . . Not there yet? Me neither. When a trial hits, I *want* to leap directly to acceptance, but often I don't. I am getting closer, though; I spend less time in denial and anger before I reach acceptance. Let's not lose sight of the goal:

"Be perfect, therefore, as your heavenly Father is perfect."

Matthew 5:48

Of course we will never reach perfection on earth. But it is my prayer for you that God will use this book to bring you one step closer to that goal.

Self-Pity

Why would anyone want to wallow in self-pity? Well, let's be honest. It may simply be easier to be a victim than a hero. Maybe we can get more attention, maybe we can avoid some responsibilities. Suffering may be a great excuse not to live up to our families' expectations, our own expectations, our bosses' expectations . . . God's expectations. It may be easy – much easier than fulfilling our God-given responsibilities and accomplishing our God-ordained purposes in life. I can speak from experience . . .

A number of years ago I was diagnosed with a chronic illness, and, well, let's just say I was pretty sick. As weak and as frightened as I was, I was also quite relieved – like a great load was taken off my shoulders – because suddenly I felt I had justification not to be productive. I had an excuse not to keep up with my responsibilities in the home or with my kids or at work. I had the perfect excuse not to fulfill my purpose in life. It was sort of liberating.

But I quickly discovered that this sense of "relief" was very superficial, and very short-lived. I had this enormous emptiness inside of me that I simply could not fill by wallowing in my selfishness. Living the life of a victim robbed me of fulfilling my God-given purposes, and I soon found there is just no true contentment, no genuine joy, in living a life of self-pity.

Celeste Li
Jupiter, Florida

Jesus says,

"The thief comes only to steal and kill and destroy; I came that they may have life, and have it abundantly."

John 10:10 NASB

Satan comes to attempt to steal our privileges as children of God, to kill our passion to live for Christ, and to destroy the destiny God has designed us for. One of the ways he may strive to do this is by crushing us with adversity in order to drive us into a life of self-pity.

Jesus comes as our Redeemer and our Savior to give us abundant life, life full of meaning and purpose and contentment and joy. Don't settle for a life of self-pity when what God has in store for us is *abundant* life. He has such purpose for us, regardless of our illness or pain or suffering or loss; all He desires is our fully committed hearts. We must give Him our hearts, and let Him handle the rest.

Self-pity. Pity for self. Bemoaning our problems, lamenting our pain and suffering, wallowing in pity for ourselves. Self-pity. Me, me, me. One look at our Savior dying on the cross can take our minds right off ourselves and fix them on God, where our focus belongs.

"For even the Son of Man did not come to be served, but to serve, and to give his life as a ransom for many."

Mark 10:45

We are here to love God and to love others. We are here to bring God's message of mercy, forgiveness, and salvation to a lost and hurting world. We are here to serve God by serving others. I see no room for selfishness in that calling.

Guilt

If only I had quit smoking, if only I had exercised more, if only I had not lived such a wild life, if only, if only . . .

My friend would call this an "Itty Bitty Should-Have Committee" that is riding on your shoulders. [4]

"And you should have done this, and you should have done

that, and you should not have done this, and you should not have done that . . ."

This "Committee" may be shouting so loudly that it can become impossible to hear anything else. Impossible to hear the love of others. Impossible to hear God's voice. When I first recognized my Committee, it was so huge that some of it had to ride on the other shoulder.

Getting rid of our Committees can enable us to more clearly hear the voice of the Lord. But how do we get rid of our Committees? First, we must differentiate between true guilt, and false guilt. Listen to how Paul differentiates between the two.

Godly sorrow brings repentance that leads to salvation and leaves no regret, but worldly sorrow brings death. See what this godly sorrow has produced in you: what earnestness, what eagerness to clear yourselves, what indignation, what alarm, what longing, what concern, what readiness to see justice done.

2 Corinthians 7:10-11

Before we investigate these types of guilt, I would like to give you an overview.

1 - True guilt. Corinthians calls this **Godly sorrow** in the NIV, or **sorrow that is according to the will of God** in the NASB.
2 - False guilt. Corinthians calls this **worldly sorrow** in the NIV, or **sorrow of the world** in the NASB. Within false guilt I see two categories:
   a - Deliberate pretended guilt.
   b - Imposed guilt. This is guilt that we, the world, and other people impose upon ourselves.

Let's explore.

1 - *True Guilt (Godly Sorrow)*

Godly sorrow, sorrow that is according to the will of God, can produce repentance. This is true guilt. I believe that God wants us to feel guilty *until* we admit our sin, mourn our sin, repent from our sin, and accept His forgiveness. This verse instructs us to be repentant, not merely remorseful. Take a look at the difference. Remorseful can be explained as "a selfish dread of the consequences . . . but with no effective change of heart." [5] It indicates that we're sorry because of the repercussions of our actions, but, given the same set of circumstances, we would probably do it again. This is the thief in jail crying because he got caught, who, when released from jail, goes and robs another bank. It is regret for the punishment, regret for the consequences, without a deep change.

Repentance is vastly different than remorse. Repentance is a 180-degree turn. Repentance is a total change of heart, leading to a change of emotions, attitudes, thoughts, and actions. Repentance is a complete about-face, a choice to leave that sin behind. My Word Study Dictionary says that it "involves regret or sorrow, accompanied by a true change of heart toward God." [6] I have invited Lisa to describe a time of true repentance in her life.

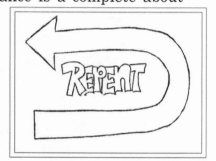

Immersion in a Bible study forced me to search the deepest recesses of my heart, mind, and soul, to analyze how closely I am following God's Word, or if I am even following it at all. Studying His Word forced me to admit an ignored offense, and with God's grace I have completely eliminated my sin. What surprised me was the immediate response from God: He poured His strength into me to

enable me to do it His way! I had a 180-degree turn, a total
change of heart.

Lisa
Denver, Colorado

I think Second Corinthians is telling us that true guilt does serve a purpose. It can produce **earnestness**, "diligence" and "haste"[7] to clear ourselves, to set the issue right as best we can. It can lead us to call it what God calls it: not a mistake, but a sin. It can lead to **indignation** and **alarm**: appropriate anger at ourselves for our sin, and alarm that we have erected a barrier hindering our connection with God because of our sin. Finally, it can lead to **longing** and **concern**, driving us to **see justice done**, to work to make restitution for the pain that we have caused someone.

Godly sorrow, sorrow that is according to the will of God, true guilt, **leaves no regret**. I think **no regret** means that when we have Godly sorrow, we take the necessary steps to repent, to make restitution, and to change. We accept God's forgiveness, and then we do not look back. We can then remove that member of the Committee, choose not to listen to him anymore, and free ourselves from carrying around the guilt.

2 - False Guilt (Worldly Sorrow)

a - Deliberate Pretended Guilt

This type of false guilt involves being pretentiously sorry in order to escape consequences or to manipulate for selfish gain. We may fool other people, but God, who searches our hearts, is not deceived by our masquerade.

As all sin does, this pretended guilt can interfere with our connection with God.

b - Imposed Guilt

This type of false guilt is a less intentional sin. It can be guilt that the world imposes upon us through movies, television, music, magazines, the internet, or other forms of media. It can be guilt that other people, even family and friends, may impose on us. It can be guilt that we may impose upon ourselves. Sometimes, we may accept this guilt because we simply don't know God's truth. Other times, we may be at least partially aware of the truth, and our acceptance of this guilt is more deliberate; we *allow* people and the world to impose this guilt on us.

Are you guilt-ridden from what you have heard from sources such as these? Perhaps you have heard comments like this:

- "You should be spending more time with your family."
- "You should coach the soccer team."
- "You should have spent time with your relatives, instead of having a romantic dinner with your spouse."
- "You should keep more up to date with world news."
- "You should stay later at work. You don't appear dedicated and will probably lose your job the next time the company lays workers off."

Or perhaps you have been perusing some magazines and now feel guilty that you are out of shape.

Or perhaps the neighbors just bought their teen a car and you feel obligated to buy your teen a car.

Or perhaps your friends are trying to send you on a guilt trip because you did not contribute to their favorite charity.

Or perhaps you feel obligated to volunteer every time you are asked, and feel guilty if you decline a request to volunteer.

How can we know if our guilt is true guilt or false guilt? We can't always know. Submerging ourselves in Scripture and prayer can draw us closer to God and help us to discern if it is God calling us to repentance, or the world imposing false guilt upon us. Realize that God's truths do not produce oppressing guilt. If it is Godly sorrow, we will sense conviction, not guilt. As we repent and receive His forgiveness, He can lift the burden, bring us His peace, and give us the power necessary to accomplish His will.

Second Corinthians says false guilt **brings death**. False guilt can hinder our connection with God. False guilt is sin. It is not of God; it can drive a wedge between God and us; it can hinder our fellowship with God. When we are carrying false guilt, we cannot be in right relationship with God.

How do we remove these members of the Itty Bitty Should-Have Committee? The first step is recognizing the Committee. The second step is repenting of our sins relating to the issue. The third step is plunging into God's Word, allowing the Holy Spirit to root out Satan's lies and replace them with God's truth. The Holy Spirit can then enable us to make the choice not to listen to this Committee anymore, and can free us from carrying around the guilt and the weight of the Committee. At first, we may need to actively choose every day, many times a day, to take every thought captive (2Cor 10:5), to refuse to listen to the Committee, to choose not to dwell on the past, but to live in today. And, as we continue to walk in Christ, His Spirit can blast every member of the Itty Bitty Should-Have Committee off our shoulders and out of our lives.

Depression

Many people who are enduring hardships deal with depression right alongside their suffering. Now before you say, "Not me!" I would like to share with you what depression may look like. You may think of depression as constant tears, feeling mired in pain and despair with no means of escape. Yes, this can be depression. However depression may masquerade with some more subtle looks, some that even trained physicians may miss: [8]

- Apathy, losing interest in activities or people that you used to care about
- Guilt, blaming yourself for everything
- Trouble concentrating
- Memory problems
- Feeling that your spouse and family members and friends don't love you
- Inability to feel any love for family and friends
- Extreme fatigue
- Excessive sleep
- Inability to complete the tasks of everyday life
- The sensation that you are in slow motion or stuck in the mud
- Or the opposite: racing around at breakneck speed but not really accomplishing anything
- Immersing yourself in your employment, volunteer work, work around the house, care of everyone else but yourself, or some other form of busyness so that you have no time to feel your emotions

I'm not going to delve into a medical study of depression, but I do want you to understand that even some of great faith were depressed, such as Moses and Elijah. In the Book of Numbers, when Moses was leading the Israelites through the desert, he was being hit with criticism from both sides: The Israelites were **wailing** and **the LORD became exceedingly angry** (Num 11:10). Moses was caught between two storms here. Petrifying! I would not want to be in his shoes. Moses cried out to the Lord,

" . . . the burden is too heavy for me. If this is how you are going to treat me, please go ahead and kill me."

Numbers 11:14-15

Do you hear his desperation? This is the man who walked the Israelites through the Red Sea! He is so desperate he is ready to give up and die.

Let's jump to Elijah. In First Kings, God commanded Elijah to build an altar of sacrifice and flood it with water. He did as commanded, and God sent down fire that burned up the sacrifice, the wood, the stones, the soil, and the water included. You're wondering about now, why is Elijah *depressed*? I'm wondering the same thing. Suddenly Elijah found himself fleeing for his life from wicked Queen Jezebel.

[Elijah] prayed that he might die. "I have had enough, LORD," he said. "Take my life; I am no better than my ancestors."

1 Kings 19:4

Satan can use depression the same way he attempts to use self pity: **to steal, kill, and destroy** (Jn 10:10), to try to rob us of our God-given purpose, to kill our desire to serve and glorify God, to destroy any remnant of the calling God has on our lives. Sometimes he is successful. Yet Moses and Elijah, although they were so depressed they wanted to give up and die, rose above their anguish and went on to do God's will. Moses led the Israelites for forty years through the desert to the Promised Land; Elijah confronted kings in their sinfulness, and trained up his protégé Elisha before his death.

You wonder, How did they do that? How did they rise above the depression and despair? How did they stay connected to the Lord, and do His will?

Perhaps Moses and Elijah realized what Psalm 139 teaches,

All the days ordained for me were written in your book before one of them came to be.
Psalm 139:16

My friend Pamela has composed a very personal poem about depression that has opened my understanding of this verse. She has agreed to share it with us.

I Used To Wish To Die

*I often wish to die
And depart this miserable life
But death is not the answer
For what of your life thereafter?*

*I often wish to die
So passive and puny am I
But death is not the answer
Just stop for a bit and ponder*

*See your life is not just about you
There are people to whom you're assigned
Your struggles are not just for you
How you handle them can save someone's life*

*I used to wish to die
So foolish and selfish was I
For that's already been done
And the victory won
By God's only begotten Son.*

*Pamela Jo Wilson
Author of Isaiah54Woman.com
Palm Beach Gardens, Florida*

What strikes me most about Pamela's poem is her realization of the selfishness of her depression. My guess is that this realization was a critical turning point for her. Pamela has come far since that desert time in her life. She now has this smile that fills up the whole room, and eyes that sparkle like glistening dewdrops. Like Moses, like Elijah, Pamela has risen above her own pain and has gone on as a single mother to raise two young boys. She has also founded Isaiah54Woman, a ministry that reaches out to single mothers, to draw their focus to Christ.

Some Keys to Overcoming Depression

Again, we are not delving into a full treatment plan for depression. But I do want you to see some of the deep heart work that seems critical to truly conquer depression:

- Knowing God deeply and surrendering to Him completely.
- Trusting in His care and love for us.
- Setting our minds on things above.
- Accepting *His* plan for every part of our lives.
- Seeking His revelation of any lies that have ensnared you. (For Pamela, I think "so foolish and selfish was I" hints at the lies that had trapped her.)

You too are suffering, yet you are still alive – instead of giving up, just waiting to die, *reach out for God*. Open your heart to Him. Work to seize His purpose for you, for He has tremendous purpose for *all* His people, hurting or not. *All your days were ordained before even one of them came to be.* You are simply not leaving this planet until every ordained day is completed. As Pastor Tom Mullins of Christ Fellowship teaches, "Are you breathing? Then God's got work for you!"

Worry and Anxiety

Are you a worrier? Do you believe that if you think about a problem enough, you will come up with an answer? Are you up all night "thinking?" Are you unable to focus on work or everyday tasks because you are "thinking?" Read the statements below[9] and see if any apply to you.

- "If I think about this enough, I should feel a sense of certainty."
- "If I can just think this through, I won't have to feel this way."
- "If bad things happen, it is my fault."
- "If it feels likely, it is likely. If it feels dangerous, it is dangerous."
- "Mistakes mean I blew it because I was not in control."
- "Bad things will happen to me and I will not be able to deal with it."
- "Worry shows how deeply I care about my children."
- "Because I have a thought, it is important and I must give it my full attention."
- "Worry prevents bad things from happening. It keeps me from being blindsided. It keeps loved ones safer."
- "I am out of control. I am making myself sick. I have got to stop worrying."

Worry can be manifested by obsession with our suffering and the impact it has on every aspect of our lives. It can be churning around in our minds our misery, our loss, and how life is completely different because of our loss. It can be believing that *we* must take care of everything, instead of surrendering our lives to God's control. Worry is self-centered; it is focused on me, me, me.

We're going to go medical here. Worry, anxiety, stress, and fear can further destroy our health. These unpleasant emotions can cause our bodies to produce a massive amount of stress hormones. These stress hormones can be very damaging to our bodies. I compare it to running our cars all day long with the accelerator down to the floor; the stress hormones can run our bodies into the ground with exhaustion. The result? These stress hormones can:

- Thwart physical healing
- Compromise our immune system, putting us at risk for additional diseases
- Decrease our pain tolerance, making it even more difficult for us to cope with the pain

Yet Jesus has a different plan. In the Sermon on the Mount, He speaks against worry five times (Mt 6:25-34). *Five times.* I think He repeats Himself so that we do not miss it.

"Can any of you by worrying add a single hour to your life?"

Matthew 6:27

This word **worry** is merimna in the Greek. As I studied merimna and related words, the definitions that leapt out at me were "disunited" and "divided." Merimna describes an emotional state so fragmented that it brings "disruption to the personality and the mind." [10]

Merimna is translated "worry" here in Matthew 6, but is translated "anxiety" in other passages. Worry, anxiety, and panic attacks are not exactly the same, but worry can lead to anxiety and anxiety can lead to panic attacks. Although I can comprehend anxiety on a "medical level," learning from those who themselves suffer with anxiety and panic attacks helped me to better grasp the inner workings here. My friend Kim G. (you'll meet her below) speaks from personal experience. She explained to me the differences:

- Worry fears realistic scenarios that *could happen.*
- Anxiety imagines unrealistic worst-case scenarios, and lives in fear that those worst-case scenarios *will happen.*
- A panic attack can cause fear to grip your body because your mind and body are convinced that those worst-case scenarios really *have happened.*

Kim G. went on to explain that anxiety is more than simply worrying. Anxiety is the debilitating obsession with "what ifs." Those suffering with anxiety can recognize that their thinking is completely illogical, but they generally can't help but continue to think those illogical and imagined thoughts. When people are suffering from anxiety, the escalating stresses and worries of life will lower their ability to control their thoughts, and a full-blown panic attack may occur.

In order to help us to understand this process more clearly, I have asked Kim G. to describe her journey from anxiety and panic attacks to freedom and peace.

I have struggled with anxiety all my life. Having grown up in an abusive home, I was always on edge. As I grew into adulthood, the anxiety only increased, and when the stress of life was too much, I would have full-blown panic attacks. Relaxation techniques and psychologists helped minimally.

All through my life I had some friends that were born-again Christians. Each and every one of them had a sense of peace, a very calm way about them. Even when things were difficult in their own lives, they would still radiate an inner peace.

By February of 2009, the stress I was living with was out of control. My husband had been out of work for more than six months; we lost our home, we lost our medical insurance for the kids, and we were struggling with some legal issues. I was the only one supporting my family, and we were barely making ends meet. The weight of the world was on my shoulders, and I felt as though I was going to be crushed underneath it all. I had reached a point of such desperation and my anxiety was so high that the slightest worry would trigger a full-blown panic attack. At night I would sit in a chair and shake, fear gripping every single cell of my body.

Through a Christian friend and a Pastor at a church I had attended a few times, I realized I wanted to turn to God. From the moment I gave my life to Christ and received Him into my heart, I felt as though the weight I had been carrying was lifted. The issues I have still exist, but it is all right, because I know it is all part of God's plan, and I have given it all to Him.

Soon after I came to Christ, God gave me the first Bible passage that ever spoke to my heart: **"Who of you by worrying can add a single hour to his life?"** *(Mt 6:27). I have taped it to my computer at work as a daily reminder that now I am walking in His peace.*

Kim G.
Loxahatchee, Florida

Let's go to First Peter to help us understand more clearly what happened in Kim G.'s heart.

All of you, clothe yourselves with humility toward one another, because, "God opposes the proud but shows favor to the humble." Humble yourselves, therefore, under God's mighty hand, that he may lift you up in due time. Cast all your anxiety on him because he cares for you.

1 Peter 5:5-7

Humble yourselves, *then* cast. It seems to me the order here is very significant.   It makes me realize that simply "taking every thought captive" is not going to be enough, that attacking the problem by trying to *force* your mind to stop worrying is not going to bring complete relief from anxiety.

Let's look at Kim G.'s story in more detail. "The weight of the world was on my shoulders." She realized that she was carrying what was not hers to carry, that she was trying to control what she had no control over. Her humbling entailed surrendering to God's control. As she released her problems and fears to God, she even felt as though the weight she had been carrying was lifted. And indeed it had been. She was set free and received His peace.

Notice Kim G.'s comment, "The issues I have still exist." Surrender to Jesus did not make her problems disappear. Jesus simply took her troubles on His capable shoulders and provided His peace. He now walks *with her* through her hardships, and now *He* is the One who is carrying the load.

Notice also that Kim G. alludes to the *journey* she is now on as she refers to the Scripture verse that is her daily reminder. Although there was an initial first time choice to surrender, all her worry and anxiety did not necessarily disappear completely in that single moment. As she continues her walk with Christ, she will repeatedly surrender her worries to Him on a day-by-day, even minute-by-minute basis. And, the more she surrenders to Him, the more the Holy Spirit will grow her trust in God. The more she relies on His strength and receives His peace, the more the Spirit can enable her to walk more easily and more assuredly in that peace.

The World's Peace vs. God's Peace

Is there a difference? Jesus says there is. He explained to His disciples just before His death,

"Peace I leave with you; my peace I give you. I do not give to you as the world gives. Do not let your hearts be troubled and do not be afraid."
John 14:27

The world's peace is a sense of calm that comes when everything *externally* is going well: when our finances are secure, when our health is strong, when our boss is pleased with us or our grades are good, when our relationships are without conflict, when our kids are on the right track. The world's peace is fragile; it can be easily shattered when the money disappears, when our disease symptoms flare up, when we lose our job or are struggling in school, or when our son announces he is getting a divorce.

God's peace, however, is the only peace that can truly overcome worry. The Greek word for peace is eirene, a beautiful word whose Old Testament equivalent is shalom.[11] Shalom is derived from a word meaning "to be safe."[12] This kind of peace can only come from God, when there is no barrier between us because we are in right relationship with Him. Psalm 85 puts it poetically,

Righteousness and peace kiss each other.
Psalm 85:10

God's peace comes from our confidence that our salvation and eternal life are secure. We can have this confidence because we know that we are clothed in Jesus' righteousness (2Cor 5:21). Jesus' righteousness is perfect, sinless, holy. Human righteousness is not. Righteousness does not mean that we never sin; righteousness means we are living in right relationship with God; we are repentant of sins, forgiven by God, and surrendered to Him – *and* we are clothed in the righteousness of our Savior.

Righteousness and peace kiss each other. You have probably found out through experience that the peace which the world offers generally cannot survive trials. But the peace that God offers *transcends* hardships. God's peace has nothing to do with the circumstances of life; with God's peace we are safe because our relationship with Him is secure.

How can we have peace in the midst of tribulation? Let's travel to Taiwan to hear Dr. Shih describe it.

As a busy and talented orthopedic surgeon, I was very active with my career, family, and children, when I was suddenly hospitalized for endocarditis, an infection on my heart valve. After many days in the hospital and multiple antibiotics, I was still very weak, with constant fever and chills; they had run out of options to treat me, and I was terrified. I lay in that hospital bed, a powerful surgeon who had saved countless lives, now unable to save my own life.

On the eleventh day of my hospitalization, some of my Christian relatives came to visit me. I used to go to church "socially;" I had head knowledge about Christ, but no heart commitment. My Christian relatives read to me from Philippians 4:6-7: **Do not be anxious about anything, but in everything, by prayer and petition, with thanksgiving, present your requests to God. And the peace of God, which transcends all understanding, will guard your hearts and your minds in Christ Jesus.** *I realized how desperately I needed Jesus and the peace that only He can offer. I cried and cried and gave my heart and my life completely into His hands, to live only to follow His will. Right then and there God gave me that peace which transcends all understanding. It was such an unexpected peace, because physically I had no assurance I would ever recover.*

But although Jesus delivered me from the terror and worry, He did not immediately cure me. The complications continued, and I suffered a few strokes and then rectal cancer. *As I lay on the PET scan table, I realized the Lord had still given me this amazing peace, and unbelievable joy. Peace in Christ does not mean everything on the outside is good. It does not mean you feel good. In Christ, in the midst of the biggest storm, you can have peace.*

They removed the rectal cancer, but the complications continued: surgical complications, and infection after infection. Because of the persistent fevers and chills, the doctors sent me home on oral antibiotics. Still possessing this peace that is beyond comprehension, I lay in my bed at home, reading my Bible every moment I was awake. One week later, I was miraculously cured! My fevers were gone, all my tests normalized. The doctors were amazed by my rapid recovery.

I now have a completely different point of view of life, and totally different values. I have taken a one-year leave from my practice to travel internationally and share my testimony: how God transformed me from a powerful surgeon to a humble Christian.

Li-Yuan Shih, M.D.
Chang-Gung Hospital
Linko, Taiwan

Lying in a hospital bed with endocarditis, strokes, and rectal cancer, yet possessing **the peace of God, which transcends all understanding**. I think Dr. Shih would agree that trust in God unlocks the door to that peace:

You will keep in perfect peace those whose minds are steadfast, because they trust in you.

Isaiah 26:3

Having our minds steadfast on God, trusting Him, living in right relationship with Him, can bring us to perfect peace.

Fear

Are you afraid?   Afraid of being unable to support yourself or take care of your family, afraid of becoming an invalid, afraid of becoming dependent upon other people? Are you terrified of possible upcoming pain? Are you afraid of abandonment of family and friends? Are you petrified of dying? We are going to look at three tools to defeat fear, and then I'm going to give you a peek at how my friend Betsy utilized these tools.

First Tool: Understand What Causes Fear

False

Evidence

Appearing

Real

False evidence. A belief system built on Satan's lies. These lies can appear real, they can appear to be truth, for Satan is not only a liar, he's a *good* liar. He is the father of all lies. He is so good at lying, he can talk our socks off. He can make us believe anything, *anything*, that will drive us away from God. If we let him.

Fear can be a normal response when we are confronted with the unknown. A problem can arise when we allow fear to dominate our lives, when we allow it to paralyze us. Understand that allowing fear to overwhelm us can hinder our fellowship with God because we are not trusting Him. Fear can also hinder us from hearing from Him clearly. The first step to handle fear is to ask the Holy Spirit to reveal the lies that are driving the fear. Then, root out the lies, and through studying God's Word, replace the lies with God's truth.

Second Tool: Perfect Love

There is no fear in love; but perfect love casts out fear, because fear involves torment. But he who fears has not been made perfect in love.

1 John 4:18 NKJV

Perfect love casts out fear. Do you think it is God's perfect love for us, or our perfect love for God? I'd say it's both.

The word **love** used here is not any futile type of feel-good kind of love. It is the Greek word agape. Agape involves "God doing what He knows is best for man, not necessarily what man desires."[13] Pause and chew on that a moment. What is *best* for us – not necessarily what we *want*. And meditate on it a bit deeper: Do you *really* believe that God knows what's best for you better than *you* do?

Agape is how God loves us, freely, unconditionally, no strings attached. Agape is God so committed to us that He will do whatever it takes to meet all our needs, particularly our spiritual needs. Agape is God giving us what He knows is *best* for us, not necessarily what we *desire*, or what we *deserve*. Agape is Jesus dying for us: a completely selfless love. As we grow to know God more deeply, we can come to know in a large measure the depth of His agape. Knowing His love more deeply can enable us to cast off our doubts, to trust Him more, and to fear the terrors of life less. Knowing God's perfect agape can be a pivotal tool to displace fear.

Yet, I think to cast out fear, God also calls *us* to demonstrate perfect love to *Him*. The basic meaning of this word **perfect** means completed, mature, fulfilled, having reached its goal.[14] Hmmm . . . sounds like developing that kind of mature love will be a slow growth process. Listen to the contrast: immature love leads to insecurity, anxiety, doubts, and fear. Mature love, or perfect love, leads to boldness, confidence, faithfulness, and trust in God.

Of course we will never fully attain perfect love on earth. Yet the more we love God with spiritually mature agape, the more it can dislodge fear. What does it mean to love God with agape? It means unconditional, freely given love, and faithful, selfless serving, regardless of whether we are living a life of comfort, or a life of suffering.

How *exactly* do we love God? How do we love a God we cannot see or touch? Jesus teaches us how.

"If you love me, keep my commands."

John 14:15

Obedience proves our love. So our agape means our unconditional obedience, willingly given, regardless of the circumstances of our lives. The more we grow in Christ, the closer we can reach this perfect love. More obedience, more perfect love, less fear. It seems to me to be a direct correlation.

Third Tool: The Spirit of Power, Love, and a Sound Mind

For God has not given us a spirit of fear, but of power and of love and of a sound mind.

2 Timothy 1:7 NKJV

God did not give us a **spirit of fear**. I don't believe that this means that we will never fear, because fear can be a normal response to the unknown. But I think a *spirit of fear* implies that we are paralyzed by fear, overwhelmed by fear.

The Greek word for **fear** here can also be translated "cowardice."[15] Realize that we can be overcome with cowardice when our faith is not strong. We demonstrate ourselves to be faithless when we live in cowardice. When we are not courageous enough to trust that God is working for our good, when we do not accept the sovereignty of His plan, when we do not believe Him to be with us always, we may possess this spirit of cowardice.

What does God offer us to conquer fear? Go back to that verse:

- His **power**, the power of the Holy Spirit, dynamis in the Greek. I really grasped the extent of the meaning of this word dynamis when I learned that our word *dynamite* is derived from it.[16]
- His **love**, His agape, His faithful, unconditional, selfless love.
- A **sound mind**. Sophronismos. This is a complex and spectacular word. Let's take a look at it.

I think the Amplified Bible gives us the most comprehensive translation: **a calm and well-balanced mind, discipline and self-control**. That encompasses quite a few elements! I'll share with you what I see in my study of this word and its derivatives.[17]

- Sound judgment and wise decision-making
- Self-discipline and determination to hotly pursue Bible study, prayer, and your church family
- Singlemindedness necessary to ensure that your three-legged stool is stable
- Discipline to take every thought captive

- Refusal to allow your mind and emotions to dwell in fear

I'll take a moment to summarize all we have learned from 2 Timothy 1:7. In order to vanquish fear, we must believe in and accept God's agape. We trust that He is giving us what He knows is best for us. We leave behind the sins of our minds and emotions and discipline ourselves to meet regularly with God, to pray, to go to church, and to read His Word. This heart work can invite the Holy Spirit in as dynamite to blast those fears out of our hearts and minds.

Betsy Burden is on my *Triumph* Servant Leadership Team. Over the years, she has led many *Triumph* classes in two different churches. A shining example of a life lived victoriously in suffering, she admits her own struggle with fear when she was first diagnosed with breast cancer.

My children were eight and eleven when I was diagnosed with breast cancer. I first had to identify and confront my biggest fears relating to dying: that I would leave my children alone, and that I would suffer much physical pain. I felt the only two things I needed were my Bible in one hand and a box of Kleenex in the other. After several days and nights of praying and studying the Bible, I finally concluded that my precious children were a gift from God, and I simply gave them back to Him. I found that I had to trust God with both my children and my physical pain. Once I surrendered both of these to God, I was able to relax and face what I had to do.

Betsy Burden
Triumph Servant Leader
Christ Fellowship Church and Church in the Gardens
Palm Beach Gardens, Florida

Let's evaluate how Betsy used some of these tools to conquer fear. The first tool we discussed was uprooting Satan's lies and replacing them with God's truths. Betsy hints at this when she says, "I finally concluded that my precious children were a gift from God." Satan tries to convince us that we have ownership of many things, yet God reminds us, **"Everything under heaven belongs to me"** (Job 41:11). Once Betsy accepted that truth, moving into surrender came easily, "simply," as she phrased it.

The second tool she utilized was perfect love. She loved God with unconditional agape, freely given regardless of the circumstances. She demonstrated that love by her obedience as she surrendered her children and her physical body to God. Notice that she obeyed despite the uncertainty of the situation: Betsy did not know how much pain she would experience, and she did not know if she would even survive to take care of her children.

The third tool she used was power, love, and a sound mind. Notice what she needed: her Bible and a box of tissues. She did not stuff her emotions, but let them flow freely, and gave them to God to heal. She spent several days and nights praying and reading the Word – she kept her tripod strong, and emerged from her time of prayer and surrender with a calm and well-balanced mind. This is what equipped her to trust in God's agape. This is what enabled her to truly believe that He was working for her good, that He was giving her not necessarily what she wanted, but what *He* knew was best.

I think Betsy's final sentence really demonstrates the power of the Holy Spirit manifested in her: "I was able to relax and face what I had to do." Relax and face. Note the trial did not end with her surrender. But the peace of the Spirit rested on her and the power of the Spirit strengthened her to walk the path set before her, trusting that He was always with her, to lead and to guide each step of the way.

Handling Emotions

I believe that many people have stuffed their emotions most of their lives and are afraid to express them. Emotions that are suppressed often mushroom, while those that are expressed often diminish. If we try to ignore those painful emotions or pretend they don't exist, they may simply come out at other inappropriate times, in inappropriate ways. Then something minor may trigger an intense emotion.

Understand that *you* are in charge of your feelings. No one can "make you" feel a certain way. You *choose* how you want to feel. Take responsibility for your own emotions. Realize that when you believe that someone is making you angry, you are *giving away* your power and control to that person.

Learning to appropriately experience and express your emotions, especially the unwanted ones, may take much time and practice. Here are some steps that may help:

Pray for healing. Unpleasant emotions can arise from your pain. True, deep, everlasting wholeness comes only through Jesus. He is the One who can release His healing touch to your wounded heart.

Accurately identify your emotions. This may be difficult, especially if you have mostly stuffed them. Make a decision to allow yourself to identify your emotions. Learn to put an accurate name to how you feel. Don't simply call it "upset." Could it be that you are feeling angry, humiliated, threatened, betrayed, disrespected, insignificant, used, or misunderstood? Sometimes I search the internet for a list of emotions to help me accurately identify what I am experiencing. Some people find that immersing themselves in emotion-packed movies, books, or music helps them to feel and identify their own emotions in a safer way, and teaches them to put an accurate name to those feelings.

Identify without judging yourself. Remember:
- We are made in God's image; He has powerful emotions, so we also may have powerful emotions.
- Emotions are neither right or wrong, they just *are*.
- God already knows that we have these emotions, so we might as well admit them and use them to encounter Him.

Ask the Spirit for revelation. Since these suppressed emotions may come out in inappropriate ways, something minor may trigger an intense emotion. You know that the level of emotion is inappropriate for the circumstance, and you're afraid of saying or doing something that you may later regret. It's a very realistic fear. Additionally, if you have witnessed or have been the recipient of hurtful anger, you may be afraid that you will do the same. Seek the Holy Spirit for revelation. Ask Him to reveal what past event is triggering emotional memories in this current situation.

Forgive. Unforgiveness is frequently a root of ungodly emotions. If you are holding on to resentment, bitterness, or revenge, you may be unable to resolve the painful emotions. Seek to forgive and ask Jesus to heal painful memories. (We will discuss forgiveness in more detail in Chapter 7.)

Involve a friend. Ask someone close to you to walk with you through this growth period. That may be your spouse, a family member, or a close friend of the same gender. Identify your emotions out loud with this person, and ask them for confirmation that your identification is accurate, or correction if you are off track.

Journal. We clearly want to express these emotions in ways that are not sinful, and won't hurt anyone. A journal is an excellent way. We can privately pour our hearts out to God, knowing that He will never reject us or ridicule us. When we are journaling, He may reveal to us the deep issues triggering the intense emotions, and give us His wisdom to handle the situation.

When difficult emotions surface, learn to *respond* instead of *react*.

> 1 - Pause before speaking. Breathe a quick prayer to God to lead you through *His* response.
> 2 - Try taking deep breaths through the emotional turmoil.
> 3 - Try saying something like, "I'm feeling angry now. I'm not completely sure why, and it may have nothing to do with you. I need some time to process this emotion and to figure out my next step."

Your Emotions Can Lead to Encounters with Christ

Don't suppress these difficult emotions. Don't miss out on the radiance of your pleasant emotions by crushing the unpleasant ones. Come to God in total honesty about your feelings. Allow yourself to feel your emotions – all of them. The key now is to choose which ones you want to hold in your heart, and which ones you want to wash over you and move on. When we learn how to channel those intense emotions, harness them, and seek God's heart, He can use them for His Kingdom work.

Understand that these passionate emotions can lead to passionate encounters with Jesus. These emotions can drive us to seek God with an intensity we do not always have.

I want to introduce you to another member of my *Triumph* Servant Leadership Team, Joan Hoffpauir. If you could meet her in person, I think you would agree with me that what is most striking about her is the depth of her trust in God. It would not be long before you realized that this trust has been born in adversity, tested and tried, and built solidly on the Rock of Christ. This trust didn't develop without a good deal of hardship, coupled with intense seeking of the Lord in her trials, deeper and deeper surrendering, and encountering Him again and again in her pain. Let's listen in on one of her encounters with the Lord.

I had been diagnosed with non-Hodgkins lymphoma, stage four. I had left my young sons and traveled to Texas to begin tests and treatment. Terrified, I began to pray, telling God I was standing on His promises, and I thought about literally standing on His Word. I got out my Bible and stood on it, begging Him to fulfill His promises, to give me strength and never abandon me.

The next day, as I approached the hospital, I was so petrified I could hardly walk. I found myself praying from Isaiah, "Those who hope in the Lord will renew their strength. They will soar on wings like eagles; they will run and not grow weary . . ." It was all of the passage I could remember.

Somehow, clinging to those verses, I walked through those doors. Somehow, trusting in Him, I surrendered to the barrage of tests. Somehow, standing on His Word, I survived those ten hours of tests.

I waited all day for a huge infusion of energy, and it never came. I had stood on His Word, I had prayed for strength, and . . . nothing. At the end of the day, about to collapse, I just curled up in the exam room and bowed down my head. "I am so disappointed in You, Lord!" I cried out to Him. "I cannot do this without You, and You have bailed out on me! I am not soaring on wings like eagles! I am not running and not growing weary!"

I heard God's voice in my head, as clear as day, "Well, you walked and did not faint."

I realized that I had. With His strength, I had simply put one foot in front of the other. And I knew that this would be the way He would lead me through this entire ordeal.

Joan Hoffpauir
Triumph Servant Leader
Christ Fellowship Church
Stuart, Florida

Do you not know? Have you not heard?
The LORD is the everlasting God,
The Creator of the ends of the earth.
He will not grow tired or weary,
And his understanding no one can fathom.
He gives strength to the weary
And increases the power of the weak.
Even youths grow tired and weary,
And young men stumble and fall;
But those who hope in the LORD
Will renew their strength.
They will soar on wings like eagles;
They will run and not grow weary,
They will walk and not be faint.

Isaiah 40:28-31,
emphasis added

What Drives These Difficult Emotions?

Anger, self-pity, guilt, depression, worry, fear – what is driving these difficult emotions? Most likely pain. Physical pain, mental pain, emotional pain, spiritual pain.

The first step in healing involves honesty. Generally, no healing can take place until we are completely honest about our pain. Tread carefully here! It is okay to feel the pain, but don't let the pain define you. Simply admit the magnitude of the pain, and your disappointment that life isn't turning out as you wanted. Then what?

Remember, if we are thinking ungodly thoughts and experiencing painful emotions, those thoughts may be arising from a belief system built on Satan's lies. Satan's lies about pain and suffering. Satan's lies that may be telling you that God has refused to heal you, or is not powerful enough to rescue you, or just doesn't care enough about you to intervene. Satan's lies that may be telling you that you must have somehow disappointed God, that if God loved you more, He would lift that suffering from you. Satan's lies that may be telling you that you are abandoned, that God has forsaken you, and that He does not hear your cries for help.

When we reach a place of honesty, and rest on the truth of His Word, then we can begin to put the pain behind us and allow God to begin to heal us. We will do much work over the length of this book to uproot false beliefs such as these, to stop lying that everything is all right, and to replace lies with truth. The truth that we *are* in pain, that we *are* hurting, that we lost something so important to us, that we lost part of ourselves. The truth that we cannot heal ourselves, that we are totally dependent upon the Lord for His healing. The truth that God is with us, He loves us, and He is always working for our good. The truth that He is, at all times, in complete control of *every* aspect of the universe.

When I am rip-roaring furious, or so terrified I can't even breathe, or feeling completely utterly frighteningly alone even while still in the midst of people, or in the darkest most bottomless moments of hopelessness and despair, I know I must come to Him in total humility and honesty. I must admit my emotions, and confess my sins relating to the situation. So I run to Him, overcome with these emotions, and allow Him to console me. In His comfort is when I can become quiet; I can be still and know that He is God. Then, I can hear Him. When my heart is open to His voice, ready to listen no matter how painful His words are, ready to repent no matter how much I think the other person needs to repent, ready to obey no matter how difficult – it is then that He may reveal to me a piece of His heart.

Chapter 3
Surrender

urrender? Are you talking to *me*? I mean, I already surrendered my life to Christ long ago.

Yes, me too. And yet, surrender is not merely a one-time thing. At our first surrender, our salvation, we surrender to the depth of our level of spiritual understanding. And, as we grow more in Christ, He may call us to deeper and deeper surrenders – of related areas of our lives, of completely different areas, and even of deeper surrenders of the *same areas*. The same areas? Yes; it's possible we took them back again. But other times, we may not have taken them back, but we *have* grown up in the Lord, and are now ready for a deeper surrender in those places. At our salvation, we make the first choice to surrender, and then we embark on a lifetime of surrendering. We co-labor with God in an on-going lifelong process.

I must admit, I have lost count of the number of times the Spirit has revealed to me an unsurrendered area. Sometimes, I find it easy to surrender it pretty quickly. But other times, I decline to surrender it, then wrestle with God until I finally lay it at His feet. Sometimes, the wrestling takes a few minutes. Sometimes, a few hours.

Sometimes, a number of days. I am not proud of those times of defiance and rebellion.

If you have never taken the first step of surrendering your life to Christ — or maybe don't even know exactly what that means — the purpose of this chapter is to help you to explore what it means to *know* Him, to enter into *relationship* with Him. I want you to truly understand the *choice* that He offers to you.

If you do understand surrender, the purpose of this chapter is to take you deeper in your understanding, and deeper into your *level* of surrender. I believe that no matter how close our walk is with the Lord, we can always come closer, and surrender can be a door to more penetrating intimacy.

Throughout this chapter, I will be talking to both those who are weighing a first time surrender, and those who are considering a deeper surrender. There will be times when I will direct this message to the first-time-surrenderers, and at other times to the deeper-surrenderers. But throughout this chapter this message will speak to both of you, so keep your minds and hearts open.

The Holy Spirit may be speaking to some of you about an area of your life already. Others may be feeling there is nothing you are holding back. Sometimes, we can be blinded. If you cannot see any unsurrendered area just yet, stop and ask the Holy Spirit to reveal what He may be calling you to surrender right at this time. What area of your life you are trying to control, instead of giving it over to God's control? It may be your kids, your spouse, or your friendships. Possibly your job, your position or status. Maybe your health, your beauty, your body. It could be your possessions, maybe your grades, where you live, or even how you spend your time. Perhaps it's your reputation — at work, at school, in your home, with your friends, out in the community. Maybe it's your desire to focus on the things of the world instead of the things of God. It could be the approval of others, your concern about how others are assessing you or even judging you, your work to impress them, your dependence on the image you present to them. Or maybe it's *your* plan for your life, your own path, your hopes and dreams and desires. And for some of you, it just may possibly be your entire life.

Infinite Love

From what I have experienced with surrender, it all starts with *His* love. I know that may sound backwards. It sure did to me at first. I had felt that I needed to earn His love, that I needed to get my heart and my life right *first*. But that is Satan's lie. Scripture tells us the truth: **We love because He first loved us** (1Jn 4:19). We can't love Him, obey Him, surrender to Him without receiving His love first. So let's start by positioning ourselves to be drenched in His love. We are going to begin to uproot lies – lies that God does not love you, that He does not care about you, that He has forsaken you. Lies that He is not pleased with you, that He is disappointed in you, that you let Him down. Lies that you missed what He had for your life, that you blew it too hugely to be of any use to God, that it is too late. We are going to start this uprooting by being washed with the truth of His Word.

So come with me to Ephesians. We are going to read through these verses, asking the Spirit to breathe life into them.

Praise be to the God and Father of our Lord Jesus Christ, who has blessed us in the heavenly realms with every spiritual blessing in Christ. For he chose us in him before the creation of the world to be holy and blameless in his sight. In love he predestined us for adoption to sonship through Jesus Christ,

in accordance with his pleasure and
will – to the praise of his glorious
grace, which he has freely given
us in the One he loves. In him
we have redemption through
his blood, the forgiveness of
sins, in accordance with the
riches of God's grace that
he lavished on us with all
wisdom and understanding ...
In him we were also chosen,
and . . . When you believed,
you were marked in him with
a seal, the promised Holy Spirit, who is a
deposit guaranteeing our inheritance ...

Drenched in His Love

Ephesians 1:3-8, 11, 13-14

Breathtaking! God has blessed us in the heavenly
realms with every spiritual blessing in Christ. In the
heavenly realms – so we're not referring to simple earthly
blessings that will disappear when we die. We are
referring to eternal blessings, our treasures in heaven.
Let's dive into the details of these heavenly blessings.

Chosen to be Holy and Blameless

We are **chosen** in Christ. Chosen. Before the
foundation of the world, we are chosen. Whatever His will
and pleasure and purpose is, whether we can understand
it or not, God has *chosen* us. Spend a few moments
meditating on that concept.

What were we chosen for? Chosen to be **holy and blameless**. The root word for **holy**, or hagios, is "pure." Some other key parts of this definition involve "separation... set apart from a common to a sacred use."[1] God has chosen us to be set apart for Him. Blameless is literally translated "without spot or blemish."[2] Blameless does not mean without sin. Blameless means reconciled to Him, repenting and receiving forgiveness and salvation. *Chosen to be holy and blameless.*

Adopted

We are **adopted to sonship through Jesus Christ.** This word adoption is an ancient Roman legal term.[3] As children of God, we are now members of His family, members of His household. That gives us astounding rights and privileges – we are heirs of God, joint-heirs with Christ, inheriting the Kingdom of Heaven and also the earth (Rom 8:17, Rev 21:1-7). Sonship also gives us serious responsibilities and obligations. **"As the Father has sent me, I am sending you"** (Jn 20:21).

Redeemed

This word **redeem** is to give something in exchange. To pay a ransom price in order to release a captive.[4] What was the ransom price that Jesus paid? **Redemption through his blood.** His life, His blood, was the ransom price He paid to free us, to forgive our sins. He died in our place.

Only the blood of the Lamb, shed in the tortuous, ignominious death on the cross, could make a way for our forgiveness, could make a way for us to enter God's presence. It is only through Jesus' blood that we are saved, set free, rescued from the Kingdom of Darkness and transported to the Kingdom of Light. God wants relationship so desperately with you that He left the everlasting to come to earth for the purpose of pouring out His blood to the very last drop. And if you were the only one on the planet, I believe He would have done it *just for you*.[5]

Marked With a Seal

Ephesians explains that we are **marked . . . with a seal, the promised Holy Spirit**. What is the significance of this sealing?

Seal is another ancient Roman legal term. I'd like to read to you some parts of its definition: "to seal, close up and make fast with a seal signet . . . for the sake of security . . . and a token of its authenticity."[6] Let's go to the natural world to better understand the spiritual.

When my daughter Jenna was a little girl, she would write letters to her friend, close them with melted wax, and press her personal identifying mark into the wax. Like a signet ring seal of ancient times, Jenna's seal:

- Prevented her friend's nosy brother from taking anything out of the envelope.
- Identified that the letter was from her.
- Proved the letter's authenticity.

Draw the parallel.

- We are sealed with the Spirit to prevent Satan from stealing us away or attempting to claim us for his own.

- We are sealed with the Spirit to identify us as belonging to the Lord Jesus Christ, to mark us as His possession.
- We are sealed with the Spirit to prove that we are genuine. When we manifest the fruit of the Holy Spirit, God is proving us genuine – to ourselves, and to the world. He proves us to be authentic Christians.

We are sealed with the Holy Spirit. What a staggering gift!

Grace

Before we leave this passage in Ephesians, I want to look at one more word that I find to be so infused with His love. Charis, **grace**, is interlaced in all these verses. It is a precious word whose definition in my Word Study Dictionary spans three pages. Here are some highlights: "a favor done without expectation of return . . . unearned, unmerited favor." It is an "absolutely free expression of the loving kindness of God;" His only motivation is His goodness.[7] There are no strings attached; grace is a gift from God simply because of His graciousness and mercy. We have no right to it; we are unworthy of it. God gave us this gift because He just *felt* like it. The **riches of God's grace that he lavished on us** because his agape motivated Him to extend it to us. He has given us every spiritual blessing; He has chosen us to be holy and blameless; He has adopted us as His children; He has redeemed us and forgiven our sins; He has sealed us with His Holy Spirit, marked us as His possession – because He just felt like it.

It pleased Him to do it.
It is His pleasure and will.

Piercing!   Are you feeling loved about now? This reminds me of the T-shirt I have seen years ago:

God doesn't make junk.

No, He certainly doesn't. His creation is so precious to Him that He chooses to live inside of us!

From "Without Hope" to "Alive in Christ"

Pumped full of His love yet? Hmmm . . . I think we may still be in need of some more of His love. I am going to take us to the second chapter of Ephesians. Paul is writing about what life was like for us before we came to know Jesus, during the time of our life when we belonged to Satan, when we were trapped in his Kingdom of Darkness.

As for you, you were dead in your transgressions and sins, in which you used to live when you followed the ways of this world and of the ruler of the kingdom of the air, the spirit who is now at work in those who are disobedient. All of us also lived among them at one time, gratifying the flesh and following its desires and thoughts. Like the rest, we were by nature deserving of wrath . . . separate from Christ, excluded from citizenship in Israel and

foreigners to the covenants of the promise, without hope and without God in the world.

Ephesians 2:1-3, 12

Dead in our sins. Objects of wrath. Belonging to Satan. Living for Satan's glory; living for our own glory. Without hope and without God in the world. Created so tenderly by the Master Craftsman, yet rejecting Him, turning our backs on Him, dead in our sins. This is where we were when God pursued us and snatched us from Satan's grasp.

But God, being rich in mercy, because of His great love with which He loved us, even when we were dead in transgressions, made us alive together with Christ (by grace you have been saved).

Ephesians 2:4-5 NASB

Dead yet made alive by Christ's blood, simply because of His great love with which He loved us.

You are not your own; you were bought at a price.

1 Corinthians 6:19-20

We were bought at a price – what price? God purchased us by His own death. He wanted us so desperately that He ransomed us with His own blood. I would like to add something to the back of that T-shirt:

God doesn't buy *junk.*

After paying that price, do you think God is not going to take care of you? Jesus reassures us,

"Are not five sparrows sold for two pennies? Yet not one of them is forgotten by God. Indeed, the very hairs of your

head are all numbered. Don't be afraid; you are worth more than many sparrows."

Luke 12:6-7

The very hairs of your head are all numbered. Not just counted. *Numbered.* I can almost hear God, on His mighty throne, "Morgan just lost hair #956,726 . . ." What unbelievable love is this? We cost more than all the riches that the world could buy. Yes, *we* are God's treasure. Since we are His treasure, His heart is with us, His love and tenderness and compassion and mercy.

Are you still doubting the depth of His love for you? Questioning whether He would want you at all – or wondering whether He would want you back? I'd like to take you to one more passage. Better yet, I'm going to let a little 13-year-old girl take you there.

Although I had not abandoned the spiritual disciplines and I was faithfully reading my Bible, praying, and going to church, I had hit a time of spiritual dryness. I began to think God had forgotten me. I even started to wonder if God really loved me. I mean, He died for everyone else, too.

*Then one day, when I was having my time alone with God, I read from Isaiah, "**I will not forget you. Behold, I have inscribed you on the palms of My hands.**" (Isa 49:15-16 NASB) It was all the love I needed.*

Jenna Li
Jupiter, Florida

Are You Afraid to Meet Him?

Some of us may be afraid to come to the Lord. We may fear His wrath, or we may fear He will turn His back on us, or we may fear the look of disappointment or disapproval that we think we will see in His eyes. I want you to know that if you are feeling condemnation, shame, embarrassment, disappointment,[8] disapproval, fear, or condemning guilt, those feelings are *not* from God. I'm going to say it again. Condemnation, shame, embarrassment, disappointment, disapproval, fear, and condemning guilt are *not* from God.

God's Spirit brings *conviction* as He gently leads us to repentance. Repentance means that we honestly and humbly tell God we blew it and we want to be right with Him. When we repent and ask His forgiveness, He will wash us clean, give us a fresh slate, and put our sins as far away from us as the east is from the west (Ps 103:12). He may not remove the *consequences* of our choices, but when we surrender to Him, He will walk with us through the pain. Only He can bring beauty from the ashes in a way we cannot possibly even imagine (Isa 61:3).

Condemnation, shame, disappointment is not who God is. But don't take *my* word for it. Go right to *His* Word.

Jesus' Life Reveals Who God Is

"The best clue we have into how God feels about human pain is to look at Jesus' response," declares Philip Yancey. "He seemed unusually sensitive to the groans of suffering people, and set about remedying them. And he used his supernatural powers to heal, never to punish."[9]

If we want to know what God is like, if we want to know His heart, we can look at Jesus' time on earth, and His tenderness and compassion for humanity. Imagine the sea of humanity, the multitudes with their sins, pain, diseases, and suffering, who gathered around Him begging for

forgiveness and healing. His heart went out to them; He
was deeply moved in spirit; His heart ached to heal them
all (Mt 23:37). Let's read about some of Jesus' encounters
with those who were hurting, ostracized, marginalized,
broken-hearted, or awash in sin.

**When he [Jesus] came down from the
mountainside, large crowds followed him. A man
with leprosy came and knelt before him and said,
"Lord, if you are willing, you can make me clean."
Jesus reached out his hand and touched the man.
"I am willing," he said. "Be clean!" Immediately he
was cured of his leprosy.**

Matthew 8:1-3

Leprosy is a disease that causes gangrene of the body.
Parts of a leper's body actually die and fall off. Gangrene
is horrid looking and putrid smelling. In Jesus' time,
lepers were required by law to keep a distance of 100 yards
from people – a football field away. Yet Jesus did not shun
this man. He reached out His hand and *touched* him.
Jesus, who does not shy from lepers, does not shy from us
in our states of suffering or sinfulness. No, no. Instead,
He reaches out to us.

I would like to read to you one of my most favorite
passages in the Bible. No matter what your sin may be,
put yourself in the adulteress' place as we read, and open
your heart to receive Jesus' tender mercy, forgiveness, and
compassion:

**The teachers of the law and the Pharisees
brought in a woman caught in adultery. They
made her stand before the group and said to Jesus,
"Teacher, this woman was caught in the act of
adultery. In the Law Moses commanded us to stone
such women. Now what do you say?" They were
using this question as a trap, in order to have a basis
for accusing him.
But Jesus bent down and started to write on
the ground with his finger. When they kept on**

questioning him, he straightened up and said to them, "If anyone of you is without sin, let him be the first to throw a stone at her." Again he stooped down and wrote on the ground.

At this, those who heard began to go away one at a time, the older ones first, until only Jesus was left, with the woman still standing there. Jesus straightened up and asked her, "Woman, where are they? Has no one condemned you?"

"No one, sir," she said.

"Then neither do I condemn you," Jesus declared. "Go now and leave your life of sin."

John 8:3-11

What an earth-shattering story of Jesus' compassion. He alone was without sin, yet He cast no stones. There is no condemnation in Christ (Rom 8:1), not for this woman, and not for us. In Christ there is only love, mercy, and forgiveness. **"Neither do I condemn you; go and sin no more"** (Jn 8:11 NKJV).

God loves you so much. He loves you so, so much. You are His treasured possession. He wants to impress this message into your soul: "I love you so deeply." God is overflowing with love for you. Don't build a wall around yourself in an attempt to keep His love out. Throw open the door and let His love flow in, and He can lead you on your journey from anger, guilt, pain, and fear to acceptance, peace, comfort, and trust.

I believe that it is much harder for our compassionate God to stand by and let us suffer than it would be for Him to remove our suffering. Follow me to the tomb of Lazarus and see if you agree with me.

So the sisters [Mary and Martha] sent word to Jesus, "Lord, the one you love [Lazarus] is sick." When he heard this, Jesus said, "This sickness will not end in death. No, it is for God's glory so that God's Son may be glorified through it."

. . . **So then he told them** [his disciples] **plainly, "Lazarus is dead, and for your sake I am glad I was not there, so that you may believe. But let us go to him."**

. . . **When Mary reached the place where Jesus was and saw him, she fell at his feet and said, "Lord, if you had been here, my brother would not have died." When Jesus saw her weeping, and the Jews who had come along with her also weeping, he was deeply moved in spirit and troubled. "Where have you laid him?" he asked. "Come and see, Lord," they replied. Jesus wept.**

John 11:3-4, 14-15, 32-35

Jesus wept. **Jesus wept.** He was **deeply moved in spirit and troubled.** Why? Why did Jesus weep? He knew what He was about to do. He knew that He was going to raise Lazarus from the dead. He knew He was going to unite Mary and Martha with their brother in a matter of moments. So why did He weep?

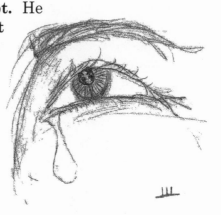

Scripture doesn't say, but I think that Jesus was weeping for Mary and Martha. I believe that He was deeply moved in spirit and troubled because of their pain, the pain that He knew He caused them by staying where He was for two more days. Even though He knew that this miracle was going to take their already huge faith and grow it in a massive way, even though He knew that nothing else could even come close to expanding their faith and knowledge of Him the way this miracle would do, He wept for the pain He was causing them during this trial. He wept for their suffering. His heartache was immense. He felt their pain. We are one with Jesus, just as the Son and the Father are one (Jn 17:22-23). He feels our pain.

Jesus wept.   The shortest verse in the Bible, but perhaps the most significant for us who are suffering. **Jesus wept.** I do not want you to forget that verse.

Take a moment to be still and know that He is God. Bow your head, close your eyes, open your heart, and give Him time to speak to your soul, to tell you, beloved of God, how much He loves you.

Yes, Jesus is weeping for our suffering, but He still may choose to allow our trials to continue. Not that our physical suffering is unimportant, but our spiritual state far outweighs the physical in importance. For He knows the greater plan. He may be using our tribulations to bring us to come to know Him deeply. He may be using our afflictions to bring *others* to come to know Him deeply.

We are suffering. God is weeping. Yet we are not abandoned, for He will never leave us or forsake us (Heb 13:5). When we surrender to Him, to His perfect plan, He lavishes His grace upon us, simply because of the great love with which He loves us. Surrender can bring down the barrier that separates us from the outpouring of His love. Not that He doesn't love us when we are unsurrendered – for His love is infinite and eternal and unchanging. But we may be unable to *receive* that love when we have erected a barrier by our refusal to surrender. His love is colliding with the door of your heart . . . waiting for you to open the door . . . searching for a crack to ooze into . . . knocking, pounding, crashing . . .

Are you ready for the next leg of the journey? **We love because He first loved us** (1Jn 4:19). We are going to explore *our response* to His infinite love next. Keep the tears of God as your anchor as we continue through this chapter.

How Do You Respond to Infinite Love?

When I really take it all in, the only possible response to His infinite love is my surrender. Let's look at this call a little more closely.

From one man he made all the nations, that they should inhabit the whole earth; and he marked out their appointed times in history and the boundaries of their lands. God did this so that they would seek him and perhaps reach out for him and find him, though he is not far from any one of us.

Acts 17:26-27

God determined your appointed time, the times set specifically for you, the exact dates you would be born and die, and He also determined the exact places you would live. Unbelievable! God determined *that*?! Why? Because He is a controlling God and He just wants to control everything? I don't think so. God did this in the hope that you might *seek Him and perhaps reach out for Him and find Him.* Whether you are working towards a first time surrender, or a deeper level of surrender, understand that God placed you here, in this exact time, at this exact location, in this specific set of circumstances, *because* He desires you to come to Him! To give you every opportunity to find Him! And God promises He will reveal Himself to you when you seek Him with an all-absorbing, hold-nothing-back search:

> **"You will seek Me and find Me when you search for Me with all your heart."**
>
> Jeremiah 29:13 NASB

God promises to give you every opportunity to find Him, *and* He promises to make Himself findable when you seek Him passionately. I believe that God is addressing both a first time surrenderer and a deeper surrenderer. As I say it again, realize that I am talking to both of you: God promises to give you every opportunity to find Him, *and* He promises to make Himself findable when you seek Him passionately. But whether you embark on that extreme search or not is completely up to you. It is your choice. *His* actions are certain. But *your response* is up to you. **Perhaps** you may reach out for Him and find Him. He gives you free will.

You met my friend Kim G. in the last chapter. She is the one who gave us an education about worry and anxiety. She has a powerful story of how God placed her in an exact time at an exact location, and then orchestrated the particular events in her life in order to give her every possible opportunity to find Him. I've asked her to share what happened that day.

One day I was online chatting with one of my Christian friends, telling her how much my family was struggling financially, how out of control and desperate I felt, and she once again mentioned to me how God had helped her. I thought to myself, I wish He could help me. As we continued chatting, I received a friend request on Facebook from a man I didn't know. I looked him up and learned he was Pastor David Helbig, the Online Pastor of Christ Fellowship Church*, a church I had attended the past two Christmases. I thought it was a coincidence and I sent him an e-mail stating as such. He e-mailed me back and said every once in a while he randomly sends out friend requests to those who belong to Christ Fellowship's Facebook group.

---

*Gochristfellowship.com

I told him I was considering turning to God. He answered all my questions and concerns, and his answers seemed just right to me. By the end of our conversation, I was ready to receive Christ. Pastor David led me through a prayer and I received Christ into my heart.

Since giving my life over to God, God has opened my eyes to the path that He is laying out for me. I am doing my best to follow it and I am amazed everyday at how God is working. Every day is a new opportunity to hear Him, through a passage I read in the Bible, through prayer and listening, or through situations and people. In addition, God has brought some amazing Christian women into my life, women I would never have met had it not been for Him, women who have helped me and taught me so much.

Kim G.
Loxahatchee, Florida

Coincidence? Hardly. I don't believe there are any "coincidences" with God. As I've heard it said, "There are 'God-incidences,' but no 'co-incidences'." Kim G. and I both believe that God clearly orchestrated these events, hoping that she would feel her way toward Him and find Him — and she did just that.

Do you believe that it is possible to really know God, to know Him intimately and deeply? To talk to Him — and have Him answer you? To know who He is, to grasp some understanding of what He is about and what His heart is? To gradually come to know Him more and more, and through knowing Him to understand His plan for your life? I crave that for you. I long for you to reach out for Him and find Him. He put you here, in this time, in the exact place you live, in your exact circumstances, *explicitly* so that you would find Him. *Specifically* for you to come to know Him deeper. *Undeniably* to invite you to surrender. It is no coincidence that you are reading this book.

The Barrier That Keeps Us From God

What is the barrier that keeps us from knowing God in a deep intimate way? That barrier is sin. God tells us in Isaiah, **your sins have cut you off from God** (Isa 59:2 NLT).

"I don't sin – or at least not much," you might say. Yet God says, **"There is no one righteous, not even one"** (Rom 3:10).

No one? That's right. God says **no one**.

We are given chances every day to choose sin or to choose God. We can choose to lie, or to tell the truth. We can choose to encourage our spouses, or to criticize them. We can reach down to help someone in need, or we can walk right by. We can choose to spew out hurtful words, or keep our mouths shut.

I want you to understand that although by the world's standards we may be "good people," by God's standards, we are not. God says that all our righteous acts are like filthy rags (Isa 64:6). Even if we do the right thing, our motives may be impure. We *may* be doing a good deed, but we *may not* be doing it solely to glorify God. Our sinful motives may include making ourselves look good, or assuaging a guilty conscience, or capturing that "feel-good" sensation in our hearts that can come from helping someone in need. Good actions, impure motives. God calls that sin (Pr 16:2, 1Cor 4:5).

God's definition of righteousness is so far above what humans call righteousness that He says even *thinking* of a sinful act is just as sinful as doing it! (Mt 5:21-22, 27-28).[10]

God is so holy, so completely perfect, so absolutely pure; His purity is beyond our comprehension. I have heard God described as a pure glass of spring water. If I put a drop of motor oil into it – just a drop – would it still be pure? Come on, it's just a drop – you can barely see it! We can still call it pure, right? Wrong. Its purity has been destroyed.

In the same way, if we would come into God's presence in our filthy rags of our own brand of righteousness, we would destroy His perfect purity. God's purity defines Him, and if His purity was marred, God would not be God.

The Holiness of God

"God is a consuming fire."

Hebrews 12:29

Who can come anywhere near an all-consuming fire?

"Who of us can dwell with the consuming fire? Who of us can dwell with everlasting burning?" Those who walk righteously . . .

Isaiah 33:14-15

He who is righteous can enter God's presence without being consumed by His fire. However Romans says **there is no one righteous** (Rom 3:10). Isaiah says that **all our righteous acts are like filthy rags** (Isa 64:6). If we entered His presence in our sinful states, His fire would simply consume us.

We may seek to make ourselves pure, by following the Ten Commandments, praying, going to church, reading our Bible, doing good deeds. Although these are important disciplines, they will never mask our sins, they will never break through the barrier of our sin that separates us from God. God says **no one will be declared righteous in God's sight by the works of the law** (Rom 3:20). All our human efforts will never bring us to the state of purity our holy God demands in order for us to enter His presence. On our own, we can never reach the perfect purity necessary so that His holy fire will not consume us.

Not only do our sins bar us from God's presence, and not only are we completely unable to make ourselves pure and righteous on our own, but God also states in Romans that **the wages of sin is death** (Rom 6:23). The penalty of sin is death. Physical death plus spiritual death, being separated from God here on earth, and being separated from God forever in hell. "It's not fair!" you may scream. But He is God, and He gets to make the rules.

It hurts, doesn't it? At first, yes. But let this wash the pain away: God loves us so much, even in our states of repulsive sinfulness, that He made a way for us to become perfectly pure and thus be able to enter His presence. That way is the Lord Jesus Christ. God says the penalty to be paid for sin is death. *And* God says, "I love you so much, I don't want you to pay that price. I, God, the Lord Jesus Christ, will die in your place. I will pay that penalty for you."

"For God so loved the world that he gave his one and only Son, that whoever believes in him shall not perish but have eternal life."
John 3:16

This is how much God loves us: He gave us His only Son, gave Him to us to torture and viciously murder, so that we may enter God's pure and holy presence and spend eternity with Him. Jesus did not die for us because we were holy or good or kind or righteous. He died for us **while we were still sinners** (Rom 5:8); He died for us simply because He loves us. This love is just beyond human comprehension. Fair for us is eternal punishment, not eternal life. I'll take "not fair" any day.

Jesus answered, "I am the way and the truth and the life. No one comes to the Father except through me."

John 14:6

No one enters God's presence except through Jesus. Through Jesus, we are clothed in Jesus' righteousness (Gal 3:27, Isa 61:10), we wear His perfect sinless purity, so God *sees* us as pure, as righteous:

God made him who had no sin to be sin for us, so that in him we might become the righteousness of God.

2 Corinthians 5:21

We can **become the righteousness of God**? Sounds crazy, doesn't it? But remember, He is God, and He gets to make the rules. His rules say that we, the drop of motor oil, clothed in Jesus' righteousness, can enter the pure spring water of God's presence. Clothed in Jesus' righteousness, we can live with the holy fire without being consumed.

What Does "Through Jesus" Mean?

"No one comes to the Father except through me." What exactly does "through Jesus" mean? How do we become clothed in Jesus' righteousness? Does it mean we pray and go to church and read our Bible and do good deeds? No, there is *much* more to it than that. **"Whoever *believes* in me shall have eternal life."** Well, that sounds simple. Hmmm. . . we're going to cover that word "believes" in a minute.

Step One: Repent

First we will start with Jesus' own words,

"Unless you repent, you will all likewise perish."
                                                    Luke 13:3 NASB

Perish is to be separated from God eternally in hell.
You may be wondering if hell really exists. Cliffe Knechtle
in *Give Me an Answer* reassures us that many people have
that same question.[11] Jesus talked more about hell than
anyone else in the Bible. Hell is a real place. Revelation
calls it **a lake of fire** (Rev 20:15) and a place of **no rest
day or night** (Rev 14:11). Thessalonians says hell is
eternity without God (2Th 1:9). What is it like without
God? God is everything good, hell is an absence of God, so
it is an absence of God's goodness. An eternity of **blackest
darkness** (2Pet 2:17), of agony and unrest, an eternity
devoid of purpose and meaning, an eternity of futility and
hopelessness. "Eternal aloneness"[12] in the lake of fire.

Does it sound mean and vindictive, God "sending"
people to hell? Hold on a minute, listen to these verses:

**The Lord is . . . not wanting anyone to perish, but
everyone to come to repentance.**
                                    2 Peter 3:9, emphasis added

**"Do I take any pleasure in the death of the
wicked?" declares the Sovereign LORD. "Rather, am
I not pleased when they turn from their ways and
live?"**
                                                    Ezekiel 18:23

God does not "send" anyone to hell. God does not want
anyone to go to hell. Hell was not made for people; Jesus
tells us it was made for Satan and his demons (Mt 25:41).
Yet God gave us free will. If we tell Him that we are good
enough to stand before Him alone (2Cor 5:10), if we tell
Him that our own righteousness is good enough, if we tell

Him that we have no need of Jesus as our Savior, if we tell Him that we don't need Him here on earth – then God will not violate our free will in all eternity. Knechtle phrases it this way: "On the judgment day God will say, 'Based on your own decision to live life separately from me, you will spend eternity separate from me.' That's hell."[13] If we have chosen life without Him on earth, we will spend our life in all eternity without Him as well.

Unless we repent, we will all perish. We talked about repent in Chapter 2, that 180-degree turn, a total change of heart, leading to a change of emotions, attitudes, thoughts, and actions. Repentance is humbly telling God there is nothing we can ever do to make up for our sins. Repentance is accepting Jesus' redeeming work on the cross as the price paid for our sins. Repentance is turning *to* God and *away* from our sins. There is no way to go **through Jesus** without first repentance from sins.

And for those who are seeking a deeper surrender, I don't think I need to tell you that repentance is our first step.

Step Two: By Grace Through Faith

What else does "through Jesus" entail? Jesus said, in Matthew,

"Not everyone who says to me, 'Lord, Lord,' will enter the kingdom of heaven, but only the one who does the will of my Father who is in heaven. Many will say to me on that day, 'Lord, Lord, did we not prophesy in your name, and in your name drive out demons and perform many miracles?' Then I will tell them plainly, 'I never knew you. Away from me, you evildoers!' "

Matthew 7:21-23

Not everyone who calls Jesus "Lord," not everyone who calls themselves "Christian," will enter the Kingdom of Heaven. Only those who *know* Jesus, who are doing the will of His Father. Hmmm . . . back to good deeds? It can't be, for Ephesians tells us,

For it is by grace you have been saved, through faith – and this not from yourselves, it is the gift of God – not by works, so that no one can boast.

Ephesians 2:8-9

We are saved, brought into right relationship with God, invited to enter His presence, by grace through faith. Let's look at those two words. Remember grace is that free, undeserved, gift from God. Unearned, unmerited favor. We didn't deserve it, and we could never earn it. Jesus died in our place, simply because He loves us. Accepting God's grace means admitting that we cannot be righteous on our own. It means accepting that Jesus paid the penalty for our sins, and receiving God's forgiveness.

By grace through faith. Faith in the Greek is pistis. You will also see pistis translated in your Bible as "believe." As I read through my Greek study tools, what leaps out at me is that pistis is derived from a word meaning "to rely on; to trust."[14] Pistis is vastly more than just head knowledge or lip service. Pistis is deep in our hearts (Rom 10:10). Pistis is an action word – it means we believe something so deeply, we *live* like we believe it. Pistis is our lives lived out in trust of our beliefs. If we truly, deeply trust what we say we trust, our actions will reflect that trust. Faith is not good works, but the *proof* of our faith is our good works. Jesus said,

"By their fruit you will recognize them. Do people pick grapes from thornbushes, or figs from thistles? Likewise every good tree bears good fruit, but a bad tree bears bad fruit."

Matthew 7:16-17

If we repent, and truly deeply accept Jesus as our Lord and Savior, it will be evident in our lives: we will be doing the will of the Father. Only Jesus saves, by the gift of God's grace, but it is our lives lived out in trust of God that prove our faith is genuine. The evidence of our belief is that we live our lives in accordance to God's will. Living in obedience to God proves that we have received this grace. Jesus said,

"Whoever believes in me will do the works I have been doing."
John 14:12

Faith, or belief, is so deep that it just bursts forth as doing what Jesus had been doing: living to glorify the Father. Loving God and loving others. Serving God by serving others. Bringing God's message of mercy, forgiveness, and salvation to a lost and hurting world. That is *God's* definition of faith.

I want to really make these concepts concrete, so I've invited Shirley to describe her first time surrender to the Lord. Shirley and I had been out of touch for a number of years, but I have known her since we attended an all-girls Catholic high school together. Imagine our delight to discover that our faith journeys have taken us both to the same place: right into the heart of God.

I had the feeling that I didn't belong anywhere, so I left the country. I felt lost and insecure; I had no purpose; something was missing in my life, and I thought, maybe hoped, I would find it in England.

My greatest desire was to have a family of my own. I had lots of money saved, I was about to sign a lucrative contract and planned to buy a house, start the adoption process, and have enough money at the end of the contract to take some time off and bond with my adopted children. It was a good plan. But it wasn't God's plan.

A little more than a year after moving to England, I found myself being called back home. I had no question in my mind or heart that, for the first time in my life, I heard and recognized God's message to me. I did not know why I needed to go, or why I needed to go now, especially since just two weeks before I had finalized the sale of my house in the States, but God told me to go home.

So at age 42 I quit a job that I loved. I moved back to the States and in with my brother and his family. As I once again had the privilege of watching my brother and his wife raise their children with strong Christian faith and values, and, I was forced to examine my own life. I was raised Catholic and always felt I believed, but now I was compelled to ask myself, am I living out what I say I believe?

Within a few months of returning to the States, I was diagnosed with breast cancer, and had a mastectomy. I thought, "God, there are so many other ways You could have gotten my attention. But breast cancer?" Yet even as I thought those words, I knew I had needed to be shaken up.

Being diagnosed with breast cancer led me into an even deeper evaluation of my beliefs. I realized, I am not afraid of dying, I am afraid of living. My plan is gone. What I thought was most important, a family, I am unable to attain. So why am I here? I still felt lost, I still had no purpose, and I was still so insecure.

I came to realize that faith is not just a belief; faith is how you live your life. I suddenly realized that what I was missing, that what I went to Europe to find, was a true relationship with God and a genuine faith in Jesus. I knew now was the time to make a decision to live out my beliefs in every aspect of my life. I came to accept that it's not about my plan; it's about God's plan. Obviously what I had in my mind was not His plan. I arrived at this turning point with much tears, but my fear melted away when I let my plan go and started focusing on His plan.

In the years since I made that choice, my faith has continued to grow. I have become more thoughtful in my interpretation of the Bible and in prayer, and I have been comforted during my most difficult, painful times by prayer. I realize how instrumental my brother and his family and friends were in my decision, and I, too, have learned to be an example of Christian faith lived out. My life is nothing if I have not impacted others for Christ. I know God has a purpose for me; I may not know it now, but at some point I will know it. Maybe it is to be an example to others of Christian faith lived out. Maybe it is to be an aunt dedicated to helping her brother raise his children in Christ. Maybe it is to be an inspiration to other cancer survivors who feel their plans have been forever changed by their illness, and who need to know that God has a plan for them. And maybe . . . it is to reach the hundreds of children with cancer out there who are lost and in need of comfort.

Shirley
Romansville, Pennsylvania

I love this testimony! I could read it a thousand times. I would like to tease out a few highlights – directed at both the first time surrenderers and the deeper surrenderers.

Notice Shirley's focus on her plan vs. God's plan. She foreshadowed it at the beginning: "It was a good plan. But it wasn't God's plan." See her tears as she came to that realization. Feel her pain as she surrendered her "good" plan for God's perfect – but as yet unrevealed – plan. She is saying "yes" without even knowing what she is saying "yes" to! [15]

And watch closely the result of her surrender: "My fear melted away when I let my plan go and started focusing on His plan." Her fear melted away. She is blessed with peace, security, and eternal purpose – even without knowing the path ahead of her. I believe that no amount of money, no human relationships, no fulfillment of earthly dreams, could *ever* bring this kind of peace, security, and purpose.

Let's take a moment to review. **"No one comes to the Father except through me."** *Through Jesus* involves three steps. Step one is repent. Step two is by grace through faith. And now we will move into step three, surrender.

Step Three: Surrender

"For God so loved the world that he gave his one and only Son, that whoever believes in him shall not perish but have eternal life."

John 3:16

And he died for all, that those who live should no longer live for themselves but for him who died for them and was raised again.

2 Corinthians 5:15

Second Corinthians 5:15 shows us what it means to live out John 3:16: those who live, those who are given eternal life, are to no longer live for themselves but for Him who died for them. This means that we live for Jesus and not for ourselves; we live to glorify Jesus and not to glorify ourselves; we make Jesus the *Lord* of our lives; we give Him *control* of our lives. I call this surrender.

Is surrender to God like surrender in war? Yes, and no. Let's do a comparison.

How is surrender in war the same as surrender to God?

Surrender in War	Surrender to God
Give up everything	Give up everything of earthly value
Often put to death	No longer live for ourselves but for Christ – this means to die to self and live for God

How is it different?

Surrender in War	Surrender to God
You have no choice; you are forced to surrender because you have lost	It's your choice to surrender; you have free will; God will not force you
All your abilities, gifts, and talents are wasted	All your abilities, gifts, and talents are used to the utmost
All your suffering and pain is wasted	All your suffering and pain is given meaning and used fully
You are killed or imprisoned with no further purpose in life	God reveals to you His purpose and enables you to fulfill it completely
Lose everything, get nothing	Lose everything, receive astounding gifts

When we choose to surrender to God, we give God everything and receive many astounding gifts, such as these:

- All of our sins are completely forgiven (1Jn 1:9, Eph 1:7).
- We are given eternity in heaven, and heavenly rewards and responsibilities beyond our wildest imaginations (1Pet 1:4, Mt 25:14-28, Rev 22:5).
- We are given amazing spiritual treasures while still here on earth – such as peace that surpasses all understanding (Phil 4:7), joy beyond measure regardless of our circumstances (1 Pet 1:6-8), and a personal relationship with the Creator of the Universe (Rom 8:15).
- We are given God's Spirit, who enters into our heart and gives us encouragement, wisdom, guidance, conviction, comfort, courage, and strength (Jn 14:16-17).

Surrendering to God is dying to ourselves and living for God. It is giving God control of money, possessions, school, work, status, reputation, and relationships: spouse, kids, and friends. Surrender is putting Jesus in the driver's seat in all aspects of our lives, including the really difficult areas of our time, our dreams, and our plans. Surrender is choosing to live for God's vast eternal plan, His Kingdom, His purpose for us in this world – instead of living for our own dreams, wants, and desires. Surrender is consecrating ourselves to Him, living a life completely devoted to Him. Surrender is making Jesus our Number One.

My friend Rhonda, a highly educated yet very humble woman with a dual doctorate in Rehab Medicine and Neuropsychology, was faced with this exact choice: to serve the world, or to serve God. Let's hear her decision.

Life with three happy, healthy, beautiful and accomplished state-ranked tennis-playing children was every mother's dream. Add to that a husband who was a physician and myself a Ph.D. in the medical field . . . Life was very busy and I loved every moment of it. So why was there this little something not quite right . . . a void maybe? Why, oh why, was I making myself so busy?

Through all of this I missed the most important thing in this world and the next: a personal and dependent relationship with Jesus our Lord and Savior. The saddest part was that I thought that I had everything – what more was there? What I did not know is that it's one thing to believe and love Jesus, but it's another to surrender to Him and let Him be Lord of your life, to spend quiet time with Him, to worship Him and put Him first in your life. I have surrendered to Him and that void is filled, as I focus on Him and on sharing His Word with others.

Rhonda
West Palm Beach, Florida

Rhonda had been deceived. Rhonda had grown up in the church, and she thought she had a personal relationship with Jesus, for she did "believe and love Jesus." But "believing" and *surrendering* are completely different. As she later recognized, she did have beliefs, but she was not living her life in trust of those beliefs. And "love" in a human feel-good kind of way is completely different from *agape*. We learned in Chapter 2 that agape means our unconditional obedience; agape is surrender. Rhonda discovered that she had "no personal and dependent relationship with Jesus," for she had never made Him the Lord of her life. She had never surrendered.

I am also seeing a second level of deception in her story. By the world's standards, she had everything. "What more was there?" It was the perfect life. And she loved it – or so she thought. For many decades she had managed to hide from herself and others that gaping void in her heart. But God removed the scales from her spiritual eyes and revealed her true heart, inviting her to surrender to Him. She accepted that invitation.

I'd like you to hear my daughter Jenna's struggle with surrender. Perhaps you can relate.

I was in first grade when I came to know Christ. After that commitment, I was growing in Him, studying my Bible, serving in church, learning to pray. But when I was 11, God revealed to me that I was putting things in my life on the throne in my heart – putting things before God. I was putting dance, my mom, and what other people thought of me before God. I did not want to give them up and let God be on the throne in my heart, to direct and reign in my life, to be in charge of me. But God wrestled with me and finally changed my heart. I have put God above dance, my mom, and what other people think of me, and now I am fully submitted to God; He rules completely throughout my life.

Looking back, I see that when God called me to surrender these three things to Him, He did not test the sincerity of my surrender on all of them right away. It was the attitude of my heart that really mattered. The only thing He immediately tested me on was what other people thought of me. That very day of my surrender to Him, He gave me a ministry: to welcome lonely people both in church and in school. This remains one of my ministries even today.

It was not until two years later that God called me to demonstrate the sincerity of my surrender of dance. He called me to the mission field, and two years in a row I gave up my annual dance performance to go on mission trips, first to Bolivia, and next to the Dominican Republic.

As for the surrender of my mom . . . that didn't come for three years. God called me on a three-week mission trip to the Dominican Republic; I had never been away from my family for so long. It was hard to leave my family for such a lengthy time, but God had a higher calling.

Jenna Li
Jupiter, Florida

I remember very well her "wrestling." It spanned two days, evoked floods of tears, and occupied her family praying in intercession. The fruit of her surrender is precious Kingdom work in school, in church, and on the mission field.

"Through Jesus"

No one comes to the Father except through Me. In summary, "through Jesus" means by

- Repentance, the 180 degree turn away from our sins.

- Grace, the free undeserved, unmerited gift of Jesus dying in our place. Admitting our need for a Savior, accepting Jesus' death as paying the price for our sins, and accepting God's forgiveness for our sins.
- Faith, believing so deeply that we live like we believe it; living in trust of Him.
- Surrender, giving our lives over to God's control, putting Him first, living for Christ and not for ourselves.

When we first choose to surrender to Jesus, God rescues us from Satan's Kingdom and transports us to the Kingdom of Jesus Christ (Col 1:13-14). Our sins are forgiven, we have stepped into a deep relationship with Jesus, and we are given eternity with God in heaven. We are sealed with the Holy Spirit (Eph 1:13). No one can snatch us from His hands (Jn 10:29).

Choosing to surrender your life to Jesus, whether it is the first time you have ever surrendered, or whether it is entering into a deeper level of surrender, can be a very heavy, very difficult decision. Repenting, leaving sins behind, sins that seem to somehow make your life easier at this time, is often not an easy decision. Putting Jesus first in your life can be daunting. Abandoning your own dreams and desires and choosing to live for God's Kingdom, for His will and His plan, is probably not a decision you can make lightly. You don't even completely know what He is calling you to do! Choosing for Jesus is costly. Listen to how Jesus describes surrender.

And He was saying to them all: "If anyone wishes to come after Me, he must deny himself, and take up his cross daily and follow Me."

Luke 9:23 NASB

Are You Ready To Surrender?

Have you ever surrendered to Jesus? Have you ever repented of your sins and turned over *everything* to His control? Have you admitted your sin and desperate need for a Savior? Have you received His grace, His mercy and forgiveness for your sins? Are you right now demonstrating by your faith, by your trust in Him, that you belong to Jesus? Is He first in your life? **"Not everyone who says to me, 'Lord, Lord' will enter the Kingdom of Heaven."** When you arrive at heaven's gates, will Jesus say to you, **"Well done, good and faithful servant!"** (Mt 25:21)? Or will He say, **"I never knew you. Away from me, you evildoers!"** (Mt 7:23)?

And if you *have* surrendered in the past, are you living a fully surrendered life now? What will Jesus say to you when you stand before Him to give an accounting? Understand that when you first surrender to Jesus, you surrender all that you understand at that moment. However, you are not finished with surrender then; you have merely embarked on a lifetime of surrendering. As you come to know Jesus more, He may call you into a deeper and more complete surrender of things you did not even know you were holding back. Each deeper level of surrender positions you to receive a more intimate revelation of our Savior. It is a lifetime of growing in Him. As you become more surrendered to Him, as He reveals Himself more and more to you, as your relationship with Him becomes a richer and more precious treasure, you may wonder why you were holding those things back at all!

What If You Are Unable to Surrender?

I understand. Sometimes, I get stuck, too. When I am stuck, this is how I pray: "Lord, I am willing to be made willing to surrender. Please do whatever it takes to enable me to release these things to You." God knows my heart. He knows how desperately I desire to live fully surrendered to Him, and I trust Him to honor that request.

Are You Feeling a Tug at Your Heart Right Now?

That may be God, calling you. Calling you to a very first surrender, or to a new level of surrender.

If you are ready to surrender everything to Jesus as your Lord and Savior, if you understand the decision and accept the cost, I invite you to answer God's call. If you are ready to repent of your sins, to put God above everything else in your life, and to allow Him free access into every aspect of your life, I offer you an opportunity to do that right now. If you are ready to accept Jesus' death as paying the penalty for your sins, if you are ready to surrender everything to His control, to live for Jesus and not for yourself, to believe, to have faith, to trust Him completely, to live for His glory and not your own, to put Him first in your life, I invite you to pray with me right now:

> *Oh Heavenly Father, I see so clearly my sins, and I repent and choose to leave them behind. All my good deeds can never make up for my sins, and I accept Jesus' death on the cross as the payment for my sins. Thank You, Heavenly Father, for your overwhelming mercy and grace. I surrender everything to You, I give you control of every single aspect of my life. You have offered me a choice, and I choose to believe, to have faith, to trust You with every part of my life. I choose to give my*

life over to You; I choose to put You first in my life; I will no longer live for myself, but will live for my Lord Jesus Christ. Amen.

I would love to know of your decision to surrender! E-mail me at CJL@triumphoversuffering.com so I can rejoice with the angels in heaven and encourage you and pray for you.

PART II: ABSOLUTE SOVEREIGNTY

Understand Why We Suffer

Chapter 4
God Is Sovereign

Why? Why me? What did I do to deserve this? Why do some righteous people suffer while some of the wicked enjoy good health and riches and power and fame and success? Why do bad things happen to good people? Whose fault is it anyway?[1]

I know you're ready to leap all over these questions. After all, we're in Chapter 4 already. Believe me, I can't wait either. Yet before we tackle these questions, we must come face to face with one of God's attributes, an attribute that many of us would probably rather not think about, yet one that we cannot escape if we are going to wrestle with the questions of why we suffer. Let's go to the Book of Job, for it asks the age-old question, "Why me?"

> Then the LORD said to Satan, "Have you considered my servant Job? There is no one on earth like him; he is blameless and upright, a man who fears God and shuns evil."
> "Does Job fear God for nothing?" Satan replied. "Have you not put a hedge around him and his household and everything he has? You have blessed the work of his hands, so that his flocks and herds are spread throughout the land. But stretch out

your hand and strike everything he has, and he will surely curse you to your face."

The LORD said to Satan, "Very well, then, everything he has is in your hands, but on the man himself do not lay a finger."

Then Satan went out from the presence of the LORD.

Job 1:8-12

Interesting. As Philip Yancey expresses it, sounds like a combination of "Satan inflicts the pain, but only after obtaining God's permission."[2] All Satan wants us to know is the half-truth, that he is the **prince of this world** (Jn 14:30). Yet we learned when we studied Satan's tactics in Chapter 1 that a half-truth is a lie. When we take the whole counsel of the Bible, we learn that Satan cannot even *sneeze* without God's approval. He must ask *permission* to wreak his evil. He is completely subject to God. God is in charge.

Satan doesn't want us to know this, but let's get one truth crystal clear in our minds: God has no opposite. Do not imagine God and Satan as two angels grappling on the ground, the more powerful one to win this world. Satan is merely a created being, a fallen angel. And God? God is the Uncreated One . . . the Alpha and the Omega . . . the first and the last . . . He who was and is and is to come . . . the Blessed and only Sovereign . . . who alone possesses immortality and dwells in unapproachable light (Rev 1:8, 1Tim 6:15-16). *No one* created Him. He always was and always will be. Before He created the universe, God was here – *forever*. God is in complete and utter control of everything, great and small, from wars to famines to how much traffic is piled up on the highway today.

But don't just take *my* word for it. Go right to *His* Word.[3]

Is God Responsible for Suffering?

The LORD said to him [Moses]: "Who gave human beings their mouths? Who makes them deaf or mute? Who gives them sight or makes them blind? Is it not I, the LORD?"

Exodus 4:11

These are things our hearts bleed over. An innocent child born blind or deaf. A man suffers a stroke and can no longer speak. God states here in black and white, **"Is it not I, the LORD"** who causes these things.

"I have wounded and it is I who heal."

Deuteronomy 32:39 NASB

God wounds? Does that mean as in car accidents, land mines, terrorist bombs? God *wounds*? Why would He ever even claim responsibility for such things?

The lot is cast into the lap, but its every decision is from the LORD.

Proverbs 16:33

The Lord controls the lot, the roll of the dice, the game of chance. Surprising? This might be bad news for those in Vegas. God is even controlling the roll of the dice.

The LORD Almighty has sworn, "Surely, as I have planned, so it will be, and as I have purposed, so it will happen . . . For the LORD Almighty has purposed, and who can thwart him? His hand is stretched out, and who can turn it back?"

Isaiah 14:24,27

No one can turn back His hand.

"I form the light and create darkness, I bring prosperity and create disaster; I, the LORD, do all these things."

Isaiah 45:7

God *creates* disaster? As in earthquakes? Tsunamis? Hurricanes? Tornadoes? This is the hand of the Lord? If God is good, why would He **create** disaster?

Is it not from the mouth of the Most High that both calamities and good things come?

Lamentations 3:38

Calamities? From the mouth of the Most High? Does it really say that?

"I will repay you for your conduct and for the detestable practices among you. Then you will know that it is I the LORD who strikes you."

Ezekiel 7:9

"I the Lord who strikes you." He takes all the blame.

> **"Praise be to the name of God**
> **for ever and ever;**
> **wisdom and power are his.**
> **He changes times and seasons;**
> **he deposes kings and raises up others.**
> **He gives wisdom to the wise and**
> **knowledge to the discerning.**
> **He reveals deep and hidden things;**
> **he knows what lies in darkness,**
> **and light dwells with him."**

Daniel 2:20-22

He changes times and seasons. He raises up kings and deposes them.

What is God telling us here? Listen to these verses! From good things to calamities, from deafness to prosperity, from seasons to the roll of the dice, God is telling us that *He* is in control. He is completely sovereign over all the heavens and all the earth. Sovereign. An attribute of God that we may rather not think about, yet it is so crucial that God uses it for His very Name: Adonai.

"Sovereign" is the Hebrew word Adonai, which means "Lord." This Name "points to the supreme authority or power of God." Adonai derives from a root word meaning "to rule." Adonai is "controller, lord, master, owner."⁴ Adonai is our Lord and Master, the Matchless Controller, the One who possesses supreme authority and unlimited power, who reigns completely over all of heaven and all of earth. *Sovereign* is surely a word we can use to summarize these verses.

Let's go right back to Job. God gave Satan the nod of approval, and . . .

. . . **Satan went out from the presence of the LORD. One day when Job's sons and daughters were feasting and drinking wine at the oldest brother's house, a messenger came to Job and said, "The oxen were plowing and the donkeys were grazing nearby, and the Sabeans attacked and carried them off. They put the servants to the sword, and I am the only one who has escaped to tell you!"**

While he was still speaking, another messenger came and said, "The fire of God fell from the heavens and burned up the sheep and the servants, and I am the only one who has escaped to tell you!"

While he was still speaking, another messenger came and said, "The Chaldeans formed three raiding parties and swept down on your camels and made off with them. They put the servants to the sword, and I am the only one who has escaped to tell you!"

While he was still speaking, yet another messenger came and said, "Your sons and daughters were feasting and drinking wine at the oldest brother's house, when suddenly a mighty wind swept in from the desert and struck the four corners of the house. It collapsed on them and they are dead, and I am the only one who has escaped to tell you!"

Job 1:12-19

There are no words to describe this devastation.

So . . . is God responsible for man's suffering? Job sure wants to know. He spends chapter upon chapter railing against God, demanding an answer and a reason why. God doesn't leave us hanging. He answers, all right: four chapters worth. Listen to a bit of God's answer.

"Who is this that obscures my plans with words without knowledge? . . . I will question you, and you shall answer me. Where were you when I laid the earth's foundation? . . . Who shut up the sea behind doors when it burst forth from the womb? . . . Have you ever given orders to the morning, or shown the dawn its place?"

Job 38:2,3,4,8,12

✳   God doesn't explain Himself. What He does do is take on full responsibility. His answer is that *He* is the Almighty One, *He* is in charge of heaven and earth, and *He* knows what He is doing. **The LORD has made everything for his own purposes** (Pr 16:4 NLT).

Are We Puppets?

I don't know about you, but right about now I'm feeling like a mere puppet. All this talk of "free will" seems like nonsense if all these verses are true.

How exactly can God *decree* but not actually *do* it? How can He work out everything for His own purposes *without* violating man's free will?[5]

Let's go back to Job for some answers. Recall that Satan asked God for permission, which God granted. Now who, or what, caused Job's sufferings? On the first level, desert

winds and evil people did. It appears no one coerced the
Sabeans or Chaldeans; they were out to perform wicked
deeds of their own evil devices. On the next level, Satan
was the culprit. Satan planned it all. Yet on the final
absolute level, God decreed it. God took full responsibility
for Job's suffering, fulfilling His own ends, with plans that
He never explained to Job. Yet look closely how free will
was never violated. Both Satan and the evil men acted
freely.

This is frightening. It makes God out to be some kind
of sadist. Why would He *plan* for us to suffer?

Right now you may be justifying a few things in your
minds, thinking, Okay, maybe God plans some trials.
Maybe God planned my broken leg because then I met this
doctor in the hospital who soon became my husband . . .
but decreeing murder and amputations and child abuse?
That is going too far.

Hold on for a minute. Let's go to a few more verses:

**Who can speak and have it happen if the LORD
has not decreed it?**
                                                      Lamentations 3:37

**"Men of Israel, listen to these words: Jesus the
Nazarene . . . delivered over by the predetermined
plan and foreknowledge of God, you nailed to a
cross by the hands of godless men and put Him to
death."**
                                                      Acts 2:22-23 NASB

**"Lord, You are God . . . truly against Your holy
Servant Jesus, whom You anointed, both Herod and
Pontius Pilate, with the Gentiles and the people of
Israel, were gathered together to do whatever Your
hand and Your purpose determined before to be
done."**
                                                      Acts 4:24, 27-28 NKJV

God's hand and purpose decided Jesus' death *beforehand*? Jesus' death was by the *predetermined* plan and foreknowledge of God? What exactly does that mean? What does **decree** mean anyway?[6]

To Decree

To decree is "to determine . . . beforehand."[7] I have heard it paraphrased this way: to decide an issue in advance and make sure that it happens as planned.[8] Let's hear that again: to decide an issue in advance and make sure that it happens as planned. This does not mean to *invent* the evil, but to decide in advance what evil will be *permitted*, and then to ensure that it happens *according to the plan* – the plan that only the Creator of the Universe knows in its entirety, the plan that completes the Kingdom.

So there is no easy out here. These verses clearly state that *God* planned Jesus' death – not men, not Satan. God, the Trinity, the Father, Son, and Holy Spirit, decreed Jesus' death. Jesus decreed His own death. The Trinity decreed all the people involved, as well as the exact means, the crucifixion. God ordained it, willed it, determined it, decreed it, planned it. We can't get away with saying, "A loving God could never decree horrible acts of sin and violence."[9] Our backs are to the wall. We are really in trouble now. Nothing, *nothing* happens outside of the will of God. With our finite brains struggling to comprehend God's infinite plan, we may never understand His reasons, but if we accept that the Bible is God's word, we must accept that God is in charge. In things large and small, wonderful and heart wrenching, God has planned it, decreed it, willed it. Did God *invent* crucifixion? No. Romans explains that when God gives wicked men over to depravity, they invent evil (Rom 1:30). They invent evil, however, with God's predetermined plan and foreknowledge. God planned it would happen and knew *how* it would happen, Jesus agreed to it before He came from heaven, and God ensured it happened in such a way that would fulfill His purposes, for His Kingdom and His glory.

Again you may ask, where is the free will? Pause a moment and think of Judas. Remember, he was responsible for his sins. Jesus says of him,

"The Son of Man will go as it has been decreed. But woe to that man who betrays him."

Luke 22:22

This is so hard. Can we really concede that God is in complete control? It's frightening to think that God decrees the carnage of wars, exploding mines, and atomic bombs. That He determines rape and incest and child abuse. That He ordains paralysis and murder and cancer. It's so frightening to think in these terms. We wonder, *Is He really in control?*

I think at this point I have to agree with Joni Eareckson Tada when she writes, if God *"didn't* deliberately permit the smallest details of your particular sorrows . . . [then] your suffering itself would be meaningless."[10] **The LORD has made everything for His own purposes** (Pr 16:4 NLT). *Everything.* The pleasure as well as the pain, the comfort as well as the adversity, the mountaintop as well as the valley. He has made it for His purposes. For His eternal plan. Our suffering is *not* meaningless.

How Can God Have Sovereignty And We Have Free Will?

Good question. I'm glad you asked.

No sin happens that God does not determine in advance. He decrees it, He ordains it, He decides it in advance and makes sure it happens as planned. Yet He does not *originate* the sin. Evil occurs in the *absence* of God, when men reject God and He gives them over to depravity. Men sin when they follow Satan and suppress the truth and invent evil (Rom 1:30, Jn 8:44, Jer 19:5, 32:35). God merely directs Satan and people so that they accomplish the evil they intended, but at the same time fulfill His own eternal plan. I like how Joni Eareckson Tada puts it: "God sees the evil already there and *steers* it to serve his good purposes and not merely Satan's viperous ones. It's as if he says, 'So you want to sin? Go ahead – but I'll make sure you sin in a way that ultimately furthers my ends even while you're shaking your fist in my face.' "[11]

How can He do this? *Who knows?* With our little pea-brain minds we think we know the infinite eternal inscrutable mind of God? Ecclesiastes states it so graphically,

As you do not know the path of the wind, or how the body is formed in a mother's womb, so you cannot understand the work of God, the Maker of all things.

Ecclesiastes 11:5

How a body is formed in a mother's womb. I just need to be silent on that one.

The Bottom of the Tapestry

When a craftsman is creating a tapestry, little children may gather around to watch. Because they only see the bottom side, from their perspective down below, it looks like a mess. They generally cannot comprehend, cannot

even imagine, what its final beauty will be. When he is
finished, and turns it over for all to see, the artwork is
glorious to behold.

We are like those children down below, looking at the
back of God's tapestry that He is so carefully, painstakingly
weaving. We cannot possibly imagine what He is creating
— we only see the strings and the knots and the loops! Yet
at the end of the world we will see His Kingdom in all its
glory, and *then* we will understand. Occasionally, He may
allow us to glimpse the top side that He is working on, and
we watch, spellbound, as He works. More often, we only
see the bottom side. It is then that He calls us to trust His
heart, His hands, and His great love for us.

I would like to introduce you to a real powerhouse for
the Lord. Struggling with accepting God's sovereignty,
Brittany spent quite a few years angry, frustrated, and
embarrassed by an uncontrollable event in her life. It
wasn't until God let her peek at the top of the tapestry
that she was truly able to bow to His perfect plan.

*I failed third grade. It ate away at me my whole life.
All throughout my school years, I endured taunts because
I was considered stupid. I thought all of that would be
behind me when I left school, but the tormenting persisted
into adulthood, as people discovered that the year I
graduated college matched their graduation year, and then
were shocked to find we were not the same age.*
*But one season God showed me the top of the tapestry.
I was used by Him as He brought 42 people into His
Kingdom. Had I not failed third grade, I would never have
been in that place at that time to be His chosen instrument.
He made it so clear to me that if I had not failed third
grade, I would not have been so strategically positioned to
be His mouthpiece during that season, and those 42 people
would not have come to know Christ. I am embarrassed
at the number of times I cried out to Him in anger and*

frustration because I had failed third grade. I will never again question the humiliation of failing that year, and I would endure it all again for those 42 people!

Brittany
Philadelphia, Pennsylvania

I can relate to Brittany, for at times I fight against His sovereign hand. Like Job, I may demand a reason why. Sometimes, God in His graciousness will give me a glimpse of the top of the tapestry. My goal, however, as I mature in Christ, is to bow my heart to His sovereignty even *before* the glimpse. My aim is to trust that God is working for my good, to trust that He may be equipping me or "strategically positioning me" for His Kingdom work.

Jacob's son Joseph knows something about being "strategically positioned." He was sold into slavery by his brothers, then imprisoned for years for a crime he did not commit (Gen Ch 37-41). Upon interpreting Pharaoh's dream predicting an impending famine, Joseph was released from prison, set over all the land of Egypt, and given charge of storing food for the upcoming famine. Psalm 105 explains that when Abraham's descendants were few in number, God called for a famine upon the land. But God had already sent a man before them, Joseph, who was sold as a slave. Joseph arranged for them to move to Egypt to survive the famine, and while in Egypt God caused His people to be very fruitful, so that over 600,000 men (plus women and children) crossed the Red Sea traveling back to the Promised Land (Ps 105:12, 16, 17, 24, Ex 12:37).

God sent Joseph ahead of them. Joseph did not meet his brothers again until years after they had sold him into slavery. Expressing his forgiveness, Joseph said to them, **"You meant evil against me, but God meant it for good in order to bring about this present result, to preserve many people alive"** (Gen 50:20

NASB). Joseph accepted God's sovereignty. Joseph understood that he had been strategically positioned.

The Potter Crafts Our Days

All the days ordained for me were written in your book before one of them came to be.
Psalm 139:16

We studied this verse in Chapter 2, as we looked at our number of days here on earth. This time, we are going to look at the word **ordain**. To ordain is the Hebrew word yatsar – this is a beautiful word with the idea of "Potter" stamped all over it. Listen to what my Word Study Dictionary says:

> To form, to fashion, to shape, to devise. The primary meaning of the word is derived from the idea of cutting or framing. It is used of God's fashioning man from the dust of the ground; God's creative works in nature and in the womb; the molding of clay; the framing of seasons; the forging of metal; the crafting of weapons; the making of plans. It also signifies a potter; a sculptor; of the Creator.[12]

God has skillfully crafted every one of our days, as a Potter shapes a vase, as a Sculptor carves a figure, as a Silversmith forges a cup. There is meaning and purpose in each moment that He has crafted for us, whether the moment is pleasurable or painful.

Remember that to "decree" or to "ordain" means to decide an issue in advance and make sure that it happens as planned. Remember also that God does not invent the evil. Now I want you to recognize that when God decrees tribulations for us, He does not let Satan run rampant through our lives (Lk 22:31, Job 1:11). He allows only that which will accomplish His plan for us and for His Kingdom. But why would He decree *hardships* for us? We will explore this deeper in upcoming chapters, but let's get a glimpse right now. God can use suffering to

- Advance His Kingdom
- Prepare us for His Kingdom work on earth
- Prepare us for our rewards and responsibilities in eternity with Him

God ordains adversities that are tailored perfectly for each one of us. He *handpicks* these trials.

I have asked my friend Dawn to wrap up this chapter describing her collision with God's sovereignty, and the unexpected blessings that came out of a time of great torment.

I went to a mental health clinic, seeking help for depression. The doctor there asked me if I was going to kill myself. I told him that I am a Christian and would not do that, but sometimes I wished God would take me home. He Baker Acted me – had me admitted to a locked ward against my will. He wrote down lies that I said I was going to kill myself – things I never said. They told me I could not leave until they said I could – I was at their mercy. It was an awful, horrible experience. I felt like I was in prison. I was scared to death, but I knew God was with me.

I prayed and prayed – and I realized that God put me there to speak to some girls in my room about Him – so I did. It would never have been my choice to be in that mental hospital, but if that was God's will, I was ready to be used by Him.

Months later, I learned that my stay in the mental hospital is what got me approved for permanent disability. God put me in that mental institution to reach those girls,

but also to give me the blessing of money for my permanent
disability.

Dawn
Wake Forest, North Carolina

Yes, He ordains. Yes, He decrees. But see His hand
of protection. Feel the immensity of His love. Recognize
that we do not know the future, nor can we control it; He
knows every moment, and holds our lives in His hands.
First Corinthians describes it as the contrast of seeing
something in a dark mirror vs. seeing clearly:

Now we see things imperfectly, like a puzzling
reflection in a mirror, but then we will see everything
with perfect clarity. All that I know now is partial
and incomplete, but then I will know everything
completely, just as God knows me now.
1 Corinthians 13:12 NLT

Even when God gives us a glimpse of the top of the
tapestry, realize that it is still only a glimpse. Our little
pea-brains cannot fathom His plans, His purposes, or the
depth of His love. He doesn't expect us to understand.
What He does call us to do is to trust His love through the
pain. To trust *Him*.

When God, in His omniscience, has placed us where
we do not want to be, we can spend that season fighting
against Him. We can spend the entire time immersing in
self-pity, or railing against Him in anger, or wallowing in
hopelessness, despondency, and depression. Or . . . we can
work *with* Him. We can trust the tenderness of His love.
We can bow our hearts to His sovereignty. We can humbly
ask Him what *He* would like to accomplish in our hearts
and in our lives during this season of His making.

If God has decreed that the illness will continue, that
the trial will rage on, that the suffering will persist, it does

not mean that our faith is not strong enough, or God is not powerful enough, or we are not righteous enough. It simply indicates that our spiritual growth and His Kingdom work are much more important to Him than our comforts here on earth. It simply reveals that He is working a plan that is more immense than we can possibly imagine, whose purpose is for *His* glory – and for *our* good (Rev 4:11, Rom 8:28). What He is concerned about is our *response*. The question He poses to us is, "Will you work with Me, or will you fight against Me?"

We serve an Almighty Sovereign God, a God who declares, **"I have wounded and it is I who heal"** (Dt 32:39 NASB), yet who loves us so passionately that He came to earth to be ruthlessly murdered so that we could spend eternity with Him. Infinite love plus absolute sovereignty. What an extraordinary combination! Maybe, at this point, we cannot possibly imagine the purpose of our suffering. Yet we can choose to bow to His sovereignty, while trusting His heart.

Chapter 5
Suffering Can Work To Conform Us To the Image of Christ

*M*y son Alec is in physical therapy as I write, just beginning a six month rehab of a torn ligament and meniscus in his knee. His physical therapist explained to him, "The definition of suffering is pain without knowing the reason why. You know why you have pain, so although your rehab will be very difficult, it won't be overwhelming."[1] That really struck me. I realized how desperately we desire understanding, and how that understanding can make seemingly unbearable pain become bearable.

I also realized that for many of us, the *physical* reasons why we suffer may simply not be enough to assuage the pain in our hearts. Alec may know that his knee hurts because he just had surgery, but he may not know why God sidelined a very active 19 year-old guy, who was studying hard in college, had started his own business, and was planning a summer internship – and turned his life upside down on its head.

Sometimes, when we ask why, we receive this answer:

For my thoughts are not your thoughts, neither are your ways my ways," declares the LORD. "As the heavens are higher than the earth, so are my ways higher than your ways and my thoughts than your thoughts."

Isaiah 55:8-9

It's the answer God gave Job. No wonder we cannot even *imagine* the top of the tapestry! The limited trying to fathom the Limitless. Yet, I truly believe there are many times God *desires* to give us a glimpse of what He is working. He loves us so much, and He knows that we may need a ray of hope to persevere in the trials. With deep reverence and awe, and while bowing to His sovereignty, let's ask the Holy Spirit for a deep understanding of some of the causes of our sorrows.

Understand that some of what we study may relate to you right now, some may relate to you at other times in your walk with Christ, and some may not relate to you at all. Allow the Holy Spirit to be your Teacher. As we seek revelation by studying His Word, we will realize our limitations, and we will depend on the Holy Spirit to speak to us. As we work through these chapters, there are three truths I want you to keep in mind.

- Afflictions are not a "punishment" for sin. If we are imagining God on His almighty throne aiming lightning bolts at down at sinners, we may be confusing Him with Zeus (Jn 9:3, Ps 103:8-10).

- A key in triumphing over suffering is to face forward. If our poor choices played a role in our anguish, it is imperative that we recognize them in order to repent and to avoid those mistakes in the future.

However, our *focus* must be on what is ahead. In God's hands, our suffering is *not* meaningless.

- Revelation is through the Holy Spirit. He is the One who will reveal to you what God is working through your agony.

Though we may not always be able to comprehend His plan, He calls us to trust His heart. Infinite love plus absolute sovereignty.

God's Definition of Good

Paul was persecuted, beaten, stoned, imprisoned, shipwrecked, and eventually martyred (2Cor 11:23-27); yet he has a good handle on the infinite love plus absolute sovereignty concept. Listen to what he writes in Romans:

And we know that in all things God works for the good of those who love him, who have been called according to his purpose. For those God foreknew he also predestined to be conformed to the image of his Son . . .

Romans 8:28-29

Look at this verse closely. What exactly does **good** mean? Good is the Greek word agathos. There are a lot of layers of meaning to this word; let's read a few definitions which I think are relevant here: "useful, beneficial, profitable."[2] Agathos implies useful and profitable blessings that are what we *need*, not necessarily what we *want*. Agathos is *not* ice cream for your child for dinner just because you want to put a smile on his face.

I see agathos as Jesus in the temple, chastising the merchants in order to set things right in His Father's house (Jn 2:14-16). I see agathos as God allowing us the consequences of our sin in order to bring us back to right relationship with Him. I see agathos as the good that God is always working in our lives to accomplish His goal.

What *is* His goal? Read that verse again: **to conform us to the image of his Son**. Stop right there. This is *God's* definition of good. Anything that conforms us to Jesus' image. That might not match up with our definition of good. No wonder we have trouble understanding Him! No wonder we don't accept our suffering! God is giving us what we *need*, not necessarily what we *want*. Realize, though, that as we are conformed more and more to Jesus' likeness, as our heart becomes His heart, what we *want* will come closer to what God has determined we *need*.

In *all* things God works for the good. All things. Let's get **all** crystal clear in our minds. This word **all** means *all*. Every, everything, completely, always, continually, the whole universe, forevermore. In other words, all. In beautiful circumstances and treacherous ones, God is working for good.

For everyone's good? No, it doesn't say that. It says **for the good of those who love him, who have been called according to his purpose**. Those who love Him. Love. Agape. We discussed this word in Chapter 2. God is working for good to those who give Him agape, who give Him unconditional, freely given love, who fulfill their purposes with unconditional obedience, no matter the circumstances. For me, agape means that when I am in the depth of misery, I am not wallowing in anger or self-pity, but I am coming humbly to Him with my heart open to His transforming power, ready to be conformed to the image of His Son.

Faith Can Be Proved Genuine in Suffering

Let's read from Peter, James, and Paul, who all address trials. Peter reminds us to rejoice *despite* our trials because of the reward awaiting us in heaven, and then he says,

In this [our heavenly rewards] **you greatly rejoice, though now for a little while you may have had to suffer grief in all kinds of trials. These have come so that the proven genuineness of your faith— of greater worth than gold, which perishes even though refined by fire—may result in praise, glory and honor when Jesus Christ is revealed.**

1 Peter 1:6-7

This analogy is right on target. Our trials are fire. Our faith is similar to gold, but more valuable because it is imperishable. We discussed faith in Chapter 3, pistis, an action word that means we believe so deeply that we live like we believe it. We know God's heart and will, we live out our lives in trust of our beliefs, and even in times of trouble we never stop trusting Him. It seems to take time, experiences, and tests and trials to grow our faith and to prove it genuine. Deep faith generally does not just appear overnight.

When gold is thrust into the fire, the impurities and unwanted materials rise to the surface and are removed. Similarly, when our faith is thrust into the fires of our trials, the unwanted materials can rise to the surface. Only God knows what is in our hearts (Jer 17:10, Ps 139:23-24). Pride, selfishness, idolatry, rebellion, independence, unforgiveness, control, stubbornness, refusal to trust Him, are just a few of the many sins that may be lurking in our hearts. When these sins are exposed, we now have the opportunity to repent and to invite God to purify us.

I'd like to introduce you to Helen and Edmund. This dear couple has been part of my husband's life since he was very young, and as another set of parents they have spoken into both of our lives over the years. Edmund's story brings to life the concept of faith in the fire. As he speaks, watch how the fires of the trial cause his lack of trust in God to surface, and how gently God leads him to a new level of trust in Him.

My wife was fighting for her life, hospitalized for pneumonia, her condition deteriorating slowly with no hope in sight. Each time I entered the hospital I went into the chapel, knelt, and flipped the pages of the Bible to a random section. Each time the words were startlingly profound, amazingly relevant, and mysteriously soothing. Each time I prayed for a miracle, and waited for a sign from heaven that Helen would recover.

On Sunday, the priest spoke about calling upon God for help when we are sick. "The granting of our prayers enforces our faith," he said.

*That night, as I was driving to the hospital, my headlights reflected a sign on the rear bumper of a pickup truck. The reflection became brighter and brighter, brilliant as a neon sign on Times Square. The sign, three times the size of the license plate and ringed by bright silvery stars, announced, "**Expect a Miracle**." The sign was so bright it was blinding, bringing tears to my eyes, and as I watched, it reflected every color of the rainbow.*

The following day Helen's fever broke. For the first time in seven days she was able to talk without gasping for air. Helen would soon recover.

The trial, the unmistakable sign from God, and the miracle of answered prayer strengthened my shaky faith in an amazing way, bringing me to trust God more deeply and to recognize that God was always watching over me.

Edmund
Stuart, Florida

From "shaky faith" to "trust God more deeply." I suspect that somehow, the faith development wouldn't have happened without the trial.

I want you to notice something else here. Edmund was not the one in the hospital. Helen was. Sometimes, we have no idea why we are suffering. Sometimes, it could be to grow *someone else's* faith. His ways, higher than our ways . . .

Dokime

It can be easy to say that we trust God when life is smooth. But we read in First Peter that it is *the trials* that prove our faith genuine. Genuine. Dokime. Examining the Greek, what comes through most clearly to me about this word is the idea of *tested and proved*. Tested and proved genuine. Listen to some of the definitions:

- "Proof of genuineness, trustworthiness."[3]
- "Tested"[4]
- "Tried, and approved"[5]
- "Proving whether something is worthy or not"[6]

Dokime is a word used to describe metals that are "tried by fire and thus purified," so pure that they are "without alloy."[7] Figuratively, dokime means "approved to be acceptable men in the furnace of adversity."[8] Specifically, that means one has been commended not by men, but *by God*.

Dokime. Tested and proved genuine. I have heard it said that in Jesus' time, clay pots were tested by fire, and those that did not crack were stamped "Dokime," or "Genuine," on the bottom. When we, as earthen vessels, are thrust into the fire, and we hold fast to God with

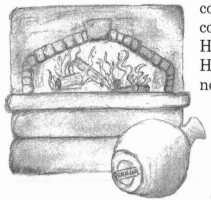

courage and faith, when we continue to believe that He is who He says He is and will do what He says He will do, when we do not abandon trust in Him, we can emerge from the fire intact and strengthened. Then, like those clay pots, we can bear that seal, "Genuine."

Trial by fire can be petrifying. Yet listen to God's promise when we are in the fire of our trials:

> But now, this is what the LORD says . . .
> "Do not fear, for I have redeemed you;
> I have summoned you by name; you are mine . . .
> When you walk through the fire, you will not be
>   burned;
> The flames will not set you ablaze . . .
> Since you are precious and honored in my sight,
>   and because I love you."
>
>   Isaiah 43:1,2,4

When we are in the fire of our trials, Jesus is with us. We will not be burned because we are precious, honored, and loved. Could we ask for more?

The Goal of Our Trials: To Bring Glory To God

The final result of the trials? Peter writes that the deepening of our faith results in **praise, glory, and honor of God.** How exactly does that happen? How can something as hideous as our suffering bring glory to God? I have some thoughts.

- In the midst of our woes, we can choose to turn to God and worship. When we worship in suffering, we worship Him not for comforts and pleasures on earth, but for *who He is*. This is the purest form of worship, the worship that pleases Him.

- If our hearts are open through our hardships, God can reveal our sin to us, giving us a chance to repent and to allow Him to conform us to Jesus' image. Our faith can then be refined, and Jesus can be revealed through us in a deeper and more glorious way.

- Praising God in the midst of the agony can have a phenomenal impact. People may pay no attention to praise of God when things are going well for the praiser. Yet when the one who is praising is suffering, it can be awe-inspiring! People may stop to listen, to find out what someone who is suffering has to praise about.

- Finally, as our faith is deepened through the trial, if we remain ready to obey, God may give us work for the Kingdom that we may not have been able to do if we had remained in a state of weaker faith. God calls this "equipping" (2Tim 3:16-17, Heb 13:20-21).

Responding to Trials With Joy

Let's see what James says about trials.

Consider it pure joy, my brothers, whenever you face trials of many kinds . . .

James 1:2

Hold on – this is different than First Peter. God tells us in First Peter to rejoice *despite* our afflictions because we are focused on heavenly rewards. Yet God is telling us in James to consider the trials *themselves* pure joy. Joy, in suffering? Are You sure? Let's read that again.

Consider it pure joy, my brothers, whenever you face trials of many kinds, because you know that the testing of your faith produces perseverance. Let perseverance finish its work so that you may be mature and complete, not lacking in anything.

James 1:2-4

Note the definiteness of suffering here. James doesn't say "if you face trials" or "maybe possibly if you happen to have a trial," but he says **whenever you face trials**. There is no question we will be facing them. The question is, will we respond as God desires? And what does God say our response should be? **Consider it pure joy.**

We can consider our trials to be joy because it is God working to conform us to Jesus' image by testing our faith. During times of adversity, James says we can learn perseverance. Check out the depth of meaning in this word in the Greek, hupomone. It can be translated "patience, endurance, constancy under suffering in faith and duty."[9] I would call it steadfastness without succumbing under trial.

My Word Study Dictionary also emphasizes for hupomone the *peace* in the midst of the suffering, "bearing evils and suffering with a tranquil mind."[10] And *joy* is also a part of this word: "cheerful or hopeful endurance."[11]

Perseverance is bearing up under with courage and trust. Perseverance is enduring under tremendous weight without succumbing. Perseverance is clinging to Jesus when the circumstances of our life are crashing around us. This is how our faith can be matured. It seems to me that faith that has not been tested is not real faith; it is merely words. Faith that has been tested and persevered can become authentic faith, faith in action, faith that is alive and vibrant.

I'm going to ask Betsy back again to talk about what genuine faith means to her. You met Betsy in Chapter 2; she is an unwavering soldier on my *Triumph* Servant Leadership Team.

I had never really had anything bad happen to me before I was diagnosed with breast cancer. God used this time of suffering to grow me to become more spiritually mature and to become a better person. There were so many Scriptures I did not understand until I went through this valley. I began to understand how we must go through fire to be refined and shine like gold, or how we must be beaten and threshed like grain to become wheat. I felt I had "fast-forwarded" to meeting Jesus; nothing else was important.

I have definitely become a kinder, gentler person; I know what my priorities are, and I take one day at a time. I have seized Jesus' words, "Do not worry about tomorrow, for tomorrow will take care of itself. Each day has enough troubles of its own" (Mt 6:34).

I heard more than one survivor say that breast cancer was the best thing that had ever happened to them. I first thought they were crazy, but as I traveled along the journey, I slowly began to understand what they meant. I truly became more spiritually mature and I think a better person because of the experience. And if it took getting cancer to meet the people I have met, then it was truly worth it.

Betsy Burden
Triumph Servant Leader
Christ Fellowship Church and Church in the Gardens
Palm Beach Gardens, Florida

Having mature faith is being certain deep in our hearts that God is working for our good because we are those who love God. It is to trust that He is working, always working, to grow us to be more like Christ, even if it does not make sense right now. Deep faith can require courage, huge courage, because having faith is daring to believe that things are not always as they may seem to be to the outside observer. It is daring to believe that God is working everything for good, even when we cannot see Him at work, even when it *appears* that nothing good could ever come of this, even when we only see the bottom of the tapestry.

Peter and James have weighed in on suffering. Let's read what Paul has to say.

We exult in hope of the glory of God. And not only this, but we also exult in our tribulations, knowing that tribulation brings about perseverance; and perseverance, proven character; and proven character, hope; and hope does not disappoint, because the love of God has been poured out within our hearts through the Holy Spirit who was given to us.

Romans 5:2-5 NASB

In this passage, God instructs us to exult in two things: our tribulations, and the hope of the glory of God. If, when we are suffering, our hearts are open to God to be transformed to be like Christ, we can develop perseverance, or hupomone, which then can develop character. Character is dokime, the same word as genuineness from First Peter. Now how does all that lead to hope? That sounds like a far stretch to me.

Hope in the Greek is elpis; its definition spans three pages in my Word Study Dictionary.[12] If I had to summarize these pages in just a few words I would say confident expectation. As I study these pages, I see elpis is not simply wishing. Elpis is hope with the complete confidence of the end result; expecting, trusting, *knowing* that God will make it happen according to His plan. Elpis is a sure thing, a certainty, but a certainty that has not yet happened.

Realize that elpis includes patience: waiting on God's perfect timing for that certain outcome. And most importantly, we must recognize that *God* determines the outcome. His plan, not ours. Our hope is sure, because it is dependent upon the only One who can make it happen. Our hope is not dependent upon us.

When I read that word **hope** in the Bible, I have my mind trained to think, "courage to trust." And if I want a clearer picture, I think, "courage to trust while I wait on God's timing for His promised outcome."

Now what exactly are we hoping for? What is His promised outcome? Look back at that verse: **we exult in hope of the glory of God.** It is a sure thing that our trials will bring glory to God – *if* we are persevering and allowing our character to be proven, and allowing God to pour out His love into our hearts by the Holy Spirit.

But what if . . . what if the trial is too much for us? What if we can't persevere through it? God knew you would ask. As you read His answer, realize that the word **temptation** in this verse can also be translated **trial.**[13]

No temptation [or trial] **has overtaken you except what is common to mankind. And God is faithful; he will not let you be tempted** [or tried] **beyond what you can bear. But when you are tempted** [or tried]**, he will also provide a way out so that you can endure.**
                                                         1 Corinthians 10:13

Joyce Meyer, nationally known author and speaker, explains it this way: "With God, you never fail a test. God just keeps administering it until you pass it."[14] I like that thought. This is much better than school. God administers the tests and trials necessary, never abandoning us, never giving up on us, but patiently leading us through what He knows is vital to bring us closer to Him.

We are suffering; God is working. God defines tests and trials as **good** because they are necessary to grow our faith. Now *that* is an entirely new perspective. That is *God's* perspective. His thoughts, higher than our thoughts (Isa 55:9).

He Is the Potter; We Are the Clay

The Potter is molding us, shaping us, conforming us to Jesus' image.

But who are you, O human being, to talk back to God? "Shall what is formed say to the one who formed it, 'Why did you make me like this?' " Does not the potter have the right to make out of the same lump of clay some pottery for special purposes and some for common use?

Romans 9:20-21

Did God just call us lumps of clay? He sure did. And you think being a lump of clay is bad? In Isaiah God calls us *potsherds*:

"Woe to those who quarrel with their Maker, those who are nothing but a potsherd among the potsherds on the ground."

Isaiah 45:9

A potsherd is "a sharp fragment of broken pottery,"[15] a practically useless broken chip of earthenware. Pause a moment and look at the potsherds pictured on the spine of this book. Think about the Potter tenderly taking His potsherds and shaping them for His glory.

Now look at the cover. Take in His scars, feel His infinite love. Do not forget that the King of all Kings came to earth from the everlasting and *died* for us potsherds. Do not miss the fierceness of His love. And now, drenched in His infinite love, bow your heart to His absolute sovereignty.

Only the Potter knows how we should look, for He chooses our purpose. He wants us to be soft and flexible, because the shape He desires us to be in today is not necessarily the shape He desires us to be in tomorrow.

Today, His purpose for me may be to bring the gospel message to someone who does not know Him. But tomorrow, His purpose for me may be to clean up a patient's vomit in clinic. If I am not soft and pliable in His hands, I am useless, and He may choose to use trials and sufferings to bring me back to that soft and pliable state. He demands that I trust His workmanship, knowing that I will only be useful to Him when I am in the shape He has planned for me. For He determines my purpose, and only He knows if the person whose vomit I cleaned up today will be the one I bring the gospel to tomorrow.

Chapter 6
Suffering Can Open Our Eyes To Our Sin

e have been exploring what God says in His Word about why we suffer, and we have learned three possible reasons for our tribulations and trials:

- To conform us to Christ's image
- To grow our faith and prepare us for more difficult kingdom work
- To glorify God by bringing us to a more pure worship of Him

As you read the title of this chapter, your heart might have done a little flip-flop. I want to tread very gently here, for I know that some of you may be suffering deeply as a result of *others'* sins. You may wonder, how can God be talking to me about some minor sin of mine, when someone else's major sin has raged on unchecked, seemingly without consequences, seemingly ignored by God?

I know exactly how you feel. I have been there. But what I want you to understand at this time is that no sin, great or small, escapes God's notice. God commands us to focus on our *own* relationship with Him, and to trust Him to be fair and righteous Judge. This chapter is about getting *our own hearts* right with God.

Is My Sin the Cause of My Suffering?

Allow me to clarify. I want you to really understand that although sin in general is the cause of pain and suffering, and although we may certainly suffer consequences because of our sins or poor choices, our personal sufferings are *not* matched up on a "one-to-one correspondence" with our own sins. I'll say it again. Our sufferings are not matched up in one-to-one correspondence with our sins.

Read what Jesus says to the man born blind from birth, and the explanation that follows.

As he went along, he saw a man blind from birth. His disciples asked him, "Rabbi, who sinned, this man or his parents, that he was born blind?"
"Neither this man nor his parents sinned," said Jesus, "but this happened so that the works of God might be displayed in him."

John 9:1-3

I like the way Joni Eareckson Tada explains it:

> Lest anyone misunderstand, John 9:1-3 and the Book of Job make it clear that our sufferings don't bear a one-to-one correspondence to our sins. In other words, just because I am diagnosed with cancer today doesn't mean that I recently sinned worse than my neighbor who is healthy. But we are all sinners by both birth and choice,

and so experience the sentence of suffering pronounced upon our race by God in Eden. God's reasoning in deciding how to distribute suffering is often a mystery.[1]

Do not think that because you are crushed with more hardships than someone else it means that you are a greater sinner. God's method in decreeing adversity for each of us is far beyond our ability to fathom. Hold these truths in your heart as we proceed through this chapter.

Let's spend some time in Romans to understand more clearly why this earth is in agony.

For we know that all creation has been groaning as in the pains of childbirth right up to the present time. And we believers also groan, even though we have the Holy Spirit within us as a foretaste of future glory, for we long for our bodies to be released from sin and suffering.

Romans 8:22-23 NLT

All creation groans. Even we Christians groan.

Clearly one of the reasons we suffer is simply because we live in a fallen world. Yet, why does the fact that the world is fallen cause us to groan? In order to answer this question, we will need to get a firm grasp on why we are here. Why did God create the universe? Why did God create mankind?

Why Are We Here?

We'll go to the Word to answer that question.

All things have been created through him and for him.

Colossians 1:16

"You created all things, and by your will they were created and have their being."

Revelation 4:11

This word **will** in my Word Study Dictionary includes "that which pleases and creates joy."[2] We were created *for Him*, for *His* glory, to *please* Him and give Him *joy*. I am deeply honored and very humbled.

For His *glory*. Glory in the Greek is doxa – its definition spans four pages in my Word Study Dictionary. Let's tease out what I think are the highlights of this definition.

The root word of doxa means "to recognize," thus doxa is "ascribing to God His full recognition." It includes "splendor, glory, dazzling light, infinite perfection, divine majesty and holiness." Doxa is "the aspect . . . which catches the eye, attracts attention, or commands recognition; the brilliance attracting the gaze."[3]

Doxa is the obvious presence of God. God in all His invincible power, His dazzling majesty, His perfect purity, His supreme sovereignty, His unchanging character, His utter faithfulness, His infinite love. God's glory is simply who He is. God's greatest desire is that mankind comes to know Him as He truly is:

- The entire universe, God's handiwork, reveals to us His breathtaking creativity and electrifying power (Ps 19:1-6).

- Jesus came as God in the flesh, to reveal to us the very character of God (Jn 14:9).

- At this time, since Jesus is no longer here in flesh and blood, God reveals who He is through *us*.

When others see God in us, we give God glory. Doxa in us. *This* is why we were created.

Did God Invent Evil?

Good question. I'm glad you asked. We touched on this in Chapter 4, but we'll go into more depth here. Let's look first at what happens when people reject God and do not fulfill their God-designed purposes.

For the wrath of God is revealed from heaven against all ungodliness and unrighteousness of men, who suppress the truth in unrighteousness, because that which is known about God is evident within them; for God made it evident to them. For since the creation of the world His invisible attributes, His eternal power and divine nature, have been clearly seen, being understood through what has been made, so that they are without excuse. For even though they knew God, they did not honor Him as God or give thanks; but they became futile in their speculations, and their foolish heart was darkened . . . Therefore God gave them over in the lusts of their hearts to impurity . . . For they exchanged the truth of God for a lie . . . And just as they did not see fit to acknowledge God any longer, God gave them over to a depraved mind, to do those things which are not proper, being filled with all unrighteousness, wickedness, greed, evil; full of envy, murder, strife, deceit, malice; they are gossips, slanderers, haters of God, insolent, arrogant, boastful, inventors of evil, disobedient to parents, without understanding, untrustworthy, unloving, unmerciful . . .

Romans 1:18-31 NASB

Romans teaches us that when people choose to suppress the truth of who God is, when men choose not to fulfill their purpose, choose not to glorify God, not to give thanks to God – then God may give them over to depravity. The literal translation of give them over is "to deliver over or up to the power of someone." Some other translations are "to yield up," or to "surrender" them.[4] God gives them over to what they themselves have chosen. God will not force Himself upon them. They *choose* not to acknowledge Him, so He steps out of their lives. And that leaves humans to live like humans live without God: **depraved**, meaning "rejected, by implication worthless."[5] All creation groans.

You ask why we suffer? Evil is the result of man's choice to *reject* God. Evil is what happens in the *absence* of God. All creation groans.

The root of all suffering is evil, sin, spiritual darkness. When Adam and Eve chose sin, suffering entered the world. Sin – our own sins and others' sins – are the cause of pain in this world today. God *did* create the perfect world (Gen 1:31), but that perfection was destroyed by sin. Initially, it was Adam and Eve's sin, but now our own sins continue to destroy His masterpiece. We have inherited sin through Adam, *and* willingly commit sins ourselves.

Therefore, just as sin entered the world through one man, and death through sin, and in this way death came to all men, because all sinned.

Romans 5:12

Suffering does not mean that God does not exist. Suffering is caused by man rejecting God: Adam and Eve's initial rejection, and our continued rejection today. Some people outright reject God. Others do seek Him in repentance. Yet all of us, even those seeking Him, are guilty of sin. And rarely does our sin affect us alone.

Does this mean that when we turn to God, all our woes will immediately disappear? We know from personal experience that this is not the case. Realize, though, that when we turn to God, although He may not remove the pain of living in this fallen world, He does offer us tremendous blessings. He heals us spiritually, and out of our spiritually healing may flow emotional, mental, and even physical healing. And if even He does not immediately heal us or instantly remove the pain, He does walk with us through our hardships. Also, as we draw nearer and nearer to Him, He can fill us with His peace, joy, and hope even in the darkest of valleys. He can enable us to walk in triumph even in the midst of adversity.

So can we blame it all on Satan? Well, Satan, *is* the father of lies, a murderer (Jn 8:44), a thief (Jn 10:10), the accuser (Rev 12:10), our enemy and adversary (1 Pet 5:8). and he can incite evil in us (1Chr 21:1). Yet Romans states clearly that we cannot simply blame it all on Satan. When humans do not glorify God or give Him thanks, when we do not acknowledge Him and come to Him in repentance, when we do not ask for forgiveness and sanctification, we can become the **inventors of evil** (Rom 1:30). All creation groans.

Clearly, God did not invent evil. Spiritual darkness is the absence of God. Satan and humans are the inventors of evil. Yet *God takes full responsibility* for the evil on this earth, as we learned from the Book of Job.   Evil exists only by God's permission. I agree with Joni Eareckson Tada when she says, "What's clear immediately is that God permits all sorts of things he doesn't approve of."[6]

We Can Multiply the Intensity Of Our Suffering

As you may have discovered, the hardships of living in a fallen world are compounded by our own sinful choices.[7]

Scripture confirms this: Psalms and Proverbs teach some tough principles.

Those who chase fantasies will have their fill of poverty.

Proverbs 28:19

A false witness will not go unpunished, and whoever pours out lies will not go free.

Proverbs 19:5

Some became fools through their rebellious ways and suffered affliction because of their iniquities.

Psalm 107:17

We can add a few of our own proverbs: A person who smokes risks lung cancer. A reckless driver invites an accident. Suffering is simply *being part of* all creation that groans (Rom 8:22). Yet we sure can multiply the intensity of our suffering by our own sinful choices.

Obedience Can Be Proven Genuine In Suffering

We don't want to live this way. We don't want God to give us over to depravity. How *do* we bring Him glory? I think I can summarize it with one word: obedience.

Take a deep breath now.   For some this may be a touchy topic. I want you to realize that obedience is a *choice*. Obedience cannot be coerced. When we obey, we accept that we are under God and dependent upon Him, so we *choose* to do His will.   Obedience is surrendering, submitting, giving God control of our lives. We choose to place *His* desires above our own.

Sometimes, we may rebel against God's laws.   We may refuse to obey His principles and statutes.   Yet

His commandments are for our *good*, they are for our protection. God created this world and the laws under which this world operates. By His Word, He reveals how the world functions, and how we can live abundantly. He outlines *His* path for us, for He knows that when we follow His ways in obedience, it will be for our greatest good.

I have asked a courageous friend of mine, Steven, to share his journey from rebellion to obedience.

I was prisoner to my addiction of homosexuality. When I gave my life to Christ, the Lord did not deliver me immediately. Although I was going to church several times a week, reading my Bible, praying, and growing in Christ in many other ways, I was still so trapped in my addiction. I contracted HIV a few years after I had given my life to Christ; shocked and humbled, I continued to struggle with my addiction. The HIV progressed to AIDS and I suffered from severe complications of the disease.

It took ten years to clear the filth out of my mind and to fill my mind with God's Word. Ten years to learn that I could not trust what the world tells me or what my own desire tells me, but only what the Word of God tells me. Ten years to uproot Satan's lies from my heart and fully embrace God's Truth. I sought counseling at L.I.F.E. Ministry* in New York, and the counselors there guided me to Jesus' deliverance from the bondage and addiction of homosexuality.

That was over twenty years ago. Jesus has delivered me completely from this addiction, not only in my actions, but also in my mind and heart. However, each day as I take my medications, my sin is ever before my eyes; it is the thorn in my flesh. I am reminded not only of my own sinfulness, but also of the tremendous love and power of God, and the mercy and forgiveness I have in Christ.

Steven
New York, New York

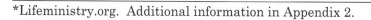

---

*Lifeministry.org. Additional information in Appendix 2.

When Steven came to Christ, His burning desire was to obey God and follow His commands. However, he was trapped in his addiction and unable to live a life of obedience. It was the complication of AIDS that opened his eyes to recognize that he could not escape this trap on his own; he needed the help of other Christians to guide him into the delivering power of Christ.

Although Jesus delivered him from the bondage of his addictions, and healed him spiritually, mentally, and emotionally, Steven is not at this time physically healed. I have watched Steven in action for many years. An extraordinary evangelist, he walks humbly with his God, living his entire life in pure worship of his Savior.

Like Steven, we may desire to live in obedience. But sometimes, we fall short. How can we grow more here? Reading Hebrews, I have learned that obedience is tied up with suffering. Listen closely.

During the days of Jesus' life on earth, he offered up prayers and petitions with fervent cries and tears to the one who could save him from death, and he was heard because of his reverent submission. Son though he was, he learned obedience from what he suffered, and, once made perfect, he became the source of eternal salvation for all who obey him and was designated by God to be high priest in the order of Melchizedek.

Hebrews 5:7-10

I can't say that I understand all the nuances of these verses, but I do know that this is referring to the Agony in the Garden. The human side of Jesus did not want to undergo this horrific death by torture, or the separation from God when He would take our sins upon Himself. He cried out to the One who could save Him from death,

"Father, if you are willing, take this cup from me; yet not my will, but yours be done."

Luke 22:42

But He **learned obedience** from what He suffered? What does that mean?

Claiming to be obedient, submissive, surrendered when life is easy is completely different than being obedient when the obedience entails tribulation. Obedience can be tested and proved through affliction. Anyone can claim to be submitted to Jesus. Yet it is in adversity when surrender can be proven genuine. In the same way that faith that has not been tested is not real faith, submission that has not been tested is not real submission. I think that both without testing are merely words. When obedience requires difficulty and suffering we can learn what authentic obedience really is.

It can be hard for us to comprehend the mystery of Jesus "learning" anything. Yet this passage in Hebrews teaches us that Jesus **learned** the true meaning of obedience when He was called to obey even when it entailed the horrific suffering of His crucifixion. Similarly, if we want to learn authentic obedience, I believe it will be through suffering.

We Invite God to Move When We Choose Genuine Obedience

Why is it important to learn genuine obedience? Look back at Hebrews 5:7-10 to see what happened when Jesus learned obedience.

- He became the source of eternal salvation for all who obey Him. Because Jesus obeyed God and died for all men, He became our way to God.

- He was designated high priest. Because He can relate to us in our suffering, He is able to perform His role as High Priest: intercessor for us before the Father.

- He was heard because of His reverent submission, **"Yet not my will, but yours be done."** (Lk 22:42). God heard and answered – not by removing the cup, but by giving Jesus the strength to endure.

Miraculous things can happen when we learn genuine obedience. Each time we choose obedience through our hardships, God's Kingdom comes into our hearts a little more as darkness is conquered and replaced by the Holy Spirit. As we surrender on a deeper level, God can reveal Himself to us more intimately, and He can use us more powerfully since we are filled more with His Spirit.

This next testimony I'd like to share with you is from a man who has fearlessly served as a leader in Student Ministries for many years. He was actually my son Alec's first Bible study teacher and mentor, and holds a special place in our family's heart. As Joe speaks, watch how his obedience opened the door for a powerful move of God.

Although my dad strived to be a good father, he was an alcoholic. I had forgiven him when I came to know Christ, and soon learned that there were layers and layers of forgiveness. As I came to know Christ more, I forgave more. Finally, I thought I had pretty much resolved this forgiveness issue.

I joined a men's Bible study group and learned what accountability meant. These men of the Lord would hold my feet to the fire and not let me get away with anything. God spoke to me through these men, and I recognized I still harbored much resentment, judgment, and unforgiveness toward my father. Through much prayer, God destroyed these strongholds and led me to a place of love and forgiveness for my father.

At this time I was leading a group of middle school boys in a weekly Bible study at my church. Many of them were struggling on so many levels, and I soon learned that 10 of the 11 boys did not have a father in their lives. God led me to recognize their desperate need for a father, and gave me a ministry to stand in as their father figure, to allow them to see a father through me. I know I was not ready for this ministry until God cleansed my heart of my sinful attitudes toward my own father. He prepared me for this ministry by exposing my sin and taking me through the fires of purification.

Joe Tardonia
Christ Fellowship Student Ministries Leader
Palm Beach Gardens, Florida

What would have happened if Joe did not choose the path of obedience? If he had remained in a place of unforgiveness and judgment? Joe recognized that had he not been through those fires of purification, he would not have been equipped to minister to those fatherless boys. And don't miss God's perfect timing: the purification right before the ministry assignment.

God May Reveal Himself When We Choose Genuine Obedience

Jesus was heard because of his reverent submission (Heb 5:7). Let's explore. First listen to Jesus' own words in the Gospel of John:

"He who has My commandments and keeps them is the one who loves Me; and he who loves Me will

be loved by My Father, and I will love him and will disclose Myself to him."

John 14:21 NASB

Keeping God's commandments equals loving God. Those who love God, God loves. Before we become too confused on this issue, recognize that from the whole counsel of the Bible, we see that we cannot *earn* God's love. Remember what we learned in Chapter 3: surrender, or obedience, brings down the barrier that separates us from the *outpouring* of His love. Not that He doesn't love us when we are disobedient or in rebellion – for His love is infinite and eternal and unchanging. But we are unable to *receive* that love when we have erected a barrier by our refusal to obey.

When we keep God's commandments, when we obey Him, Jesus promises He will **disclose** Himself to us. As He discloses Himself, we may come to know His will more clearly. The more closely we are aligned with His will, the more we may be able to pray His will, and our prayers will be heard because of our **reverent submission**. We are praying **"Your will be done,"** *and* we know more exactly what His will is.

God always demands our full and immediate obedience, whether we understand His reasons or not. Sometimes we may understand why right away; other times we may not understand until after we obey. And other times we may not understand until months or years later, or not even until eternity. God does not promise us an explanation for everything, but He does promise the strength to carry out His will, even in the most agonizing times.

I have asked my friend Nancy to share one of her many experiences of obedience. This woman is a live wire at Christ Fellowship who has co-founded our church's Cancer Support Groups and also founded our church's Ministry for the Deaf. In addition, she is a founding board member of Diane's Voice, an ovarian cancer awareness organization.

And, she and her husband are right now students in Kaleo, Christ Fellowship's School of Biblical Leadership. I believe that the reason God taps this woman so frequently is because she is *available* and *obedient*. No matter the call, whether she comprehends it or not, her answer is always, "Yes, Lord, send me."

My usual "quiet time" is around 2 AM when no phones ring and I can truly listen to God. One night, I believe God spoke to me and said He wanted me to learn American Sign Language. It was a crazy idea. I knew no deaf people. I actually argued with Him because I played guitar. Obviously, playing guitar and signing are not compatible! I was obedient, however, and now I have many deaf friends. I have been so blessed to know them. I also teach sign language and started a deaf ministry at my church. I thank God that I was obedient! The blessings have poured in on me!

Nancy Smith
Co-founder, Cancer Support Groups
of Christ Fellowship Church
Palm Beach Gardens, Florida

For the eyes of the LORD range throughout the earth to strengthen those whose hearts are fully committed to him.

2 Chronicles 16:9

The Lord's eyes are ranging to and fro, and in Nancy He has found an obedient heart that is fully committed to Him.

God Wants Us To Know Him

Why is obedience so important to God? Obedience proves our love for Him.

"If you love Me, you will keep My commandments."
John 14:15 NASB

Love equals obedience. But let's take it a step deeper:

I want you to show love, not offer sacrifices. I want you to know me more than I want burnt offerings.

Hosea 6:6 NLT

Just as we may crave to know the deepest desires and greatest pains of a loved one, I believe God wants us to crave to know *His* deepest desires and *His* greatest pains. John 14:15 says that loving God is obedience to Him. Hosea 6:6 says that loving God is knowing Him. How are these verses related? It seems that when we know Him, when we know His heart in a deep way, He can show us *what* to obey, and can also give us a *passion* to obey. If, during the midst of our afflictions, our hearts are open to His transforming power, He can teach us that kind of authentic obedience.

What an amazing God we serve. He simply wants us to know Him. To read His Word, to spend time with Him, silent, waiting, open to His call. Be still; He is calling you. **"I want you to know me."** It is the cry of His heart.

The Suffering Righteous

Let's investigate the relationship between suffering and righteousness. Righteousness is living in right relationship with God. When we accept Jesus as our Savior, God declares us righteous in Jesus; He sees us as righteous (2Cor 5:21). He then calls us to embark on a lifetime of living out this gift of righteousness (Rom Ch 6). We can grow in righteousness each time we choose obedience and invite the Holy Spirit to work in our hearts.

On one level, perhaps only in a secret place deep in our hearts, we may like to think of ourselves as the suffering righteous. We may even like to throw around words like "spiritual warfare" as the cause of our suffering because it makes us sound holy and close to God. Maybe, though, just maybe, our suffering is not some vague spiritual warfare for reasons we cannot comprehend. Maybe, it is not a test. Maybe, it is not the result of someone else's sin. I mean, are we really all that righteous? Are we *really* living solely to give God glory, to give Him pleasure? Maybe, our hardships have more to do with us and less to do with all creation groaning. Maybe . . . maybe we are suffering because of our *own* sin.

I've indulged us in a few euphemisms, as we talked about suffering to grow our faith and to conform us to Christ's image. Yes, when we are open, suffering can certainly grow our faith and conform us to Christ's likeness. Yet the deeper underlying truth of the matter is this: the areas of our lives that are not conformed to Jesus' image are areas where we are living in sin.

Conforming Starts With Exposing Our Sin

If our spirits are sensitive to His Spirit, He may expose our sins simply as we read His Word or come humbly before Him in prayer. We can receive His conviction and repent – with a complete about-face, a total change of heart. However, perhaps more commonly, we humans may naturally resist confessing, repenting, and surrendering. Often, our hearts can be hardened. Often, we can be so enmeshed in the world that we cannot see His truth, so that He may choose to resort to more drastic measures to reveal our sin to us. The process of conforming may then involve pain and suffering. I am going to let Wilfred's story put skin on those words.

I was on the streets, using drugs, diagnosed with AIDS. I was in a torture chamber of my own making. I prayed and prayed for God to deliver me, but it seemed my prayers were met with silence.

Finally, I realized that the life I lived, I became. I understood that God would keep me in this place of suffering until I humbled myself, repented, and turned to God. He would keep me here until He got me alone with Him, no one but Him and me. And I did just that. I humbled myself and repented, begging His forgiveness and deliverance. And God reached down from heaven and drew me to Himself.

Some things of my life have not changed. I am still poor, I am living with AIDS, I still live in that same difficult neighborhood. But my whole life is different, because now I belong to Christ. I have His peace, because I am living for His plan and not my plan. I am living every day for Him, reaching back to people in my neighborhood who are where I was, to bring them the message of peace in Jesus.

Wilfred
West Palm Beach, Florida

The horrors of Wilfred's life brought him humbly to Jesus. It was through his suffering that he was conformed to the image of Christ. I have know Wilfred for many years, and the new sparkle in his eyes bears witness to his transformation from despair and depression to hope and peace.

Is Suffering Punishment for My Sin?

You may be asking, "Is suffering punishment for my sin?" No, it is not. Suffering is *not* matched up with our sins, and suffering is *not* a "punishment" for our sins.

The LORD . . . does not treat us as our sins deserve or repay us according to our iniquities.

Psalm 103:8-10

So what is the difference between "opening our eyes to our sin" and "punishing" our sin? I believe the difference is in the heart attitude of God. If God's intent is to hurt us and shame us, then I think we would be correct in calling suffering "punishment." Yet God's intent is always powerful love for us. Think of His crucifixion. This is *not* a God who wants to hurt and shame us. He is always working for our good.

"For I know the plans I have for you," declares the LORD, "plans to prosper you and not to harm you, plans to give you hope and a future."

Jeremiah 29:11

As you read the stories laced throughout this book, you will hear again and again that "suffering is the best thing that ever happened to me." God so carefully handpicks our trials, just enough to open our eyes to our sin, just enough to grow us spiritually, just enough to fulfill His Kingdom work – and not one tear more. We can trust the Omniscient Creator of the Universe to know *exactly* what it will take.

Opening Our Eyes to Our Sin
Can Lead Us to Christ

Why is opening our eyes to our sin more important to God than our pleasures and comforts on earth?

How else will we see our need for a Savior? How else will we seek His salvation and sanctification? Joni Eareckson Tada answers it this way: "God is saying to you . . . 'I have permitted in your life what I hate so that something eternal and wonderful can be achieved – life, rich and meaningful on earth, and life in heaven, free of pain and full of joy.' "[8] I believe that God permits sin that grieves His Spirit and the resultant suffering that makes Him weep in order to achieve what He so fiercely desires for us: spirits prepared for eternity with Him. For He knows that we will never see the infinite and forever and spectacular wonders of heaven if we never *get* to heaven, or if we are not *prepared* for those wonders when we get there!

God in His sovereignty can use the lies spun by Satan and the evil invented by man to expose our sin. God says of the Israelites,

"I let them pollute themselves with the very gifts I had given them, and I allowed them to give their firstborn children as offerings to their gods—so I might devastate them and remind them that I alone am the LORD."

Ezekiel 20:26 NLT

"I let them." Let them sacrifice their firstborn children to false gods. Why? **"To devastate them and remind them that I alone am the LORD."** The NIV says to **fill them with horror** – horror of their own sinfulness.

"The heart is deceitful above all things, and desperately wicked; who can know it? I, the LORD, search the heart."

Jeremiah 17:9-10 NKJV

Who can know it? Who can know the depth of the sin in the darkest corners of our hearts? We do not know how wicked our own hearts are, or the depth of the evil of which we are capable. Have you ever considered yourself righteous in a certain area, thinking that you would never sin in that particular way, and then suddenly found yourself committing the very sin that you were sure you would never do? That is Lori's story. Let's hear it.

Like many, I thought I was a pretty good person. Working, taking care of my family, going to church, volunteering . . . I thought I was doing enough good deeds to get into heaven. Yet there was one thing that brought me to my knees. Decades ago, I had an abortion, and it was this sin that I could not ignore, that ate away at me until I began to see how wretched I really was in God's eyes – not only because of the abortion, but because of all my other sins as well. I do not think I would have ever come to God for forgiveness of any of my sins if I had not had the abortion. I would have been the typical American, "Yeah, I'm a pretty good person." As horrible as this sounds, I think God allowed me to murder my child because He wanted me to see how wretched I really am.

Today, I have accepted that Jesus paid the price for my sins, and I know I am completely forgiven. I speak out to any women considering abortion, telling them my story, counseling them to choose life for their child. I know my child in heaven understands that her death means life for the children of these pregnant women. Her death means eternal life for these pregnant women who come to know Jesus through me. Her death means eternal life for me.

Lori
Los Angeles, California

I know this cherished woman quite well. Unable to forgive herself and unable to receive God's forgiveness, she had been crushed with depression and hopelessness for many years. She was trapped in a snare of striving to earn her forgiveness and to attain a place in heaven. The futility of this pursuit spiraled her into further hopelessness and depression. Finally, she admitted her need for a Savior and surrendered her life to Christ; she has been forgiven and has forgiven herself. Her passion for Jesus is overflowing: because she has been forgiven much, she loves much.

"Her many sins have been forgiven – as her great love has shown. But whoever has been forgiven little loves little."

Luke 7:47

God wants us to see the sinfulness of our hearts, all the sin of which we are capable. Sometimes, that means God lets us commit the sin in order to understand that we are capable of it. Is this crazy? I don't think so. Otherwise, we may simply deny that we could ever be that sinful. God wants us to see the depth of the putridness of our hearts in order to give us an opportunity to repent and turn to Him in complete humility, begging His forgiveness for all the sins in our heart. He wants to give us heart transplants, to remove our black, sinful hearts and give us hearts that beats for Him. He wants to flood us with the power of His Holy Spirit so we are able to turn away from sin. He wants to sanctify us, to grow us in holiness, in order to enable us to bring Him glory – the very reason He created us.

Before I was afflicted I went astray,
But now I obey your word . . .
It was good for me to be afflicted
So that I might learn your decrees . . .
I know, O LORD, that your laws are righteous,
And in faithfulness you have afflicted me.

Psalm 119:67, 71, 75

The psalmist writes, *You* **have afflicted me.** God's doing. The psalmist gets it. **Before I was afflicted I went astray.** When he was not suffering, the psalmist implies that he was far from God, living in sin, unable to give God glory. However now, in his sorrows, he has grown closer to God. He keeps God's word. The psalmist goes so far as to say that it was **good** for him to suffer, so that his attention could be drawn to his errant ways, and he could repent and return to obeying God. He calls God's laws **righteous**, and he praises God as **faithful** for using troubles to bring him back to God. Faithful. Faithful to what? Perhaps this word is referring to God's faithfulness *to do whatever it takes* to bring us back into relationship with Him when we are straying. Perhaps this word is referring to God's faithfulness *to His agape* for us, giving us what we need, not necessarily what we want; meeting all our spiritual needs, whatever it takes. Perhaps this word is referring to God's faithfulness *to His promise* never to leave us or forsake us, but to walk with us through all our afflictions.

Can we reach that depth in our relationship with God? That we are grateful for adversity because it can reveal our sin and give us a chance to repent? That we are grateful because our repentance can restore our fellowship with Him, bring us into deeper relationship with Him, and enable us to glorify Him? I want to be there. I truly do.

Opening Our Eyes to Our Sin
May Prepare Us For Kingdom Work

Come with me back to Exodus, where we will pick up the story just after the burning bush. God has called Moses to a staggering job: leading the Israelites out of Egypt. Moses has set out for Egypt with his wife Zipporah and his sons.

At a lodging place on the way, the LORD met Moses and was about to kill him. But Zipporah took a flint knife, cut off her son's foreskin and touched Moses' feet with it. "Surely you are a bridegroom of blood to me," she said. So the LORD let him alone.

Exodus 4:24-26

This is another passage where I surely do not understand all the nuances. What I want you to see here is how seriously God takes sin. God had huge work for Moses to do, but it seems that Moses was not ready. He was not obedient to God. Since Abraham's time, God had required all Israelite males to be circumcised, and Moses had not circumcised his son. In order for Moses' sin to be revealed to him and the matter rectified, God, **about to kill him**, put him in such a position that I suspect Moses could not have possibly circumcised his son himself, so his wife had to do it for him. If we are suffering, could it be because of our sin? Perhaps God is working to bring us to obedience to prepare us for His Kingdom work – work that we may not be able do in our current state of sinfulness.

Do you think that God afflicting people to open their eyes to their sin is just an Old Testament phenomenon? Do you think that God afflicting people to bring them to repentance doesn't apply to us today? Let's go to the New Testament, to the Gospel of John. In this passage, at the Pool of Siloam in Jerusalem, Jesus heals a man crippled for thirty-eight years. Jesus' final words to this man are

"See, you are well again. Stop sinning or something worse may happen to you."

John 5:14

This is very grave. Hold on, we're going to First Corinthians where it gets even weightier.

. . . whoever eats the bread or drinks the cup of the Lord in an unworthy manner will be guilty of sinning against the body and blood of the Lord . . .

For those who eat and drink without discerning the body of Christ eat and drink judgment on themselves. That is why many among you are weak and sick, and a number of you have fallen asleep. But if we were more discerning with regard to ourselves, we would not come under such judgment. Nevertheless, when we are judged in this way by the Lord, we are being disciplined so that we will not be finally condemned with the world.

1 Corinthians 11:27, 29-32

Shocking. The Corinthians were not judging themselves, not judging their own sins and confessing and repenting, so God was judging them. The result of that judgment was that **many among you are weak and sick and a number of you have fallen asleep**, that is, died. This was God's way of disciplining them.

The Kindness of God Brings Us To Repentance

Now fasten your seatbelts. We're going to crank it up a notch.

You have not yet resisted to the point of shedding blood in your striving against sin; and you have forgotten the exhortation which is addressed to you as sons,

"MY SON, DO NOT REGARD LIGHTLY THE DISCIPLINE OF THE LORD,

NOR FAINT WHEN YOU ARE REPROVED BY HIM;

FOR THOSE WHOM THE LORD LOVES HE DISCIPLINES,

AND HE SCOURGES EVERY SON WHOM HE RECEIVES."

. . . **He disciplines us for our good, that we may share His holiness. All discipline for the moment seems not to be joyful, but sorrowful; yet to those**

**who have been trained by it, afterwards it yields
the peaceful fruit of righteousness.   Therefore
strengthen the hands that are weak and the knees
that are feeble, and make straight paths for your
feet, so that the limb which is lame may not be put
out of joint, but rather be healed.**

Hebrews 12:4-6, 10-13 NASB

In our striving against sin, we have not yet shed
blood!   God scourges – yes, it literally says **scourges** –
His children, those He loves. Why scourges? Why such
a graphic harsh word? If we could only realize what it
may take to uproot sin from our hearts. It may take huge
suffering! And God says, "Deal with it. I am disciplining
you – not punishing you – for your own good, your agathos
– what you need, not necessarily what you want. I am
disciplining you so that you may share My holiness." He
wants us to **share His holiness**. Can you even grasp that?

Debi, my friend of many years and a stalwart prayer
warrior of my *Triumph* Prayer Team, is going to share
a time in her life when she experienced God's discipline.
Watch the depth of her pruning and purifying, then we'll
ask her a question.

*I had surrendered my life to Christ years ago. I was
growing in Him. Well, a little. What I did not realize,
though, was how selfish I was. Life was all about me, me,
me. I was so blinded, thinking only about myself. Poor
pitiful me . . . I had diabetes . . . I had lost my job because
of my illness . . . I had lost my car because I could no longer
afford it, so now I could no longer get around . . . I was
getting ridiculous, thinking that all these earthly things
mattered, not recognizing what really matters.*

*Because of my diabetes, I developed a severe foot
infection. It never healed properly, and I'm stuck wearing
a "boot" at all times and can hardly even walk. I had
always been so independent, and now I was so frustrated.*

I could not understand why I was in this situation. I did not realize God was trying to tell me something. I could not accept His plan; I only wanted my plan.

He tried to get my attention in so many other ways, but I did not listen. He didn't give up on me, though. He didn't allow me to remain in that selfish state. I ended up in intensive care with a bleeding ulcer. It was critical. I didn't think I was going to live. I endured emergency surgery that removed half of my stomach, and spent weeks in the intensive care unit and still more weeks in the hospital.

It was a tough lesson, but now I fully understand, 100%, that life is not about me. I would have never gotten here spiritually without this bleeding ulcer and coming so close to death. God is transforming me from the inside out, changing everything about me by His grace. I am no longer aggravated; I have a whole different attitude. I am learning to sincerely care for people, to love them where they are without judging them. I now truly want to live for Jesus and not for me.

Debi Zimmerman
Triumph Prayer Team
North Palm Beach, Florida

From a front row seat, I have had the privilege of watching Debi's transformation. God has done a mighty and seemingly impossible work in her heart; she has emerged from that time of discipline exuding unbelievable peace in the greatest of trials. She seeks first His Kingdom and His righteousness; she serves with great humility, honoring others above herself. Her relationship with the Lord has moved from anger, frustration, and challenge to peace and sweet intimacy.

I posed a question to Debi and also to Wilfred, the gentleman you met earlier in this chapter who rests in God's peace despite poverty and AIDS. I asked both of them if they felt God was punishing them. "Certainly not," they declared. Wilfred explained, "God was simply getting my attention." Debi added, "God loves me too much to punish me."

Back to our passage from Hebrews, we see that when we are disciplined, we are commanded to **strengthen the hands that are weak and the knees that are feeble**, to accept our suffering, our scourging, and **be healed**. This word **healed** can mean physically healed, spiritually healed, emotionally or mentally healed, or all or any combination. "To heal, cure, restore to bodily health . . . to be healed from or of anything . . . of moral diseases, to heal or save from the consequences of sin."[9]

Somehow, in a way we may not fully comprehend, when we repent and are brought back into right relationship with God, it can release His healing. Sometimes instantaneously, sometimes not until His perfect timing. Sometimes physically, sometimes mentally or emotionally, sometimes spiritually, sometimes all areas at once. As we come closer to God, His healing may come forth.

And other times we may receive His deep peace and spiritual healing, yet live with the physical consequences of our sin for the rest of our lives. But even if He doesn't remove the suffering, Jesus promises to walk with us through it. And in Jesus, our suffering can be given meaning and purpose in a way we can't even imagine at this time.

Take time to examine yourself and ask God to shine His light into your heart. Ask Him to reveal deep and hidden things, to reveal where you have sinned or where you are still living in sin. Ask the Spirit to reveal whether the suffering is due to sin, whether God is causing your anguish to bring you back into right relationship with Him. **"I have wounded and it is I who heal"** (Dt 32:39 NASB). If sin is the issue, now is the time to confess it and repent, to accept His discipline, no matter how painful it is, and to turn to Him for healing.

The *kindness* of God leads you to repentance.
Romans 2:4 NASB, emphasis added

It is because of His great **kindness**, it is because He loves us, that He disciplines us to bring us to repentance. How else can we come to salvation? How else can we come to a deeper surrender and grow closer and closer to Him? How else can we be conformed to His image and bring Him glory? How else can we share His holiness? How else can we be ready to meet Him in eternity?

God disciplines us that He may open our eyes to our sin and bring us to share His holiness. What parts of your life are not bringing glory to God? What corners of your heart are not conformed to Christ's image? Are you harboring pride? Unforgiveness? Self-glorification? Lust? Are you lying? Gossiping? Judging? Viewing porn? Are your motives selfish? Is there an area of your life that you have not fully surrendered to God? Accept God's discipline with joy. Strengthen your weak hands and feeble knees, for God has plans and purposes for you that would blow your mind if He even gave you a glimpse of it. If you are suffering, He is up to something good. Don't miss it.

God Suffers When We Suffer

God does not enjoy seeing us suffer as He disciplines us. His heart aches so desperately for us that He collects every tear:

You keep track of all my sorrows.
You have collected all my tears
  in your bottle.
You have recorded each one in
  your book.

Psalm 56:8 NLT

His empathy goes beyond our comprehension:

In all their distress he too was distressed.

                                        Isaiah 63:9

God is grieved when He disciplines us. Yet there's more. God's pain when we are in agony goes even deeper than mere empathy. This is something that we cannot fully understand, but somehow, since God *lives* in us, when we suffer, He suffers. Follow along with me here.

"I have given them the glory that you gave me, that they may be one as we are one: I in them and you in me."

                                        John 17:22-23

. . . through his Spirit in your inner being . . . Christ may dwell in your hearts through faith.

                                        Ephesians 3:16-17

He [Saul] fell to the ground and heard a voice say to him, "Saul, Saul, why do you persecute me?"
"Who are you, Lord?" Saul asked.
"I am Jesus, whom you are persecuting," he replied.

                                        Acts 9:4-5

Wow – read that again. Jesus didn't say, "I'm Jesus, and you're persecuting My disciples." He said, "I'm Jesus, and you're persecuting *Me*." Jesus lives inside of us, so when we suffer, *Jesus Himself* suffers also. He not only walks *with* us through our sorrows, but He is *inside* us through them. He feels our very pain. Before you close this chapter, remember the tears of God. Pause for a moment and let all this sink in.

Chapter 7
Suffering Can Teach Us
Humility, Dependence, and Forgiveness

*O*ver the past few chapters we have delved into God's Word and learned some possible reasons for our trials:

- We know that we live in a fallen world and can multiply our suffering by our own sinful choices.

- We trust that God is conforming us to Christ's image. He may be growing our faith by decreeing tests and trials, and teaching us authentic obedience and what it means to truly worship Him.

- We accept that God may be opening our eyes to our sin in order to bring us to obedience and prepare us for more difficult Kingdom work.

I want you to realize that suffering may be God's greatest blessing to you. A blessing? Absolutely! When life is smooth, we may forget what is important. We may become wrapped up in worldly things like money, work, health, status, relationships, and even church and

volunteer work.   Some people who have no hardships go
through life, busy, crazily busy, thinking they will put off
their relationship with God until later . . . when they are
less busy, when work is less stressful, when the kids are
out of the house, when they are physically more healthy,
when their life is in order . . . for some, "later" never
comes. Yet our lives are **but a breath** (Ps 39:5), **a mist
that appears for a little while and then vanishes**
(Jam 4:14)!

Suffering can force us to take time out from the usual
rat race to evaluate our lives in view of eternity, and to
reprioritize our lives according to God's will. Tribulations
may be just the thing we need to open our ears to God (Job
36:15 NASB). I have called on Melva to explain just what
that means.

*I have suffered much with several different illnesses.
At times the suffering was so unbearable I thought I could
not handle it. However, I learned that God never gives you
more than you can bear (1Cor 10:13). I learned that I am
not in this alone – God is with me. If He helped me, He can
help you, too.*

*My medical problems have humbled me and made me
a better person. I have learned how to treat people with
compassion. I now understand the suffering others are
going through. I believe God has taken me down this path
because He wanted me to be able to help others who are
suffering, to be able to relate to them, to encourage them,
and to reach out to them in love.*

*Melva
West Palm Beach, Florida*

Melva was a committed Christian when we first met.
But it was trial after trial that brought her to deeply
trust the Lord. It was illness upon illness that humbled
her and brought her to focus on others, not on herself. It

was hardship after hardship that forced her to slow down and reprioritize her life according to God's priorities. And through all this, her intimacy with Jesus has developed exponentially.

Exchanging Pride for Humility

Hosea speaks about the Israelites, whom God had rescued from the oppression of slavery in Egypt, then cared for in the burning heat of the desert. You might expect them to be eternally grateful. Yet God said of them,

"When I fed them, they were satisfied; when they were satisfied, they became proud; then they forgot me."

Hosea 13:6

Watch the pattern:

- If we become fed and satisfied, comfortable in life
- Then we may become proud
- Then we may even forget God.

Nothing is wrong with being fed and satisfied, but we must recognize that these can be snares for pride. It can be easy to fall into pride. The pressures are all around us. The world tells us to be proud of our accomplishments: our promotions in work, our lavish homes, our graduation from school, our degrees and credentials, our trophies and awards, our kids' successes. We Americans may love to brag, "I came from nothing" and "I pulled myself up by my boot-straps." And we can even have condescending thoughts such as "I'm not sinning like the next person," or "I'm more spiritually mature than other people," or "God is using me more than He is using another Christian." How serious a sin is pride? Do not forget that pride was Satan's sin. Listen to what God has to say about pride:

Everyone who is proud in heart is an *abomination* to the LORD.
Proverbs 16:5 NASB, emphasis added

"God *opposes* the proud but gives grace to the humble."
James 4:6 NASB, emphasis added

Let's go to Second Corinthians to take a look at Paul, blessed by God with amazing visions – and with a thorn to keep him from becoming prideful because of these visions.

Because of the surpassing greatness of the revelations, for this reason, to keep me from exalting myself, there was given me a thorn in the flesh, a messenger of Satan to torment me—to keep me from exalting myself! Concerning this I implored the Lord three times that it might leave me. And He has said to me, "My grace is sufficient for you, for power is perfected in weakness." Most gladly, therefore, I will rather boast about my weaknesses, so that the power of Christ may dwell in me. Therefore I am well content with weaknesses, with insults, with distresses, with persecutions, with difficulties, for Christ's sake; for when I am weak, then I am strong.
2 Corinthians 12:7-10 NASB

Paul was given a thorn, **a messenger of Satan** to torment him. This is petrifying – how terrible must this affliction have been? Because Paul was a well-educated man and gifted in many ways, he could have become full of pride from his human successes. I believe that Paul was very aware of this trap – look at the words he uses, **exalting myself.** In the Greek it means "to lift above, elevate, exalt, be conceited, arrogant, insolent."[1] It means "to become exalted above measure; to become haughty."[2] We don't know exactly what the thorn was, but Paul tells us its purpose, to keep him humble. I think it also reminded him that anything we do by our own human abilities will perish, while God's work will remain forever:

Unless the LORD builds the house, they labor in vain who build it.
Psalm 127:1 NASB

I know that everything *God* does will endure forever.
Ecclesiastes 3:14, emphasis added

Perhaps this thorn interfered with Paul's capacity to use his own talents, and compelled him to depend upon the power of the Holy Spirit instead of on his own human ability. In our weaknesses, the Spirit's power can be made manifest. **When I am weak, then I am strong**. Paul is **well content** with this thorn because it kept him humble.

Being Humbled by God

I have asked Joan to share a story of humbling in her own life. You remember Joan from Chapter 2. One of my *Triumph* Servant Leaders with rock-solid trust in God, Joan is a lymphoma survivor, first diagnosed when her children were very small.

I had always found it difficult to surrender my children to God. Until I had no choice.

When I was first diagnosed with stage four non-Hodgkins lymphoma, my sons were three years and three months old. When it recurred, they were six years and three years old. As I left Florida for treatment in Seattle, I had to come face to face with the terrifying reality that I might never see them again. I thought I had surrendered them to Him the first time around, but apparently not. This time, I was holding on even tighter. God said to me, "Joan, I will be a better parent than you will ever be." That one statement crushed my pride in my parenting skills so completely that all that was left in my heart was utter humility.

Because I would not give them to God willingly, He orchestrated the events in my life to bring me to that humility and surrender. I would never have reached that place any other way. I recognize now that my only role is to point my children to God, because someday I might not be here to parent them.

Joan Hoffpauir
Triumph Servant Leader
Christ Fellowship Church
Stuart, Florida

God desired Joan's humbled heart – for her good and for His glory. Her first bout with cancer destroyed some of her pride, but there was still more heart work to be completed. Only God knew what it would take. I did not know Joan during those brushes with death. But I bear witness to the fruit of God's work: this woman walks in humility, with all meekness serving her family, serving the suffering in her *Triumph* classes, and ministering wherever God may strategically position her.

Exchanging Independence for Dependence

Pride can be linked to the sin of independence. We are going to read about a very independent man who liked to take things into his own hands, who had stolen his brother's birthright and blessing, then ran away up north in hiding: Jacob.

I would like to explain a few things before we start: Out of reverence, Hebrew writers would use the word "man" or "angel" instead of "God" at the beginning of a passage, and then later explain that this really was God. You see this in the story of Moses and the burning bush (Ex 3). Also, realize that names in Hebrew are very significant. If someone says they know God's name, it means they know Him personally, they know His character, they know who He is.

Then Jacob was left alone; and a Man wrestled with him until the breaking of day. Now when He saw that He did not prevail against him, He touched the socket of his hip; and the socket of Jacob's hip was out of joint as He wrestled with him. And He said, "Let Me go, for the day breaks."

But he said, "I will not let You go unless You bless me!"

So He said to him, "What is your name?"

He said, "Jacob."

And He said, "Your name shall no longer be called Jacob, but Israel; for you have struggled with God and with men, and have prevailed."

Then Jacob asked, saying, "Tell me Your name, I pray."

And He said, "Why is it that you ask about My name?" And He blessed him there.

So Jacob called the name of the place Peniel: "For I have seen God face to face, and my life is preserved." Just as he crossed over Penuel the sun rose on him, and he limped on his hip.

Genesis 32:24-31 NKJV

What exactly is going on here? This word **wrestle** literally means "to wrestle"[3] – why would God engage in a literal wrestling match with Jacob? This reminds me of the age-old ritual of father-son wrestling matches. It starts when the sons are wee ones, when the fathers can easily overpower them. Each year the son gains strength, and I think he assumes that when he wins, he will no longer have to obey his father's commands. Now it seems to me that these wrestling matches abruptly end when the father senses he is probably going to lose the next match.

So is this what is going on between Jacob and God? Why would it say **God did not prevail against him**? Did God give Jacob one too many opportunities, and this time did not prevail, so He resorted to the old dislocate-the-hip trick?

I think that God did not prevail because He *chose* not to overpower Jacob. I think God was calling Jacob to surrender to Him, yet God did not violate his free will. God did not overpower him – and yet, God knew the deepest desires of his heart. Listen to Jacob's cry of desperation, **"I will not let You go unless you bless me!"** Listen to Jacob's cry to know God deeply, **"Tell me Your name, I pray."**

I believe Jacob knew that he could not change himself, that he needed the power of the Almighty to change his heart. God answered that prayer, and I am pretty sure this is not the answer Jacob expected: God dislocated his hip. Jacob's *blessing* was his dislocated hip; he just didn't know it was a blessing yet. This crippled him: he walked with a limp. Was that really necessary? Remember men back then could not survive unless they were physically strong, able to hunt and farm and physically defend their family and property. A man with a limp would have a very difficult time surviving . . . *if* he was on his own. However, Jacob was not going to be on his own. God was with him. Before he could fulfill God's purpose as an amazing leader, I believe Jacob had to surrender his pride, ambition, and craftiness, and become totally spiritually and physically dependent upon God. I think God knew Jacob needed the physical dependence in order to come to a place of spiritual dependence. God *blessed* him by dislocating his hip.

My friend Betty is a steadfast member of my *Triumph* Prayer Team. I have watched her struggle with dependency on God for many years – well, I'm going to let her tell her own story.

Diagnosed with Multiple Sclerosis (MS), I walk slowly with a cane, dragging one leg. It won't be long before I am in a wheelchair.

I am a fiercely independent woman, but the MS has humbled me and made me physically dependent on other people. I recently had to move in with my daughter – how I resisted that move! However, God has truly given me peace about living with my family. I don't look back. I have honestly learned that things and people are great, but God is the greatest of them all. He is always there when I need Him. Although I struggle with anger, frustration, and depression, I know that through this disease, God is teaching me dependence on Him. Physical dependence translating to spiritual dependence.

The purpose of my MS is to grow me closer to God, to change my entire attitude, to bring me to understand that His master plan is more important than my own wishes and dreams. The results of this are twofold: I am driven to share the gospel with as many people as I can, and God has breathed new life into my prayer time. I treasure this work He gives me as His ambassador, and I treasure this time alone with Him that would never have been possible in my previous state of independence.

Betty Johnson
Triumph Prayer Team
North Palm Beach, Florida

"Physical dependence translating to spiritual dependence." Yes, this prayer warrior has learned much from her suffering. A passionate evangelist and dedicated prayer partner, she is available for God, on *His* plan, in *His* timing.

We may think that we are powerful as humans, but it is such a fallacy! The devil's own lies seared into our conscience. The truth is that what *we* can accomplish on earth is nothing . . . nothing of eternal value. Yet what *God* can accomplish on earth through us, if we are willing to humble ourselves and depend on Him, is a power that is **the working of His mighty strength** (Eph 1:19). Paul describes this in Second Corinthians:

For God, who said, "Let light shine out of darkness," made his light shine in our hearts to give us the light of the knowledge of God's glory displayed in the face of Christ. But we have this treasure in jars of clay to show that this all-surpassing power is from God and not from us. We are hard pressed on every side, but not crushed; perplexed, but not in despair; persecuted, but not abandoned; struck down, but not destroyed.

2 Corinthians 4:6-9

The more humble and dependent upon God that we become, the more we can turn away from pride and independence and admit that we are truly fragile, insignificant jars of clay. The more we turn from pride and independence, the more God may fill us with His Holy Spirit. His Spirit is our treasure, who never abandons us, who protects us from being crushed or destroyed, and who fills us with all hope.

Pride and independence can be powerful strongholds. Paul recognizes that. Listen to what it took for God to demolish those strongholds in Paul and Timothy:

[During] the troubles we experienced . . . We were under great pressure, far beyond our ability to endure, so that we despaired of life itself. Indeed, we felt we had received the sentence of death. But this happened that we might not rely on ourselves but on God, who raises the dead.

2 Corinthians 1:8-9

Are you over your head in trials? I call this "multitasking sufferings." Perhaps the hardships, far beyond the human ability to endure, are to teach you not to rely on yourself, but on God. There simply may be no other way to learn this.

I've asked my friend Dawn back again – you met her in Chapter 4 as she described her time locked in a mental ward against her will. Dawn is going to describe her journey from independence to dependence.

This world we live in is so hard! I learned what it meant to live in a fallen world from when I was a small child. With an alcoholic mother and an abusive father, my life was awful beyond words. I developed epilepsy from the beatings, and also ADHD. I gave my heart to Christ when I was a teen, and my mother persecuted me for my faith; I soon fell away from His path. I talked to God, but always on my terms. Instead of allowing God to heal the pain of my past, I turned to drinking, drugs, sex, and bulimia, and my own sinful lifestyle began to multiply the pain of my childhood.

I was married at 19, had two children, and soon divorced my unfaithful husband. When fibromyalgia and dissociative disorder compounded my epilepsy and ADHD, I realized that I could not survive without God. These sufferings were just too much for me to handle myself! This time, I turned to God. I rededicated my life to Jesus – this time for good. I have not been a backslidden Christian since.

When I turned back to God, I asked Him to take some of these illnesses away from me. I would rather just have the physical pain than the mental disabilities because I feel like I live in a "fog." Yet He did not. Since I look "normal" and people can't see these illnesses, I continue to be severely persecuted. Yet I cling to Jesus; if it were not for God and my faith, who knows where I would be today. Although God did not take away any of my illnesses, He has kept me going. Because these illnesses are beyond my ability to handle, I have learned day by day to depend on Him and Him alone.

Dawn
Wake Forest, North Carolina

Why does God want us in a place of dependence upon Him? Yes, for His glory – but also for our good. Dependence upon God can work to protect us from the lure of the world, from Satan's traps, from our own prideful failures. I am sure Betty and Dawn would agree that living dependent on God, abiding in Him, attuned to His will for every decision, is living the abundant life.

Exchanging Unforgiveness for Forgiveness

Pride and independence are two key areas God often addresses through our suffering. I'm going to leapfrog to one more area God often addresses when we are in the depths of misery: forgiveness. This is a tough topic. I know what you may be thinking: "Who is *she* to tell me I should forgive? She doesn't know how deeply I've been hurt." You're right. I don't know. However, what I *do* know is this: If you do not forgive, you may never be healed; you may never be set free and made whole. This I *do* know, because I've been there.

Forgiveness can be very confusing. We may think that forgiveness is a feeling; we may think that if we give it enough time, wait for the feeling to come upon us, wait for our heart to heal, then we can forgive. This is all backwards! Remember **the heart is deceitful** (Jer 17:9 NKJV); forgiveness cannot depend on a heart feeling. One of the translations for forgiveness is "to send away."[4] This implies a choice – a choice to release bitterness, hurt, resentment, and revenge. In order to forgive, we must first *choose* to forgive, and then over time, healing can take place, enabling us to feel the emotions of forgiveness. Don't misunderstand me here. Choosing forgiveness does NOT mean

- Denying that you were hurt.
- Convincing yourself that it is insignificant.
- Thinking it did not really matter anyway.
- Taking all the blame.
- Twisting things around to be your fault.
- Pitying.
- Excusing.
- Releasing the offender from accountability.
- Trusting the person who has hurt you.
- Putting yourself in a position to be hurt again.

What is forgiveness then? Forgiveness IS

- Accepting that you were hurt.
- Accepting that you were wronged.
- Admitting that it is important.
- Choosing to release the wrong-doer from your bitterness and revengefulness.
- Inviting Jesus in to heal your heart.

How, in the midst of all our pain, can we *choose* to forgive? It may not be easy. The Holy Spirit, present and working in our humbled hearts, in our jars of clay, can lead us to choose forgiveness.

Please understand that God is angry, *so angry*, with the person who has hurt you! His heart is wrenched and bleeding and torn because of the pain you have suffered. He is so broken-hearted over your pain that He **has indignation every day** (Ps 7:11 NASB). And yet, for reasons we may not yet fully understand, God also tells us that it is our job to forgive; it is His job to take revenge.

Do not take revenge, my friends, but leave room for God's wrath, for it is written: "It is mine to avenge; I will repay," says the Lord.

Romans 12:19

Justice will not be completed until the end of time. Whether it is revengeful actions or revengeful thoughts: leave it to God.

Come meet my friend Nancy Bustani, a practicing psychologist, college professor, and author, as well as founder of the Safe-T Counseling Center. Safe-T provides sexual abuse recovery as well as counseling for anger management, parenting, marriages, and other areas. I have asked her to detail her own personal journey of forgiveness.

My mother was abusive. She projected most of her frustrations on to me, the oldest of five children. She would beat me, slap me around, pull my hair, and scratch me until I bled. Her fits of uncontrollable rage were precipitated by anything from her lost scarf to my brother's spilled milk.

Our family secret was well guarded. My siblings and I were good students and played instruments; I was in the citizenship and the science clubs. My parents both worked; my mother was even president of the Parent-Teacher Association.

My mother didn't want to be bothered by me. She barely came to my high school graduation; she didn't know I graduated summa cum laude from my university; and I didn't even tell her when I graduated with my masters in psychology.

After my father died, the anger and hatred that I felt for my mother grew so intense I cannot even begin to describe it. I thought God had made a huge mistake, taking the wrong parent, and I told Him so. I suppressed my anger, but I was like a dormant volcano. I was a terrific mother, a serious over-achiever, and a compulsive cleaner, but I cried a lot, I had terrible headaches, and I became underweight.

Confronting my own malignant spirit, I concluded that I needed to forgive my mother. I felt like I was carrying a huge boulder inside of me that I needed to get rid of, but had no clue as to how. For the next ten years I struggled with bitterness and resentment toward her.

Forgiveness came early one morning when I was reading my Bible, and I felt an inner prompting to call my mother. "Mother, I need to ask you to forgive me."

"What on earth for?" she asked. "What could you have possibly done wrong? You were always my best child."

Boom! I had never heard that before. "Mom, it must have been hard on you, knowing for years that I did not like you. I am sorry that I have been very critical of you. As a Christian, I have learned that my only job on earth is to love others. Nothing else matters. I am so sorry."

There was silence for a brief time and I could hear her sniffling back tears. "I love you so much, Nancy," she said.

"I love you too, Mother."

Something spiritually amazing occurred that day. A huge weight melted deep inside of me. The unforgiveness toward my mother and toward God simply vaporized. That was when I learned that when people do not forgive, they are not wounding their offender. They are wounding themselves.

My mother and I did not have a good relationship the first 35 years of my life, but that does not have to dictate our relationship today. I had written 64 stories about my father, but now I wrote a story about my mother, the one person I never thought I would learn to love. I wrote a positive story about her successes in life. When I finished, I felt a tremendous relief. She had lost her hold on me. She no longer had power to control my emotions. It was a done deal. Why, it was a supernatural phenomenon!

Nancy Bustani, M.S.
Executive Director, SAFE-T Counseling Center
West Palm Beach, Florida

I like how Nancy explains it: "She had lost her hold on me." She worked to release her mother – and found that the one she had released was herself.

Now what if the person who hurt you doesn't apologize, and doesn't even ask for forgiveness? Good question. I'm glad you asked. Let's look to Jesus as our example.

When they came to the place called the Skull, they crucified him there,   along with the criminals – one on his right, the other on his left. Jesus said, "Father, forgive them, for they do not know what they are doing."

Luke 23:33-34

Do you think when His executioners were driving the nails into His body they were asking for forgiveness? We are called to forgive as Jesus forgives. Staggering.

I would like to introduce you to another college professor and published author. My friend Stephanie has agreed to allow us a glimpse of the spiritual release that occurred in her life. Her story illustrates the deep spiritual struggle as she chose forgiveness, and demonstrates how her choice set both her and the wrongdoer free.

The impetus to learn about my mother's killer came twenty years after the murder. My husband and I were attending an informal meeting at a church we were thinking of joining. The speaker, who headed a prison ministry, spoke of the inmates he worked with and the positive impact forgiveness had on their lives. While I basically believed forgiveness was a good thing for mankind, I had never considered forgiving the man who killed my mother. I had no interest in having a positive impact on a cold-blooded murderer. In fact, I strongly supported the death penalty; I was silently bitter that my mother's killer, Nathan, had only received a life sentence. As the speaker talked about prisoners committing themselves to God and turning their lives around when given forgiveness, my unexpected tears flowed out silently and profusely. I felt afraid.

That speaker at church changed the dial on my radio. I could not change it back. Articles in newspapers and magazines, shows on TV, and conversations with people all circled back to the topic of forgiveness.

One afternoon in my study, I came across an unnamed manila file. A piece of paper fell out: the telephone number of the chaplain's office at the State Penitentiary where Nathan was imprisoned. I simply picked up the phone and dialed.

I spoke to the priest. "I am trying very hard to find a way to forgive him. I also want to find out whether he feels any remorse."

"Does it make any difference if he feels any remorse?"

"I'm not sure," I said. What did remorse have to do with it, I wondered. I felt, somehow, that it should not drive my decision.

"This is a very brave thing you are attempting, my dear. You are unburdening yourself and walking in the path of our Savior." I felt uncomfortable.

We agreed he would deliver my message: "The daughter of the woman you killed in 1980 wishes to forgive you. Do you have anything you want to say in return?"

When I hung up the phone, I realized I had perspired through my shirt. I had actually done it. I wept, choking on my own anxiety, feeling desperate and unsure of myself.

When I spoke to the priest a week later, he told me that when he delivered my message, Nathan was speechless. Nathan said he needed time to think. "Nathan is dying – in fact, he can't even stand up. I am struck by your timing, my dear. That over a twenty-year period, you call now. A year ago, he was not sick and might not have received your message so openly. Six months from now, he will likely be dead and you would have missed the opportunity to do this. It only confirms my faith in the workings of the Holy Spirit."

In that moment, I realized that things were unfolding just as they were intended, according to a plan over which

I had no control. I was merely an instrument of something far greater than myself. I was trembling, laughing and crying all at the same time, realizing that for the first time since 1980, I felt at peace. I had nothing to fear. I realized I had been blindly working toward this moment for twenty years, fighting it all the way. And now I felt healed.

The priest continued, "Nathan wished me to convey how grateful he is for your forgiveness. He said to tell you he is deeply sorry for what he did. He said he is turning his life over to God and preparing for the end."

Stephanie Cassatly
Author of Call of the Sirens
Jupiter, Florida

In a way we can hardly comprehend, Stephanie's choice of forgiveness released Nathan to come to a place of surrender to the Lord himself.

God Offers Us His Forgiveness First

I want you to understand that God offers us His forgiveness first. Don't think that we have never hurt anyone ourselves. When we, deep within our hearts, really and truly realize that *our* forgiveness is total and complete for *all* of our sins, when we realize that God's forgiveness is solely because of His love and mercy and grace, not because we deserved it, not because of anything we have done, then *our* forgiveness to others can flow from *God's* forgiveness to us.

Just as the Lord forgave you, so also should you.

Colossians 3:13 NASB

Understand that unforgiveness can break our fellowship with God. We may find it very difficult to connect with God when we are living in unforgiveness.

Sometimes, forgiveness can be completed in us almost overnight. More often, especially if the injury is ongoing, we may need to choose forgiveness every single day, even many times throughout the day, before forgiveness is finally completed in our hearts. We may need to be so dependent upon the Holy Spirit for the strength to repeatedly choose.

How will we know when we have truly forgiven someone? How will we know when forgiveness is completed in our hearts?

Forgiveness often comes in layers. Leaving the revenge to God is only the first step. Some indications that you have truly forgiven someone are these:

- Bitterness, hatred, and vengeance are gone. When something bad happens to the wrongdoer, you do not rejoice.

- Your heart is broken for the offender because you know that they will be standing before Jesus for an accounting.

- You are praying for God to bring them into right relationship with Him – not for your benefit, but for theirs.

- You have moved from begging God to avenge the wrongdoer to begging God to have mercy on them. You are on your knees entreating God to forgive them for having hurt you, **"Father forgive them; for they do not know what they are doing"** (Lk 23:34).

What Can Happen When We Cleanse Ourselves From Our Sins

When we turn to God in our suffering, God may open our eyes and reveal His path of humility, dependence, and forgiveness. When we are still before Him in the midst of adversity, He may open our ears and speak to our hearts. It will probably not be easy. Spiritual growth is often painful. Yet it is of paramount importance.

> **. . . if anyone cleanses himself . . . he will be a vessel for honor, sanctified, useful to the Master, prepared for every good work.**
>
> 2 Timothy 2:21 NASB

Cleanse yourself, so that you may be a vessel of honor, holy and useful, for the Master has magnificent and challenging Kingdom work for you.

Chapter 8
Spiritual Warfare:
Suffering To Advance the Kingdom

Y ou may have a few questions by now: If our God loves us with a love that surpasses all comprehension, and He created this stupendous heaven for us, a place without pain and suffering, *why* are we still down here? If the reason He created us is to give Him glory, *why* are we still down here groaning with all of creation? If we will be able to purely glorify Him in heaven, where we are fully Christlike, untainted by sin, then *why* has He left us here?

The answer to these questions lies in understanding the Kingdom of God. Jesus said, **"My kingdom is not of this world"** (Jn 18:36). He taught His disciples to pray, **"Your kingdom come, your will be done"** (Mt 6:10). What does it mean for God's Kingdom to come?

How God's Kingdom Advances

God's Kingdom *did* come when Jesus died and rose from the dead. However, His Kingdom will not come in its fullness until the end of the world, when Jesus returns to earth, when God creates a new heaven and a new earth (Rev 21:1-4), and when God's will is done completely on earth as it is in heaven.

Right now, though, God's Kingdom . . .

- Comes a bit more,
- Is advanced,
- Moves forward,
- Comes closer to completion,

. . . whenever His will is done.

When sinners repent and turn to God, and God wrenches them from Satan's Kingdom and transfers them to His Kingdom of Light, His Kingdom comes a bit more.

When Christians read their Bibles and grow in Christ, His Kingdom is advanced.

When Christians repent of their sins and become more conformed to Christ's image, His Kingdom moves forward.

If God calls us to reach out to the sick, or help the needy, or bring the gospel message to the unsaved, and we hear and obey, God's Kingdom comes closer to completion. Whenever His will is done, His Kingdom is advanced, and God is given glory. We are at that moment fulfilling our God-given purpose.

In God's Hands,
Our Suffering Is Not Meaningless

Pause a moment. In evaluating why we suffer, we have really been focusing on some selfish things here. *My* preparation for eternity. *My* eyes opened to sin. *My* conforming to Christ. *My* faith enlarged. *My* spiritual growth. As Joni Eareckson Tada quips, "Notice all the me's. God notices too."[1] Let's get our eyes off ourselves right now and focus on God: God's heart and His Kingdom.

In God's hands, our suffering is never meaningless. Whether we are in a state of desolation because of our own sinful choices, or because of our sin piled up in our hearts, or simply because we live in a fallen world, when we fully surrender, God can give our sorrows incredible meaning and purpose – for our good, and to advance His Kingdom. When we surrender our agenda to His, when we align our hearts and our lives with His eternal plan, when we stop trying to control our lives and our destiny and put our hardships into His capable hands, then He can fully utilize every ache, every tear – for our good and for His Kingdom.

I have invited my friend "G" to explain how God used all her pain and suffering to equip her for His Kingdom work.

The youngest of twelve children, I was verbally, emotionally, and mentally abused to the extreme. My family was oblivious to how I was being abused in a private school as well. The person in a teaching position was so cruel, and I still bear the scars today.

As an adult, I worked for a private organization for prevention of abuse and neglect. My inner spirit was simply drawn there, and I found God had given me a deep compassion not only for the abused children, but more so for the parents who had done the abusing. Somehow, God had worked in my heart to help me to realize these parents just did not know any better; they did not have the necessary tools and education; and many of them simply did not have good role models. The Holy Spirit gave me such empathy for them, and a unique ability to see how hurt they had been throughout their lives. He helped me to understand that hurting people hurt people.

I could have never ministered to these parents without the extreme suffering I had endured growing up. I am completely accepting of whatever God would put me through to shape me to be a useful servant for Him.

"G"

Wake Forest, North Carolina

Suffering Can Equip Us For Kingdom Work

How does suffering interplay with God's Kingdom work? We'll look first at trials before the work even begins. Let's go to my town of Jupiter, Florida. I'm reminded of the little sea turtles that we see every summer.

When the turtles hatch from their eggs on the beach, they must travel a long, often arduous journey to reach the ocean. They may endure the burning sun and the threat of seagulls and raccoons. They can even become disoriented, end up going the wrong way, and become completely lost. Some people think they can help these little turtles by picking them up and carrying them down to the ocean. Although this allows the turtles to skip the rigors of the beach journey, they may rapidly die in the ocean because they have not built up their strength. They may be unprepared to handle the life-threatening challenges of ocean life.

Like those sea turtles, we may be tested and tried. God may take us through times of challenge and adversity to prepare us, equip us, and strengthen us before He sends us forth to do His Kingdom work. If we skip the trials of the preparation, we may not be spiritually strong enough to complete the job. We may not be equipped to do His will. We may not be prepared to handle the attack from the dark forces working to thwart the advancement of His Kingdom.

Now may the God of peace . . . equip you with everything good for doing his will, and may he work in us what is pleasing to him, through Jesus Christ, to whom be glory forever and ever. Amen.
Hebrews 13:20-21

Back in Chapter 6 you met my friend Nancy Smith, the Available and Obedient Servant of the Lord. This woman has been equipped many times and in many ways for the vast array of ministry work God has assigned her. I have asked her to share a time of equipping.

Over twelve years ago, I was diagnosed with breast cancer, and have had two radical mastectomies with reconstruction. My breast cancer diagnosis forced me to join an elite company of people that I really did not want to be part of! Why me!? Why now!? So many questions.

About a year after my surgery, a pastor's wife at my church asked me if I would start a cancer support group. I said absolutely not. I was adamant that what people needed was one-on-one support, not group support! I think I wrote a three-page treatise on why I should not start a cancer support group.

Well, God worked on me, and about ten years later I did start a Christian Cancer Support Group. In its first year it multiplied exponentially into more and more groups as many others joined this elite company. I have never been so blessed! What an honor to encourage and support those suffering with cancer, to walk beside them and be their prayer warrior during this dark time of their life.

There is no doubt God created me for this purpose, and planned it in advance for me because of His goodness and love for me. There is no doubt I could not have founded this support group without the suffering I have been through. There is no question that He who called me also equipped me by taking me through the suffering of breast cancer myself.

Nancy Smith
Co-founder, Cancer Support Groups
of Christ Fellowship Church
Palm Beach Gardens, Florida

God used the trial of her own cancer to equip her to reach other people with cancer. It seems that a powerful connection is suddenly created when one who has survived cancer meets another who is just beginning the journey. And it is those connections that have opened the door for Nancy to share Jesus' love and grace many many times.

Even Jesus was tested before God released Him into His public ministry work. I think this time of testing was to strengthen and equip Him.

As soon as Jesus was baptized, he went up out of the water. At that moment heaven was opened, and he saw the Spirit of God descending like a dove and lighting on him. And a voice from heaven said, "This is my Son, whom I love; with him I am well pleased." Then Jesus was led by the Spirit into the wilderness to be tempted by the devil.

Matthew 3:16 - 4:1

Right after He was baptized, at the time He was poised to start His public ministry, the *Holy Spirit* led Jesus into the desert for the express purpose of being tested. Of course Satan does the tempting "with the intent to make us fall." [2] God, though, already knows how we will respond to the test. God may decree the test in order to

- Ascertain that we are ready
- Equip us to do His will
- Strengthen us for the hardships and trials of the Kingdom work itself
- Deepen our faith so that we can stand firm when the spiritual warfare is raging

The Significance of the Equipping

The more agony the Kingdom work will entail, the more rigorous our preparation may be. Why is this so significant? Jesus tells us

"No one, after putting his hand to the plow and looking back, is *fit* for the kingdom of God."
Luke 9:62 NASB, emphasis added

The Kingdom work God has planned for each one of us is huge, it is difficult, it will entail pain and hardships. God wants those with **fully committed hearts** (2Chr 16:9), who will **pour themselves out like a drink offering** (2Tim 4:6), who will put their hand to the plow and not look back.

Jesus says in Revelation,

"I know your works, that you are neither cold nor hot. I could wish you were cold or hot. So then, because you are lukewarm, and neither cold nor hot, I will vomit you out of My mouth."

Revelation 3:15-16 NKJV

Jesus doesn't get any more graphic than that.

What will life look like for Christians? You have heard the Scriptures that describe the blessings and promises of life in Christ, all true and momentous and spectacular. Yet there are many other verses that we cannot ignore that also describe life in Christ.

Is Suffering Inevitable for Christians?

In order to answer this question, let's go on a tour.[3]

Now if we are children, then we are heirs – heirs of God and co-heirs with Christ, if indeed we share in his sufferings, in order that we may also share in his glory.

Romans 8:17

For it has been granted to you on behalf of Christ . . . to suffer for him.

Philippians 1:29

We sent Timothy . . . to strengthen and encourage you in your faith, so that no one would be unsettled by these trials. For you know quite well that we were destined for them.

1 Thessalonians 3:2-3

So do not be ashamed of the testimony about our Lord or of me his prisoner. Rather join with me in

suffering for the gospel, by the power of God. He has saved us and called us to a holy life . . . And of this gospel I was appointed a herald and an apostle and a teacher. That is why I am suffering as I am.

2 Timothy 1:8-9, 11-12

For if we died with Him, we shall also live with Him. If we endure, we shall also reign with Him.

2 Timothy 2:11-12 NKJV

In fact, everyone who wants to live a godly life in Christ Jesus will be persecuted.

2 Timothy 3:12

If you suffer for doing good and you endure it, this is commendable before God. To this you were called, because Christ suffered for you, leaving you an example, that you should follow in his steps.

1 Peter 2:20-21

I, John, your brother and fellow partaker in the tribulation and kingdom and perseverance which are in Jesus . . .

Revelation 1:9 NASB

Somehow, in a way we cannot fully understand, His Kingdom will not grow without the suffering of Christians. Don't be unsettled by these trials. You know quite well that we were **destined** for them and **appointed** to them. If our hearts are beating with God's, we will desire the growth of the Kingdom so intensely that we will rejoice in affliction because it may be an opportunity for the Kingdom to be advanced. Bold Christians, uncompromising Christians, will always suffer for His Name. All uncompromising Christians? Second Timothy makes it clear: *everyone* **who wants to live a godly life in Christ Jesus will be persecuted.** I can't say I fully understand this, but the Bible certainly seems clear on this connection between suffering and advancing the Kingdom.

Suffering Is Our Divine Appointment

Now I rejoice in what I am suffering for you, and I fill up in my flesh what is still lacking in regard to Christ's afflictions, for the sake of his body, which is the church.

Colossians 1:24

I believe that Paul is setting the standard of how a Christian should view adversity. If we respond to our trials by seeking God instead of turning from Him, we can become a Christlike example for others to follow. If our attitude in times of adversity inspires others in the church to answer God's call even if it will entail hardship for them, then the pain is worth it. We can **rejoice** in suffering.

It seems that we are all called to take our turn in adversity in order to advance the Kingdom, to spread the gospel, and to be Jesus' hands and feet as He saves souls. I have asked my friend Joan to bring this concept to life. You met this lymphoma survivor in Chapters 2 and 7. Joan is one of my *Triumph* Servant Leaders who possesses an immense depth of trust in the Lord.

It had been six years since I was diagnosed with non-Hodgkins lymphoma at age 31. I was feeling God calling me to some type of ministry to help people with illness, and I had mentioned it to a few people in church that Sunday. That evening, one of the pastors of our church called me to ask if I would visit a 27-year-old woman dying of colon cancer who did not know the Lord.

I do not even know how I walked into her hospital room, for the smell of cancer brought back the harsh reality of my brushes with death. I didn't know what to do; I didn't know what to say. Somehow, I went in. I shared the gospel with her, God's message of hope and salvation through Jesus Christ, and this woman accepted Jesus as her Savior right there. Very shortly afterwards, she went to heaven to be with Jesus.

I truly floated out of the hospital that evening. I realized if I had never gotten cancer, I could never have connected with her, I would have never been used by God to bring His message to her. At that moment, I realized if I had to go through it all again just for this woman to enter the Kingdom of Heaven, I would do it. I would have never picked this path, but I would never trade it either.

Joan Hoffpauir
Triumph Servant Leader
Christ Fellowship Church
Stuart, Florida

Equipped through trials. Eternally grateful for the precious experience of being used by God as He rescued this dying woman from the domain of Satan. Joan would have never picked this path, but she would never trade it either.

Why all the pain? Perhaps it is because of the spiritual warfare, Light vs. Dark. Listen to how Jesus describes it:

"This is the verdict: Light has come into the world, but men loved darkness instead of light because their deeds were evil. Everyone who does evil hates the light, and will not come into the light for fear that his deeds will be exposed."

John 3:19-20

Evil exists only by God's permission, and, as we discussed in Chapter 6, God does not *approve* of everything He permits.

Evil hates the light. **Everyone who does evil hates the light**. Those who practice evil, those who belong to

Satan – both men and fallen angels – hate those who are in the Light, those who belong to Jesus. Hatred can breed attack. This is spiritual warfare: the clash of Dark against Light. Suffering seems inevitable.

Spiritual warfare is a complex topic, and we're only going to skim the surface of it here. Recognize that some Christians may say they are "in spiritual warfare" because it makes them sound closer to God or more spiritually mature. Others may be seeing demons behind every bush, calling everything from spilled coffee to hurricanes "spiritual warfare." Truly, if you're driving recklessly and have an accident, or you fail an exam because you didn't study enough, or if you're fired because you are habitually late for work, that isn't spiritual warfare; it is a natural consequence of irresponsible behavior. If you're caught cheating on your taxes and land in jail, or you're having sex outside of marriage and end up with a broken heart or some kind of disease, that isn't spiritual warfare; it is the consequence of sin. Yet you must also recognize that it is possible to be embroiled in spiritual warfare and not even recognize that you are.

The Kingdom of Darkness
vs.
The Kingdom of Light

There are two worlds, two realms, the physical and the spiritual. The physical world is our bodies and everything in the universe that we can experience with our five senses. The spiritual realm is an eternal world comprised of two Kingdoms, God's Kingdom of Light, and Satan's Kingdom of Darkness. I have created a chart to help us visualize this (Jn 8:42-43, 1Jn 3:7-10, Eph 2:3,18, Eph 5:7).

The Kingdom of Light	The Kingdom of Darkness
God: The Trinity: God the Father, God the Son, and God the Holy Spirit	
Michael the Archangel	Satan
Michael's Army of Angels	Satan's Army of Fallen Angels, or Demons
All people who belong to Jesus	All people who do not belong to Jesus

As you can see visually from this chart, God has no opposite. He is the Uncreated One, always was and always will be. Although He is not in the Kingdom of Darkness, He reigns over *both* Kingdoms, for He is Ruler over all.

Satan was an archangel who was cast down from heaven when he rebelled against God (Eze 28:14-17, Isa 14:12-15). He took one third of the angels with him (Rev 12:3-10). These fallen angels are also called demons.

The spiritual and the physical realms are intertwined, and the spiritual directly impacts the physical, as you may understand more clearly as we travel through this chapter.

There is warfare going on in the spiritual realm. We are entangled in this conflict because the spiritual realm wages war both in the spiritual and in the physical realms. This is not a cute little metaphor! This is real! The reason for the warfare is the battle for every soul to be brought to eternity with Jesus.

For he [God] **has rescued us from the dominion of darkness and brought us into the kingdom of the Son he loves, in whom we have redemption, the forgiveness of sins.**

Colossians 1:13-14

Well, that doesn't sound much like warfare does it? Let's go to the Greek, because we have lost a lot in the translation. To **rescue** means to "drag along the ground; to draw or snatch from danger, rescue, deliver . . . more with the meaning of drawing to oneself than merely rescuing."[4] Think more in terms of damsel in distress, fire-breathing dragon, knight in shining armor.

" . . . the kingdom of heaven suffers violence, and violent men take it by force."

Matthew 11:12 NASB

There is violence, warfare, going on in the spiritual realms when the Kingdom of Light is being advanced, when Satan's house is being plundered (Mt 12:29). The Kingdom is advancing when someone is in the midst of choosing to come to Christ, or when a Christian is making a choice to surrender to Jesus on a deeper level, or to repent of a sin, or to become more conformed to Jesus' image. The spiritual warfare can also be extreme when we are stepping out to fulfill our God-given purposes.

When Light wins these battles, when we repent of that sin or when we determinedly obey God's call, God's Kingdom is advanced, His Kingdom comes a bit more as darkness is displaced a bit more from our hearts, or from the hearts of the ones we are ministering to.

For our struggle is not against flesh and blood, but against the rulers, against the authorities,

against the powers of this dark world and against the spiritual forces of evil in the heavenly realms.

Ephesians 6:12

Our struggles on this earth may appear to be against people and circumstances, but in reality, they are not. Our struggles are against the spiritual forces of Darkness. **Struggle** is the Greek word pale. Read this definition with care:

> A wrestling, struggle, or hand-to-hand combat. It was used of wrestling athletes and the hand-to-hand combat of soldiers, both of which required deftness and speed. It denoted the struggle between individual combatants in distinction from an entire military campaign. [5]

Our encounters with the forces of Darkness are hand-to-hand fights full of trickery, cunning, and strategy. The victor of these clashes takes control of spiritual territory, control of the hearts of men. I believe that Satan and his dark forces are not going to relinquish any territory without a vicious fight.

We may not fully realize the impact that our lives have on the angels and demons, but the Bible states clearly that our lives are interlaced with those in the heavenly realms.[6] As we suffer on earth, God may be teaching the heavenlies. We learn from Luke that the angels rejoice over repentant sinners (Lk 15:10). Peter tells us that angels long to watch mankind's salvation unfold (1Pet 1:12 NLT). Ephesians teaches us that the church reveals God's wisdom to the rulers and authorities in the heavenly realms (Eph 3:10). And we've talked about Job in Chapters 4 and 6. He seemed completely oblivious to the battle for control of his heart that was being waged in the heavenly realms. (You can explore more about this spiritual clash by doing Chapter 6 in the *Workbook*.)

"Consider My Servant Job . . ."

Can you imagine God saying that about you? It appears that God desires to use our lives to teach people, angels, evil spirits – and us – about Himself. What does He teach? He may be teaching about His wisdom, His power, His great love for His cherished children; He may demonstrate how He gives us strength. When in the darkest of times we experience horrific tribulations, and people on earth as well as the forces of darkness think faithfulness to God must be impossible, *the stakes are high*. When we come through, when we cling faithfully to God to the end, when we love Him unconditionally and obey Him completely, the reflection of God's glory in us may be immense. My friend Cindy's story brings this point to life.

I am not a Christian. Well, not yet, anyway. But I am watching, taking note. There is a family in my neighborhood that are Christians – always going to church, helping people, being kind. Not long ago, they lost a child in a tragic accident. I was shocked – what kind of God would do such an awful thing to such a loving family? I watched them closely to see what would happen. I expected them to leave their faith and their church, to stop being

*Christian. I expected them to be furious at God, bitter and
angry. But they are not! They still go to church and are still
Christian. They are still kind and helpful. They say God
is "good" and is taking care of them through this tragedy.
They aren't even angry – they have that same peace and joy
about them that they always had. How can this be? They
must be insane. Or else it's a façade – and in that case, it
will crack soon enough. Or perhaps . . . perhaps . . . I am
missing out on something really big.*

Cindy
Chicago, Illinois

We humans may be barely able to wrap our minds
around spiritual warfare. To us on earth, what does
spiritual warfare look like? On a superficial level, it can
simply look like suffering. We must discern if it is . . .

- A consequence of our sin
- Affliction to expose our sin for the purpose of
  conforming us to Christ and growing our faith
- A test or trial
- An attack by Satan attempting to thwart the
  advancement of the Kingdom of God
- A combination of these

We may not always know the answer, but the more
we come to know God, the more discerning our spirits can
become. We may be able to recognize spiritual warfare
more easily. When you are stepping forth to fulfill your
calling, expect it! When you are demolishing a stronghold
and repenting of a habitual sin, expect it! Part of the
battle is preparing for it and recognizing it.

Realize that Satan can only be in one place at a time.
He does, however, have an army of fallen angels to do his
bidding; one third of the angels that God created are now
in the Kingdom of Darkness (Rev 12:4).

Satan's Methods

How do Satan and his henchmen attack? Here are some possibilities:

- Disrupting relationships of those closest to us: our family, our co-workers, and our friends

- Disrupting other areas of our lives in order to distract us, such as wreaking havoc on our finances, our job, or our home

- Attacking us physically – with an injury, or a health issue

- Attacking our minds, trying to drive us into worry, anxiety, or fear

- Attacking multiple areas of our lives simultaneously – so we find ourselves "multitasking suffering"

- Leading us to believe false teachings that are not in line with God's truth

- Tempting us to sin

- Sowing seeds of doubt

Satan's seeds of doubt may tell us that we are not smart enough, righteous enough, worthy enough, or spiritually mature enough to fulfill our calling. Lies, from the father of lies. These seeds of doubt may come from people we don't even know, or from our own minds, or even as persecutions from people we trust – such as our spouse, our church, our family and our friends.

Satan's Goal in Attacking

Satan's goal in attacking us is to thwart us from fulfilling our God given-purposes. He desires to stop us from repenting and leaving our sin behind. He may discourage and distract us, driving us to forsake our faith. He also works to emotionally destroy us, to physically wear us down, and to spiritually suck the life out of us.

God's Purpose in Decreeing the Test

Here are some possible reasons God may be decreeing the test:

- To work to strengthen and mature our faith in order to prove it genuine and to bring Himself glory.

- To conform us to Christ for the purpose of advancing His Kingdom.

- To prepare us for our Kingdom work on earth and our responsibilities in heaven.

- To drive us to rely on Him, so that when our purposes are fulfilled, we, and all who witness it, recognize that it was His almighty power and not our mere human strength.

To make these concepts more concrete, I would like to share a time of warfare in my own life.

We were all new Christians. My kids, 8 and 9 at the time, made a decision to set their alarm clocks 30 minutes earlier each morning so they could read their Bibles and spend time with God.

It was a disaster right from the beginning. From alarms accidentally going off at 3:00 AM, to bad grades because the kids were just so tired, to getting to school and work late, to arguing and bickering and disrupted family relationships . . . we began to wonder if it was all worth it. Maybe we just were not going to be able to do it. Maybe reading the Bible was not really that important after all. I could not control the chain of events. There was nothing I could do.

It was not until the fourth day of this that God revealed to me the spiritual warfare, leading me to recognize Satan was prowling around like a roaring lion, looking for someone to devour. I acknowledged that I could do nothing to protect us. It was my call to pray, to repent and humble myself and ask Jesus to fight for us.

The Spirit told me that our job was to stand firm, to hold that crucial position in battle. I knew it was my job to encourage the kids to get up early every morning to spend this time with God, and to pray for the Holy Spirit to strengthen them and enable them to do it. We stood firm, Jesus intervened immediately, and peace reigned in our house.

From this vantage point, I can see that our plans caught the eyes of the Dark because they know how reading the Bible can bring an explosion in Christ. I understand why the Darkness desired to do whatever God permitted them to do to thwart the advancement of the Kingdom in these two kids' hearts.

I believe one of the reasons God decreed the test was to see if these kids desired Him desperately enough to persevere even through all the discouragements and distractions. He wanted to know if they would choose Him despite the warfare and trials. Of course He knew that answer, but He desired to strengthen their faith and their craving to know

Him. And through this battle, He taught us firsthand what spiritual warfare is, and what it meant to humble ourselves and stand firm.

Celeste Li
Jupiter, Florida

Spiritual Weapons

If we are looking through eyes of the flesh, we may only see the suffering; we may be so blinded that we do not recognize it as spiritual warfare. Yet it is paramount that we recognize it for what it truly is, because if we are trying to fight a spiritual battle with weapons of the flesh, we will lose.

For though we walk in the flesh, we do not war according to the flesh, for the weapons of our warfare are not of the flesh, but divinely powerful for the destruction of fortresses. We are destroying speculations and every lofty thing raised up against the knowledge of God, and we are taking every thought captive to the obedience of Christ, and we are ready to punish all disobedience, whenever your obedience is complete.

2 Corinthians 10:3-6 NASB

Spiritual weapons are divinely powerful, for they have God's infinite power. The purpose of these weapons is to demolish fortresses, or strongholds. The Greek word stronghold can also be translated "castle."[7] It is derived from words meaning "to fortify, to hold fast."[8]

Francis Frangipane, founder of River Life Ministries, is an international speaker who has published many books on spiritual warfare. In *The Three Battlegrounds*, he explains that strongholds are areas deep in our minds and hearts.[9] We have strongholds that belong to Jesus, areas of our heart that are submitted to Him. We also have strongholds submitted to Satan, which are beliefs, thoughts, and attitudes that are not in line with the truth of God's Word. These strongholds that are submitted to Darkness can lead us to sinful thoughts, words, and actions. It is these strongholds that we want to destroy and replace with Christ's strongholds.

God allows Satan and his demons access to areas of darkness, as Frangipane explains, "even in the darkness that still exists in a Christian's heart."[10] God may allow Satan to **sift us like wheat** (Lk 22:31) in order to expose our sin. Demolishing these strongholds of sin can enable us to more successfully fulfill our calling. Do not be afraid of the sifting. Jesus Himself will be praying for us (Lk 22:32), and He desires us to emerge purified and ready to be used by God.

How do we destroy these strongholds? Let's study the weapons listed here in Second Corinthians:

- Spiritual Weapon: **destroying speculations** – this is uprooting Satan's lies and replacing them with God's truths which we find in His Word.

"If you continue in My word, then you are truly disciples of Mine; and you shall know the truth, and the truth shall make you free."
John 8:31-32 NASB

Knowing the truth can set us free. We can replace Satan's lies with God's truth when we **continue** in Jesus' Word. When we abide in His Word, surrender completely to His Word, are obedient to Scripture, and deeply implant His Word in our hearts, we can be set free from Satan's strongholds. When we do our part, we invite Jesus in to release us from Satan's control.

- Spiritual Weapon: **destroying every lofty thing raised up against the knowledge of God** – that is destroying pride and false idols. Recognize that we are weak jars of clay (2Cor 4:7) and cannot destroy these strongholds on our own. Ask the Spirit for revelation of any idols you may have erected. What have you set up above Jesus in importance? Your family, your relationships, your health? Where is your focus? On relief of suffering, on pleasures, on your physical needs, wants, and desires? What do you trust more than God? Your money, your possessions, your prestige? Are you trusting in God's sovereign plan and His sovereign timing, or do you have an insatiable need to control?

- Spiritual Weapon: **Taking every thought captive to the obedience of Christ.** Are you thinking sinful thoughts? Remember Jesus said that everyone who even looks at a woman with lust has already committed adultery (Mt 5:27-28). And just what is occupying your mind? Yourself, or things above? (Col 3:2). Your own little hopes and plans and dreams, or God's eternal plan?

- Spiritual Weapon: **Punishing all disobedience** and replacing it with complete obedience. Obedience, surrender, giving control of your life over to God.

Using these weapons, we can submit our thoughts, beliefs, and attitudes to God. This can invite Jesus into our hearts to demolish Satan's fortresses and to erect His strongholds in their place. Jesus cautions us not leave our hearts **unoccupied** (Mt 12:43-45), but to ask God to fill us with His Spirit. We do our part by renewing our mind with the truth of His Word. As we cement our feet into His foundation of truth, Jesus can erect His own fortifications, and continue to fortify them as we persist in deeply implanting the Word in our hearts.

To see these spiritual weapons used in real life, I have invited my friend "G" back again to describe how she used them in her battle against the Dark.

Suffering from osteoarthritis, emphysema, polymyalgia, obesity, sleep apnea, diabetes, and herniated discs in my neck, I get around in an electric scooter. My neighbor often harasses me – the taunts and criticisms are so painful. Yet I recognize it is spiritual warfare. I know Satan is laying a trap for my faith, trying to get me to think hateful thoughts and fight back with harsh words. Yet I do not, because I recognize my struggle is not against flesh and blood, but against the dark forces. I use spiritual weapons. I pray and offer her kind remarks in return for her hurtful words. I destroy speculations – I refuse to believe Satan's lies about me that this woman spews forth; I know I am redeemed by Christ and loved by Him. I take every thought captive to the obedience of Christ. I see her as a lovely person made in the image of God, who is simply being manipulated by Satan.

"G"
Wake Forest, North Carolina

Notice that "G" recognized that the attack was not from her neighbor, but from the Darkness. If she had utilized weapons of the flesh, she would have perhaps tried to defend herself, or even attacked her neighbor back. But instead, she passed the test by standing firm in God's truth, and by seeing her neighbor with God's eyes of love and compassion. The battle was won in her own heart as she grew to trust her Savior more.

Peter teaches us some additional weapons.

All of you, clothe yourselves with humility toward one another, because, "God opposes the proud but shows favor to the humble." Humble yourselves,

therefore, under God's mighty hand, that he may lift you up in due time. Cast all your anxiety on him because he cares for you. Be alert and of sober mind. Your enemy the devil prowls around like a roaring lion looking for someone to devour. Resist him, standing firm in the faith, because you know that the family of believers throughout the world are undergoing the same kind of sufferings. And the God of all grace, Who called you to his eternal glory in Christ, after you have suffered a little while, will himself restore you and make you strong, firm and steadfast.

1 Peter 5:5-10

What are the weapons Peter lists here?

- **Clothe yourselves with humility.** Humble yourselves under the mighty hand of God, completely dependent upon Him. We are jars of clay – we must not fight the powers of darkness on our own.

- **Cast all your anxiety on him.** Trust Him completely. Leave behind the self-centeredness of worry and anxiety, and focus instead on God.

- **Be self-controlled and alert.** Literally stay awake.[11] Frangipane teaches that Satan is "an ancient and extremely treacherous foe . . . he has been deceiving mankind for thousands of years."[12] We are struggling against him in a hand-to-hand fight; he is using trickery, cunning, and strategy. Do not underestimate him.

- **Resist him.** Do not succumb to his lies, temptations, discouragement, and distractions. Do not allow him to fracture your relationships. Do not forget who you are in Christ. Do not fall into his traps by fighting with family and friends or worrying about your physical needs. Do not forget that the Victor has already been determined.

- Finally, **stand firm in the faith**; even in suffering, trust Him completely and obey Him unconditionally.

You may be familiar with the armor of God that Paul details in Ephesians:

> **Stand firm then, with the belt of truth buckled around your waist, with the breastplate of righteousness in place, and with your feet fitted with the readiness that comes from the gospel of peace. In addition to all this, take up the shield of faith, with which you can extinguish all the flaming arrows of the evil one. Take up the helmet of salvation and the sword of the Spirit, which is the word of God.**
>
> Ephesians 6:14-17

Stand firm is histemi, which can be translated, "to stand fast against an enemy."[13] I have heard it described as holding a crucial position in battle. Paul then concludes this list with one critical command: pray.

> **And pray in the Spirit on all occasions with all kinds of prayers and requests. With this in mind, be alert and always keep on praying for all the Lord's people. Pray also for me, that whenever I speak, words may be given me so that I will fearlessly make known the mystery of the gospel, for which I am an ambassador in chains. Pray that I may declare it fearlessly, as I should.**
>
> Ephesians 6:18-20

Prayer is *the* essential element in spiritual warfare. It is the offensive and the defensive weapon. The Kingdom will not be defended or advanced without it.[14]

Handling Spiritual Weapons

Look at some of Satan's weapons: disrupting relationships, wreaking havoc on your finances, inflicting physical illness – notice he is warring in the flesh. Do not fight back with weapons of the flesh.

- Instead of worrying about your finances, or allowing the stresses of life to throw you into an anxiety attack, use a divinely powerful spiritual weapon: humble yourself, then cast your anxiety upon God and trust Him in everything, big and small.

- If Satan has disrupted a relationship with someone you love, do not fight with weapons of the flesh. Don't try to justify yourself and perpetuate the argument. Choose a divinely powerful spiritual weapon: humble yourself and ask forgiveness for your part in the disagreement.

- If Satan is sowing seeds of doubt, do not fight back with weapons of the flesh, trying to prove yourself to Satan or to the world. Use a divinely powerful spiritual weapon: destroy speculations, and replace Satan's lies with God's truth. God's truth is this: of course you cannot accomplish the assignment God gave to you on your own strength; only God can accomplish it by His Holy Spirit working in and through you.

- If Satan is tempting you to sin, fight back with the spiritual weapon of obedience to God.

- If Satan is trying to suck the life out of you spiritually, fight back by spending more time with God, resting in His presence, allowing him to replenish you.

- If Satan is attacking your mind with worry, anxiety, or ungodly thoughts, fight back by taking every thought captive: immerse yourself in memorizing Scripture.

- If Satan is attacking you with adversity, do not become obsessed with the desire for physical healing or relief from your suffering. Instead, use a divinely powerful spiritual weapon: destroy every lofty thought raised up against God. Relief of suffering may be an idol – smash that idol and put God on the throne in your heart instead.

- Paramount to victory: prayer. Realize that you are too busy *not* to pray; set aside sacred times to meet with God, for it is during your prayer time that God may give you divine insight, unparalleled wisdom, bottomless courage, and the strength to stand firm.

Seeing Suffering Through Spiritual Eyes

I believe all Christians are called to take their turn suffering, which is following in Jesus' steps (Jn 15:20). I envision this as taking the baton in a relay race. In some countries where there is severe persecution for Christ, this may mean imprisonment, torture, or even death. In other countries where there is freedom to practice your faith, suffering may occur in other surprising ways. Spiritual attack may entail:

- Physical illnesses, or accidents that cause serious injuries
- Loss of job
- Loss of money
- Loss of possessions
- Emotional pain of abandonment by loved ones
- Physical or verbal abuse by family or friends
- Verbal persecution because of your faith

Additionally, when we are in the vulnerable position of reaping the consequences of our own sins, we may be open to attack from the Dark.

How Will We Know When Light Has Won?

When we have recognized our affliction as a spiritual attack because the Kingdom is being advanced, and we are brandishing spiritual weapons, how will we know when Light has won the battle? Light has won when we are conformed to Christ. We can assess three areas to determine victory: our response, our obedience, and our peace.

Our Response

When Satan attacks, his goal is to drive us away from God, to lead us into anger, bitterness, self-pity, and anxiety. When we turn to God praising and thanking, accepting and trusting His plan, Light has won that battle.

They overcame him [Satan] because of the blood of the Lamb and because of the word of their testimony, and they did not love their life even when faced with death.

Revelation 12:11 NASB

We overcome Satan when . . .

- We trust that the blood of Jesus has covered all our sins and has given us entrance into heaven.

- We cling to Jesus in faith, even in the most desperate times, for this is our testimony to God's love and grace.

- We hold God's Kingdom and His glory in the place of utmost importance in our lives, so that the most painful of trials, even unto death, do not sway us from our focus and our purpose.

- Instead of fighting Satan on our own, we turn to God in prayer and depend on Jesus' strength and the Holy Spirit's wisdom.

Our Obedience

Satan desires us to give up, to consider it too difficult to pursue our calling. When we refuse to capitulate, when we refuse to abandon our calling, when, in the midst of the warfare, we step out in faith and obedience – then we are victorious in Jesus.

Stand firm, then . . .

Ephesians 6:14

Our Peace

When we are being crushed with the pain of this world, yet we are still able to rest in His peace, we have overcome. When we are in the depth of adversity and are in no way alarmed by our opponents (Phil 1:28), and we are certain that He who is in us is greater than he who is in the world (1Jn 4:4), we have triumphed in Christ. The greater our trust and acceptance and the more complete our obedience, the more pervading will be our peace, and the more decisive will be Christ's victory.

Can God Use Troubles We Caused By Our Own Sins To Advance His Kingdom?

He most certainly can. God uses His entire creation, and *all* circumstances, to further *His* eternal plan, for His Kingdom and His glory. Additionally, God is always working for *our* good, even when we are disobedient to Him. Yet it seems to me that it is not until we *fully surrender* that we position ourselves to see the goodness of His work and to receive those blessings.

Yet recognize that persecution for righteousness' sake places our suffering and trials into an entirely different category than tribulations because of our own sins.

But if when you do what is right and suffer for it you patiently endure it, this finds favor with God.
1 Peter 2:20 NASB

Can His Kingdom Be Advanced Without Suffering?

Although we may not be able to fully understand this, the link between suffering and the advancement of the Kingdom is clear in Scripture. We are called to follow in Jesus' steps (1Pet 2:21). God's glory is revealed through our sufferings. Not despite our sufferings – *through* our sufferings. Don't be surprised; don't think the trial is strange:

Beloved, do not be surprised at the fiery ordeal among you, which comes upon you for your testing, as though some strange thing were happening to you; but to the degree that you share the sufferings of Christ, keep on rejoicing, so that also at the revelation of His glory you may rejoice with exultation.

1 Peter 4:12-13 NASB

Don't miss this phrase: the *degree* that you suffer. The greater the suffering, the more potential for His glory. The more God's Kingdom is advanced, the more He is glorified.

Jesus Is Passing You the Baton: You're Up

Paul seems to really be able to comprehend the connection between the degree of suffering and the potential for God's glory. We read about his thorn in Chapter 7. Paul writes that Christ's power is completed in our weakness, and Paul craves weakness and "delights" in agony so that Christ's power can work through him. **For when I am weak, then I am strong** (2Cor 12:10).

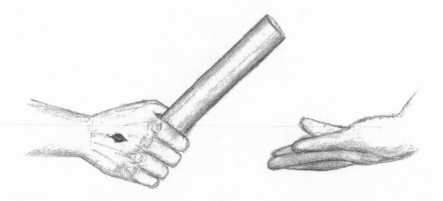

Let's get a good understanding of this concept. When we are weak through physical or emotional affliction, we can become less likely to take any glory for what Christ does *through* us, because it may become more clear that it is not of us. When we are weak, when we realize that we are humble jars of clay, then Christ can work through us powerfully because we are not trying to take the glory for ourselves. When we give God the glory, His Kingdom can be advanced twofold: advanced in the arena where He is working through us, and also advanced in our own humbled hearts.

Somehow, adversity can be God's way of declaring us worthy of bearing the name Christian. In Acts, Peter and the apostles were flogged, then they

. . . left the Sanhedrin, rejoicing because they had been counted worthy of suffering disgrace for the Name.

Acts 5:41

Stunning. Can we reach that point in our relationship with Jesus? That we rejoice in a fiery trial, a flogging, because it may be God declaring that we are counted worthy of suffering disgrace for His Name? Listen to it again in Thessalonians:

Therefore, among God's churches we boast about your perseverance and faith in all the persecutions and trials you are enduring. All this is evidence that God's judgment is right, and as a result you will be counted worthy of the kingdom of God, for which you are suffering.

2 Thessalonians 1:4-5

When we persevere in persecutions and trials, it indicates that we are **counted worthy** of the Kingdom. It is God stamping us, His earthen vessels, with the word "genuine" on the bottom. It shows that we are worthy to bear Christ's Name, to be called Christians.

In the next few chapters, we are going to be exploring our calling that can arise out of our suffering. As we embrace our purpose, God may call us to step out boldly for the Kingdom. Beware, for Satan may attempt to thwart us.

Be prepared to seize territory for the Kingdom by spiritual force. Use spiritual weapons to advance the Kingdom in your heart, and in other's hearts. When Jesus, working through you, has wrenched territory from the Dark by spiritual force, stand firm. Hold that crucial position in battle. Remain obedient. No matter how agonizing the tribulation is, cling to Jesus. Bear up steadfastly under the tremendous weight with faith and perseverance, singing His praises even when, to the outside observer, there appears to be no reason to thank and praise. Do not abandon your calling no matter how intense the spiritual warfare. Stand firm. Histemi: You are in a crucial battle position. Hold it.

God has work for you – staggering work for His Kingdom. If you have journeyed through trials, or are right now in the midst of adversity, it may be your time of equipping. Are you ready to take on your calling? Are you prepared to suffer for His Name? Are you willing to put your hand to the plow and not look back? Are you pouring yourself out as a drink offering? You are next up in the relay. Jesus is passing you the baton. Will you take it?

PART III: INTIMACY WITH CHRIST

Seize Your Purpose

Through Your Suffering

Chapter 9
Suffering Can Lead to Intimacy With Christ

*D*o you ever feel crushed with suffering? Pressed between a rock and a hard place? Broken and helpless, beyond human repair? Maybe this will explain things: the Greek word for suffering, or trouble, is thlipsis, translated "to crush, press, compress, squeeze." Wait – there's more. Thlipsis is derived from a word meaning "to break."[1] Do these words fit your situation?

Now don't miss this. I have heard that the Greek word used to describe the process of squeezing oil from olives *is exactly the same word*, thlipsis.[2]

In Jesus' time, an olive press was an enormous device, a huge millstone on top of another enormous stone. An ox or donkey would toil around in circles, turning the millstone, crushing, squeezing the olives until the precious oil oozed out. "In this world you will have thlipsis" (Jn 16:33). In this world you will be crushed with a millstone, squeezed to a pulp, until the oil drips out. Sheer coincidence, the dual implications of this word? Hardly. God understands our suffering. His signature of His love is all over that word. Stick with me here.

Jesus spent the night before He died in Gethsemane, a garden at the base of the Mount of Olives. Gethsemane is an Aramaic word meaning "oil press."[3] Jesus spent the Agony in the Garden in the *oil press*, being crushed, compressed, squeezed, as if between two millstones. Jesus can relate to our sorrows and pain. Jesus can relate to us. But . . . can *we* relate to *Him*?

Koinonia

When my teenage son hangs with his guy friends, they inevitably wind up engaging in some kind of "showing your scars" ritual. When he was in kindergarten it was the most recent scraped knee, but today it is the scars of recent knee surgery, the twisted ankle that knocked him out of gymnastics competitions for a month, or the laceration that required layers of stitches. The last time I heard him with his friends, I thought, *When are they going to grow out of this?* Not long afterwards I overheard my husband with his guy friends, displaying his scar from a motorcycle accident and one from getting skegged surfing, and I thought, *They are* never *going to grow out of this*. However, the next day I found myself sharing labor-and-delivery horror stories with another mom – and that is when I realized that this is the way people bond. We search for this fellowship, this koinonia in the Greek – a word that means "participation, communion, fellowship."[4] Koinonia is a passionate connection because two people can relate. Koinonia is also what bonds us *to Christ*.

God . . . has called you into fellowship with his Son, Jesus Christ our Lord . . .

1 Corinthians 1:9

God calls us into **fellowship** with Jesus – that's koinonia, an acute, penetrating closeness. We may reach this profound intimate connection with Him if we can relate, if we have shared similar intense, significant, defining experiences. What is Jesus' intense significant defining experience?

So His appearance was marred more than any man
And His form more than the sons of men . . .
He was despised and forsaken of men,
A man of sorrows and acquainted with grief;
And like one from whom men hide their face
He was despised, and we did not esteem Him.
Isaiah 52:14, 53:3 NASB

Marred beyond human likeness. A man of sorrows. Acquainted with grief. Despised, rejected. Jesus endured excruciating pain and unbelievable humiliation. He was deserted by all His trusted friends. He experienced deep spiritual pain, **"My God, my God, why have you forsaken me?"** (Mt 27:46). Sharing in Jesus' sufferings is a way we can bond with Him in a piercing vivid closeness, with our lives incredibly woven together.

Now if we are children, then we are heirs — heirs of God and co-heirs with Christ, *if indeed* we share in his sufferings in order that we may also share in his glory.
Romans 8:17, emphasis added

If indeed. After the resurrection, Jesus, in His glorified body, was walking through walls, breathing the Holy Spirit, disappearing and reappearing, making Himself unrecognizable one minute and recognizable the next – yet He *still* bore the scars of His crucifixion. Thomas insisted on putting his finger in Jesus' nail marks and his hand into Jesus' side (Jn 20:24-28). It seems to be the same "showing your scars" ritual. Revelation tells us that even at the end of time Jesus *still* bears these scars, He is **a Lamb, looking as if it had been slain** (Rev 5:6). I believe that even in eternity Jesus does not want us to forget what He has suffered for us, because it demonstrates, like nothing else can, His infinite love for us.

How exactly can we share in His sufferings? I would like to explore three areas the Lord may invite us to share in His sufferings. Here's an overview:

- Suffering for the unsaved
- Suffering as we die to ourselves
- Suffering for the church

Suffering for the Unsaved: Persecution for Our Faith

This area is perhaps the easiest to comprehend.

"A servant is not greater than his master. If they persecuted me, they will persecute you also."
Jesus, speaking to His disciples in John 15:20

Suffering for Jesus' name. This is the present-day martyrs in countries where speaking Jesus' name merits execution. This is the young girl in the schoolyard mocked by her friends because she goes to church. This is the man at work passed over for a promotion because "he's just too much a Jesus-freak for our company."

The early Christians suffered horrendous persecution. They were beaten, imprisoned, stoned, even crucified. They physically bore scars for our Lord. Many today also bear physical scars for Christ. Our King suffered physically, emotionally, mentally, and spiritually to the extreme. Why would we expect anything less?

When we are persecuted and stand fast in our faith without abandoning the Lord, we are bold witnesses for Jesus to those who do not know Him. When we are attacked or oppressed, and forgive our enemies and love our persecutors with the pure love of Christ, our actions

speak the gospel message to them. I have asked my friend
Jessica to share a very personal story of how God reached
her by using the way *she herself* persecuted a Christian.

*When I was in college, I did not yet know the Lord. I was
living for myself, for my own dreams and pleasures – just as
everyone else in college seemed to be doing. But there was
one girl at my college who was distinctly different. Many
of us college students went to church and claimed to be
Christian, but this girl actually lived it out. She was kind,
understanding, and forgiving. She didn't cheat or lie. She
dressed tastefully yet modestly. She had a peace and a joy
that did not depend on her grades, her relationships, or her
circumstances. And we persecuted her.*

*We made fun of her modesty, her honesty, her chastity,
and her church. She still smiled. She still treated us with
kindness. She still helped us when we didn't understand
physics. She never caved in to the pressures to cheat, lie,
undercut others, or forsake her purity. She had Godly
priorities, and she never wavered.*

*Although I had not had any contact with this girl since
college, her life impacted me twenty years later. At age 40,
as I began to seek God, I could not get out this girl out of my
mind. As I replayed in my mind again and again how she
lived during those college years, I came to realize that she
had genuine faith, and lived her life demonstrating that
faith. Twenty years after we had persecuted her, I realized
that she was the only true Christian I had ever known. And
I wanted a relationship with God just like that.*

Jessica
Pittsburgh, Pennsylvania

Jessica did eventually come to Christ and has a
beautiful relationship with the Lord just as that girl does –
but she has not found that girl again. What strikes me the
most about this story is the timing of the impact that this
girl had on Jessica: *twenty years later.* Realize that we

simply may not know the reasons for our persecution until many years later – and perhaps not even until eternity.

I wish we could have that girl's side of the story. I believe she may say something like this: It seems when God ordains persecution for us, He offers us the *privilege* of participating in His sufferings, perhaps the privilege of reaching the unsaved. He gives us the honor of koinonia, of sharing His pain, of feeling what He feels.

I believe that God is weeping over the pain in this world. His heart is broken. Yet when we share in His sufferings, He has opened the door for us to understand Him more. He has given us a little piece of His heart. Puny, insignificant humans, given a piece of the Almighty's heart. Yes, I would do *anything* for that.

Sharing in His Sufferings Can Strategically Position Us To Advance the Kingdom

Let's go to Philippians to hear Paul detail how he was strategically positioned – in prison – to advance the Kingdom. His availability and attitude gave him witnessing opportunities himself, and also inspired the brothers and sisters in Christ to spread the gospel.

Now I want you to know, brothers and sisters, that what has happened to me has actually served to advance the gospel. As a result, it has become clear throughout the whole palace guard and to everyone else that I am in chains for Christ. And because of my chains, most of the brothers and sisters have become confident in the Lord and dare all the more to proclaim the gospel without fear.

Philippians 1:12-14

Paul so rejoiced in his persecution because he realized it **has actually served to advance the gospel**! How? Paul was so intimate with Jesus, so fully surrendered to God, so completely accepting of God's plan for his life – even when that meant being beaten and imprisoned – he was not complaining and asking, "Why me?" Instead, he was witnessing – to **the whole palace guard**! In addition to the gospel being advanced right where Paul was witnessing, it was advanced in many other arenas as well, because many **have become confident in the Lord and dare all the more to proclaim the gospel without fear.** Paul's choice to embrace courage, to face forward, to live only to glorify God, and to surrender to God's almighty plan – even when it entailed persecution – impacted and inspired the brothers and sisters so powerfully.

You met my friend Joe back in Chapter 6 when he shared his journey of forgiveness of his father. To me, Joe is a modern-day Paul. Listen to his story of "imprisonment," how he witnessed to those "in prison" with him, and how the brothers and sisters outside were inspired to "dare all the more to proclaim the gospel without fear."

Too many years of football and fishing had caught up with me, and I needed a hip replacement. I was angry, and terrified – too young for this! Yet I had no choice.

After the hip replacement, I was sent to a "rehab center" – which is a fancy name for a nursing home. The patients here were ancient, with two feet in the grave. At 50, I was the "young kid" in the place. What was I doing here?

Somehow, in the midst of my pain, my self pity, and my demanding of God, "Why me?" God spoke to my heart. I realized I was here to bring the gospel message to these decrepit and precious people. Because I was "one of them," limping with them, struggling through physical therapy with them, I could relate – and I had their ear. They listened to me, because we had bonded through suffering.

God broke my heart for a very elderly gentleman, a former orthopedic surgeon. But he would not let me get close to him. But watching football together broke the barrier. We became friends, and he listened as I shared Christ. He soon turned to God and gave his heart to Christ.

While I was in rehab, my huddle group came to visit me. They learned why God had sent me here: to bring His gospel message. They realized these people would never have listened to me if I was not one of them. And my witnessing inspired some of my huddle group to step out for Christ also! One woman was sharing the gospel message with her co-workers and customers. Another woman had started volunteering in a nursing home to bring Christ's love to the elderly people there. God is truly amazing.

I know that God took me through this suffering for His specific purposes, and if I had to do it all over again, I would not hesitate to say, "Yes, Lord. Send me!"

Joe Tardonia
Christ Fellowship Student Ministries Leader
Palm Beach Gardens, Florida

When we share in Christ's sufferings, and through our pain seek intimacy with Him, the koinonia that develops can unite us with God. As our hearts are aligned with His heart, our hands can work in unison with His hands, reaching out with Him to those who are lost and hurting.

Suffering As We Die to Ourselves:
"Unless a Kernel of Wheat Falls to the Ground..."

Let's take this a step further and talk about sharing in His sufferings through dying to ourselves. I'd like to introduce you to my friend Richard Ekey, a member of my *Triumph* Leadership Team and the determined and persevering Founder of the Men's Branch of *Triumph*.

He is also the Co-Founder of our church's Cancer Support Groups.   Richard will use a powerful word picture to explain.

The Bible uses the analogy of sowing and reaping repeatedly throughout, using words like seeds, roots, fruit, and growth.   It is an apt analogy.   In order for a tree to grow, something inside, its seed, must first die.   Similarly, in order for us to grow spiritually, something inside of us must first die.   That may be our anger, our jealousy, our pride or independence, our controlling nature, our unforgiveness, or perhaps our idolatry.   When these sins die, and we surrender the pain to God to heal, the seed will then be planted.   This one seed planted in good soil can push roots downward and grow sprouts upward, and eventually produce bushels of fruit at harvest time.   The death of one habitual sin can be like that seed planted in good soil, that pushes down deep roots and grows, producing bushels of fruit of the Spirit.   And, just as there is a length of time between when the dead seed is sown and the fruit is harvested, there will be a length of time between when your sin dies and the fruit of the Spirit is harvested.

Richard Ekey
Founder of the Men's Branch of Triumph
Co-Founder Cancer Support Groups
Christ Fellowship Church
Palm Beach Gardens, Florida

This brings to mind Jesus' teachings:

"Very truly I tell you, unless a kernel of wheat falls to the ground and dies, it remains only a single seed. But if it dies, it produces many seeds. Anyone who loves their life will lose it, while anyone who hates their life in this world will keep it for eternal life."
John 12:24-25

There is no new life without death. As Richard put it, "Something inside must die." And when the seed is planted, the potential for harvest is exponential:

"Still other seed fell on good soil. It came up, grew and produced a crop, multiplying thirty, sixty, or even a hundred times."

Mark 4:8

If we are fixated on our own plans, our own way, our own comforts, it may interfere with our relationship with Jesus. If we insist on our trials coming to an end and simply wait for that day, it may hinder our openness to what God is working *through* the trial. If we are only focused on healing or resolution of the problem, we can miss the deepening of relationship that He desires. Dying to ourselves is painful. Yet it can open our hearts to receive more of His Spirit, to grow more intimate with the Lord.

Koinonia Can Lead To Pure Worship

If God relieved every difficulty that we encountered, we would probably be His people because He made life easy for us. There would really be no freedom of choice. We would probably choose Jesus for the healings and comforts and conveniences. Yet God wants us to love Him not because of the miracles He can do, but because *He is God*. This is the kind of worshipers He seeks, for Jesus teaches us,

"Yet a time is coming and has now come when the true worshipers will worship the Father in the Spirit and in truth, for they are the kind of worshipers the Father seeks. God is spirit, and his worshipers must worship in the Spirit and in truth."

John 4:23-24

How can we learn the kind of worship that pleases God? Well, it seems easy to worship when life is going our way. But in the darkest valley, when there appears to be no reason to thank and praise, and *still* we worship Him – that is pure worship. When we die to our own plans and desires, and focus on Him – that is pure worship. When we die to ourselves and live for Him – that is pure worship.

David wrote many psalms of pure worship. An example of this is Psalm 57, written while David was hiding in the caves, running for his life from Saul. Let's listen in.

> **I am in the midst of lions;**
> **I am forced to dwell among ravenous beasts—**
> **men whose teeth are spears and arrows,**
> **whose tongues are sharp swords.**
> **Be exalted, O God, above the heavens;**
> **let your glory be over all the earth.**
>
> Psalm 57:4-5

Hear his anguished cries interwoven with his praises. David was not afraid to pour out his pain and emotions to God. Yet somehow in the midst of his pain, he was still able to reach pure worship, praise in the darkest of valleys.

Paul and Silas are another profound example of worship in suffering. Let's follow their story.

> **The crowd joined in the attack against Paul and Silas, and the magistrates ordered them to be stripped and beaten with rods. After they had been severely flogged, they were thrown into prison, and the jailer was commanded to guard them carefully ... he put them in the inner cell and fastened their feet in the stocks. About midnight Paul and Silas were praying and singing hymns to God ...**
>
> Acts 16:22-25

Paul and Silas were beaten with rods, severely flogged, thrown in stocks – and were still praying and singing hymns to God! Pure worship for sure! The story climaxes as an earthquake freed Paul and Silas, and the jailer and his whole household were saved and baptized. Yes, I believe this is the deepest, purest, most profound worship we can give Him: worship in suffering.

Declining the Invitation to Surrender

Fasten your seatbelts – we're going deeper. Let's explore what happens when God is calling us to surrender, to die to ourselves, and we decline the invitation. Remember that God's plan for us is intimacy. He created us for *relationship* with Him. His greatest desire for us is koinonia – for He knows that as we draw closer to Him, we can receive more of His love and peace, and can live in deeper trust of Him. Therefore, if our attention and devotion are *not* on God, He may intervene in our lives in a way that we might call painful. Thlipsis. A breaking. His *kind intent* is to bring us to repentance (Rom 2:4).

What will it take to alert us to our precarious position far from Him? Physical illness? Loss of job? A fractured relationship? A calamity? Financial disaster? Abandonment? Destruction of our reputation? On a superficial level, these trials may appear to be consequences of our sins, or the backlash from others' sins, or simply because we live on a sinful fallen planet. But look deeper. Look higher. Is God using these hardships to get your attention and bring you to repentance? Remember, *God lets us* sin in such a way that we can exert our free will – but cannot thwart the fulfillment of His vast eternal plan.

Suffering for the Church

As we withstand persecution and watch God use it to advance His Kingdom, and as we develop deeper intimacy with Jesus by dying to ourselves, we may more fully understand the suffering Jesus endured for us. Through our koinonia, we may take on His identity, our mind becoming His mind, our heart becoming His heart. Because we are one with Him, we may develop a willingness to suffer and die for the church, **just as Christ loved the church and gave himself up for her** (Eph 5:25). I have asked my friend Kim B. back with us to share how her suffering touched the church.

I was incapacitated for a year and a half because of vertigo, forced to lie in bed because every little movement, sound, stimuli overwhelmed me with debilitating dizziness.

I had nothing – but God. I could do nothing – but pray. I could not even take care of my kids – and God humbled me and taught me that life would go on without me.

This became my time of intimacy with Christ. I had precious moments with Him that would never have happened without this illness. As I focused exclusively on Him, I became confident in the truth that He loved me and He had a plan for my life. I knew that He was not finished with me yet. I came to accept that whether I regained my health or not, I was going to remain close to my Savior, and also to my family and friends.

God also birthed a ministry work out of my suffering. People are open to me because I can relate to their pain, and I have founded a company that promotes complete wellness. Yet the most significant result of my suffering happened in my 14-year-old daughter's heart. God took her through the fire of this traumatic time and she emerged with a spiritual maturity that belies her age, a remarkable ability to relate to others who are suffering, and a tenderness that belongs only to those who have suffered.

*Now to Him who is able to do immeasurably more than
we ask or imagine . . . to Him be the glory! (Eph 3:20-21).*

Kim B.
West Palm Beach, Florida

Notice the profound intimacy with Jesus that Kim
B. developed during this season. Notice the ministry
work that emerged. And notice how her suffering was
instrumental in the spiritual growth of her daughter —
who is now a grown woman with a passionate heart for
teens and a burning devotion to the Lord.

When we are intimate with Christ, our hearts may be
one with God's, bleeding over the lost, knowing that *His*
desire is for every person to surrender to Christ (2Pet 3:9,
1Tim 2:4). When we are intimate with Christ, we may see
the church through His eyes, see the distress of the church
members and desire to do all we can to facilitate their
healing. We may desire their spiritual growth so acutely
that we may become willing to suffer for them. Paul really
grasps this, as we will read in Philippians below. Paul
wrote this letter from prison — but don't start imagining
prisons of today, with nice little cots and meals three times
a day. Think dirt floors, chains, beatings, starvation, and
cold.

**For to me, to live is Christ and to die is gain. If I
am to go on living in the body, this will mean fruitful
labor for me. Yet what shall I choose? I do not know!
I am torn between the two: I desire to depart and
be with Christ, which is better by far; but it is more
necessary for you that I remain in the body.**

Philippians 1:21-24

Remain here — suffering, beaten, imprisoned.
Unbelievable. Can we come to that extreme in our
relationship with Christ? That we desire to remain on

this earth, suffering, because it may be necessary for the spiritual growth of the body of Christ?

Understand that Paul is not contemplating suicide here. He is wondering what his sentence will be: death, or life. Of course, he realizes that God alone has the ultimate control of whether he lives or dies.

Let's focus on what Paul means when he writes that **it is more necessary for you,** for *the church,* that he remains here on earth. Let's explore this concept a bit further. Later down in this epistle to the Philippians, Paul writes about his **fellow worker and soldier,** Epaphroditis, who was sick,

... sick to point of death ... he came close to death for the work of Christ, risking his life to complete what was deficient in your service to me.
Philippians 2:27, 30 NASB

We are the body of Christ. If one member is not fulfilling his designated purpose, another member may suffer in order to fill in the deficiency. Intimacy with Christ translating to intimacy with the church. We are members of one body.

Do you think all the suffering is worth it? Let's go back once more to Philippians and read Paul's perspective.

All Else Is Rubbish

I count all things to be loss in view of the surpassing value of knowing Christ Jesus my Lord, for whom I have suffered the loss of all things, and count them but rubbish so that I may gain Christ,

**and may be found in Him, not having a righteousness
of my own derived from the Law, but that which is
through faith in Christ, the righteousness which
comes from God on the basis of faith, that I may
know Him and the power of His resurrection and
the fellowship of His sufferings, being conformed to
His death . . .**

Philippians 3:8-10 NASB

Paul possessed money, power,
influence, prestige (Phil 3:4-6) –
and he writes that these things are
rubbish, trash, *garbage* compared
to knowing Jesus so passionately, in
penetrating fellowship, in koinonia. It
seems Paul relinquished the height of
the world's glory for a life of hardships,
because he craved relationship with
Jesus.

The fellowship of His sufferings. This wording
really intrigues me. Paul doesn't say the fellowship of
sharing in the power of His resurrection, but the fellowship
of sharing in His *sufferings*. Of course we can draw close to
Jesus in times of peacefulness and rest in Him, or during
times the Lord has anointed us with His Spirit and is
using us powerfully. But it seems Paul is indicating that
a special kind of koinonia can develop with our Lord when
we are suffering. The potential is there for a unique kind
of fellowship if we seek Him with all our heart.

When our pain is so great that the world cannot
comfort us, then we can truly seek God. This is His
greatest desire for us, that we seek Him with a passion,
that we crave Him intensely, that we thirst for Him above
all else. He wants us to realize that He is *the only One* we
can completely trust. We probably will not desire Him and
trust Him above all else without pain and affliction, and
the realization that nothing in the world – no people, no
things – can comfort us. This is the love that He desires,

the love that knows with certainty that *He* is our only true Comfort.

You met Dr. Chimes in Chapter 1. I have known this warrior of Christ for many years. He is a seasoned and mature Christian, and at this stage in his walk with Christ, living out "considering it all rubbish" is as natural to him as breathing. Hear how he tells it:

When I became blind, I lost everything: my chiropractic practice, my career, my profession, my financial security. But I consider it all rubbish, because my blindness has been instrumental in my closer walk with Jesus. I have come to trust, rely, and lean on Him more. I have learned to walk by faith and not by sight (2Cor 5:7). Through my blindness, God has humbled me and made me more compassionate. Since I must depend on Him physically, I have learned to depend on Him spiritually also. God has worked in me a deep trust of Him as my Rock and my Salvation, for I simply do not know what tomorrow holds. But what I do know is that He holds my life in His hands.
Dr. Michael Chimes, Chiropractor
Palm Beach Gardens, Florida

Hear his honesty. He has "learned," he has been "humbled." I suspect this was not an easy journey.

"He Must Increase, But I Must Decrease"

Come meet one more of my *Triumph* Servant Leaders, Julie Stine, triumphing with Christ over rheumatoid arthritis. I have invited her to teach one last significant point.

As I struggle with an "invisible illness," God teaches me new truths daily as I trust Him. My calling to reach people with chronic illness has been thwarted for years because of my own illness and pain. As I wait on His timing, He has brought me to a place of pure worship, and total submission and reliance on Him. I now realize that His will shall be done in my life regardless of my physical health; I am just the vessel and it will be 100% Jesus and 0% Julie. The ultimate outcome will be complete glorification of the Father. I will be ready when God sees I am ready, for "apart from Me you can do nothing" (Jn 15:5). I am nothing without Him, and yet I can do everything with Him.

Julie Stine
Triumph Servant Leader
Stuart, Florida

I like how Julie puts it: "100% Jesus and 0% Julie." Less of me and more of Him. As I decrease, as my ego and my character and my personhood get out of the way, then people can see less of me and more of Jesus. As John the Baptist says, **"He must increase, but I must decrease"** (Jn 3:30 NASB).

Jesus becomes more prominent; I become less. He receives more glory; I receive less. Less of me can mean deeper koinonia with Him. As we die to ourselves, we can enter into such a close knit fellowship with Christ that we are engulfed in Him, our lives **hidden with Christ in God** (Col 3:3). All else can fade away and become rubbish compared to the surpassing greatness of knowing Christ Jesus our Lord.

Chapter 10
How Will You Respond
To Your Suffering?

o you feel like you have no power over your life, like you are being manipulated beyond your control? Do you think you are being manipulated by God? By Satan? We can choose to believe that we are being manipulated by some all-powerful force. We can give up and surrender to the manipulation.

Yet we do have other choices. We may not be able to choose whether or not we are afflicted with this suffering, but we can choose how we interpret it, how we *respond* to our trials. In this chapter, we are going to investigate our response to adversity and look at the choices we have.[1]

I see two paths open to us when life throws us a curve ball: to turn *to* God, or *away* from God. First, we're going to discuss what our lives may look like if we turn *away* from God. You may be surprised at what you are going to hear.

Turning Away From God In Suffering

Bitterness and Hedonism

Turning away from God may mean that we sink into a life of bitterness, unforgiveness, hopelessness, anger, self-pity, or despair. Or, it may mean that we completely give up trying to live right by God and turn to alcohol, drugs, food, relationships, gambling, sex, money, pleasures, or thrills to try to assuage the pain. This is a life of hedonism – doing whatever it takes to gratify us here and now.

Busyness

Turning away from God, however, can be subtler than bitterness or hedonism. It may mean we immerse ourselves in activities and fill up our schedules so that we are too busy to have time for God. These activities can even be seemingly good things, such as working, taking care of our family, enjoying hobbies, cleaning, or even doing volunteer work or serving in church.

Burying Our Desires, Stuffing Our Emotions, And Denying Our Pain

This scenario can be a little unclear at first whether it is turning *to* God or turning *away from* God. Let's ponder this a bit.

- Burying our desires can be insisting that we really didn't want all those dreams that are not coming true. Well, that doesn't really seem ungodly, does it?

- Stuffing our emotions can be convincing ourselves that it doesn't really matter that we've lost our "happy" family, or our health, or our financial security. That it's okay with us that life is not going according to our plan. Well, that sounds pretty stoic . . . not really a bad thing, right?

- And denying our pain can also sound pretty acceptable, like we are being good Christians and carrying our crosses without complaining.

Hmmm . . . these thoughts don't sound so bad. They're not attitudes of hedonism or bitterness or anything like that.

Back up a minute. Any belief or thought process that suppresses the truth does *not* glorify God. This choice of suppressing desires and emotions and pain in an attempt to end suffering and find happiness is falling into the deception that "everything is okay." It is living in denial. It is lying to ourselves that we have no pain. Denying will probably send us unconsciously searching for something else in the physical to quiet the pain that we won't admit that we have. Denying is saying that God is *not enough* for our contentment. I think we can see that this choice is not turning to God. Turning to God would be *acknowledging* the depth of our pain, and seeking healing and comfort *in Him*.

Praying for Relief of Suffering

This next choice can also be a little unclear whether it is turning *to* God or *away from* God. This choice involves praying for healing or for resolution of the problem. "How can *that* not be turning to God?" you ask. Time to explore.

Have you heard any of these comments?

- "Name it and claim it!"
- "You can be healed if only your faith is strong enough."
- "You must not really believe it or you would be cured."
- "Ask and you will receive."

Are these statements true?   Do we lack what we requested simply because we have not "believed?"

I think those who say "name it and claim it" may be basing their beliefs on Scripture verses, but not on the whole counsel of the Bible. As we study these verses, keep in mind that I am *not* saying, "Don't pray for healing or resolution to problems." By all means, *do* ask! We are just going to examine our methods and motives in the asking. Let's take a tour.

"You may ask me for anything in my name, and I will do it."

John 14:14

I like the sound of that.

He replied . . . "Truly I tell you, if you have faith as small as a mustard seed, you can say to this mountain, 'Move from here to there' and it will move. Nothing will be impossible for you."

Matthew 17:20

I tried that before. It didn't work.

"Ask and it will be given to you; seek and you will find; knock and the door will be opened to you. For everyone who asks receives; the one who seeks finds; and to the one who knocks, the door will be opened."

Matthew 7:7-8

I've been asking for my son to be cured since he was four years old. I'm knocking . . . why isn't the door being opened?

Is anyone among you sick? Let them call the elders of the church to pray over them and anoint them with oil in the name of the Lord. And the prayer offered in faith will make the sick person well; the Lord will raise them up.

James 5:14-15

Got elders? Got oil? Got healing?

. . . by his wounds we are healed.

Isaiah 53:5

These verses sound good – we can name it and claim it! Whoa – not so fast. Taking these verses to mean "name it and claim it" would be taking these verses out of context.

A Deeper Look

Let's go back and put all those verses into context.[2]

Asking In Jesus' Name

We will tackle that first verse in John 14 by backing up and starting at verse 12, and reading a little further into Chapter 15:

"Very truly I tell you, whoever believes in me will do the works I have been doing, and they will do even greater things than these, because I am going to the Father. And I will do whatever you ask in my name, so that the Father may be glorified in the Son. You may ask me for anything in my name, and I will

do it.. . . . If you remain in me and my words remain
in you, ask whatever you wish, and it will be given
you."

John 14:12-14; 15:7

Examine the details. In order to have our prayers
answered as we desire, there are a few conditions listed in
these verses.

- Jesus says He will do whatever we ask. Whatever
  anyone asks? No, not anyone. *Anyone who believes
  in Jesus.* And Jesus defines belief, or faith:
  **"Whoever believes in me will do what I have
  been doing."** What has Jesus been doing? His
  Father's will. So if we are doing His Father's will,
  Jesus will do whatever we ask.

- **"And I will do whatever you ask in my name."**
  What is that all about anyway? Is it simply
  attaching, "In Jesus' name we pray" at the end of
  each prayer?

Biblically, the name in ancient Hebrew meant more
than a literal name. My Word Study defines it "as a mark
or memorial of individuality . . . implying . . . character . . .
fame . . . renown, report."[3] Additionally, the name is "what
specifically identifies a person."[4]

The name is the character, the attributes, the nature of
someone. So if we are asking in Jesus' name, it means we
know Him. We know Him deeply, we know His character,
His attributes, His nature – and we know His heart. So
we are asking what Jesus would be asking His Father –
in short, we are asking His Father's will. Big difference
between "asking *anything*" and "asking *anything that is
My Father's will.*" Hmmm . . . In order to ask His will, we
need to *know* His will. That is a mighty tall order.

- **"If you remain in me . . ."** Remain, or abide, is a
  beautiful word, meno in the Greek. Let's take a look
  at some of its translations:

♦ "To stay (in a given place, state, relation or expectancy)"
♦ "To abide"
♦ "To dwell"
♦ "To remain"
♦ And my personal favorite: "to tarry" [5]

Meno is to love Jesus' company so much we want to tarry in His presence; we do not want to rush off to the affairs of everyday life. Meno is further defined as "to be and remain united with him, one with him in heart, mind, and will."[6] If we are united in His will, we can ask according to His will, and whatever we ask according to His will, He shall give to us. Kay Arthur summarizes it this way, "As you abide in Him through worship and time in the Word, His words will abide in you. Then, because you know His will, you will be able to ask according to His will." [7]

- Last condition: **"And I will do whatever you ask in my name, so that the Father may be glorified in the Son."** Giving glory to God is the reason Jesus did everything – from His miracles of healing to His death on the cross. So His Father's will is what shall bring glory to the Father. These two things are inseparably tied together. In order for our prayers to be answered as we desire, the answer must be bringing glory to the Father. We studied glory, doxa, in Chapter 6 – the obvious presence of God. Bringing glory to God is revealing to mankind the love, splendor, majesty, compassion, and faithfulness of God, leading people to recognize God as God. Could it be that at this point in time our suffering is bringing glory to God in a way that relief of our suffering at this time would not?

The Faith That Moves Mountains

Leaping to Matthew, we will take on Matthew 17:20: the faith as small as a mustard seed that moves mountains. We studied faith, pistis, in Chapter 3: an action word meaning that we believe it so deeply that we live like we believe it. **"Anyone who has faith in me will do what I am doing"** (Jn 14:12). When we are working where He is working, when we are in the center of His will, He will move mountains for us. Because our heart is His heart, because our will is His will, we will have any prayer we desire answered.

Ask, Seek, Knock

Put these verses into context by reading the entire passage:

"Ask and it will be given to you; seek and you will find; knock and the door will be opened to you. For everyone who asks receives; the one who seeks finds; and to the one who knocks, the door will be opened. Which of you, if your son asks for bread, will give him a stone? Or if he asks for a fish, will give him a snake? If you, then, though you are evil, know how to give good gifts to your children, how much more will your Father in heaven give good gifts to those who ask him!"

Matthew 7:7-11

We can see from this entire passage that the Father is not giving us absolutely anything we ask for. He is giving us **good gifts**. In Chapter 5 we studied this word good, agathos, which is what we *need*, not necessarily what we *want*. Agathos is God working to do whatever it takes to conform us to the image of His Son; in all things, He is working for good to those who love Him (Rom 8:28-29).

There is something else to notice here. We have taken these "ask, seek, knock" verses out of an even larger context: The Sermon on the Mount (Mt Ch 6-8). I would like to draw your attention to what Jesus taught His disciples in Matthew 6 just before the "ask, seek, knock" verses. He taught them The Lord's Prayer, the "Our Father Prayer." In this prayer, Jesus teaches us to pray in a very specific order:[8]

- **Our Father** . . . praying in this way is for those who know Jesus, who can call God "Father," those who have surrendered their lives to Him, who are His children.

- **Your kingdom come, your will be done.** This is how the prayer begins: with us putting God first, putting His Kingdom first, submitting to His will. Desiring only His will, craving only what He wants, thirsting for His ways that are higher than our ways (Isa 55:9). Not our thoughts, which are but foolishness to God (1Cor 3:19). Seeking first His Kingdom and His righteousness (Mt 6:33). Kay Arthur tells it like it is: "There is no adjusting God's will just because we live on an earth that does not acknowledge His rule."[9]

- Only when we pray seeking His Kingdom be advanced, only when we pray in submission to His will, does Jesus tell us to put our requests in: **give us this day** . . . How often do we truly pray like that? More likely we may burst into His throne room expecting our prayers be answered, without even a thought as to whether it is God's will or not. Jesus taught His disciples to pray for God's will *before* the "ask, seek, knock" verses. Once again we see our prayers answered as *we* desire only when what we are asking is God's will.

We Do Not Even Know How To Pray

We do not know what we ought to pray for, but the Spirit himself intercedes for us through wordless groans . . .

Romans 8:26

We do not know how to pray, and we do not know what we should pray for. Humbling. Yet the Spirit intercedes for us, taking our selfish prayers and bringing them to the Father with groanings too deep for words. We can trust the Spirit, who knows the mind of the Father, to pray the Father's will, and we can trust that the Father's will is only for our good. Here is the whole passage. You will recognize it:

We do not know what we ought to pray for, but the Spirit himself intercedes for us through wordless groans. And he who searches our hearts knows the mind of the Spirit, because the Spirit intercedes for God's people in accordance with the will of God. And we know that in all things God works for the good of those who love him, who have been called according to his purpose. For those God foreknew he also predestined to be conformed to the image of his Son . . .

Romans 8:26-29

I'm going to invite Richard back again to share about prayer. You met Richard in the last chapter. He is the Founder of the Men's Branch of *Triumph*, and also the Co-Founder of our church's Cancer Support Groups. His surprising approach to prayer can be a great lesson for all of us.

This may sound crazy to you, but I've never prayed for healing. I was diagnosed with stage four squamous cell cancer of my throat and voice box, with 19 positive nodes, and the doctors said even with the best medical treatment possible, I had only a 10% chance of surviving one year. I was young. I had kids to raise. And statistics said I would not live out the year.

I went home that night and sat out on my patio to talk to God. I simply said to Him, "I surrender. I surrender everything. I cannot carry this. It is Yours. Do with me whatever You want. I only want Your will to be done."

God spoke into my heart, saying to me, "My will is for you to take charge of your treatment. Become knowledgeable. Find out your options. I am in control."

I did just that. I researched, I learned my options, I interviewed doctors. I followed Nehemiah's method: Don't look back to find out how the wall fell down, but focus on the rebuilding. Find each breach and address it step by step.

God empowered me to do all He instructed me to do. He gave me His wisdom and knowledge to complete this God-assigned mission. God picked my team and directed my treatment. He was in control of every single part.

My treatment entailed 11 operations, and 246 radiation treatments given twice a day simultaneously with continuous chemotherapy. Many wondered how I could possibly survive the treatment, let alone the cancer.

I'm in remission since 2002. God used me at that time, and continues to use me right now, to show others what it means to suffer with dignity and respect. He is using me to show others what it means to keep walking closely with the Lord even through the deepest of suffering. He is using me to demonstrate to others true joy in suffering because I know I am never alone; I have Jesus, my best friend.

Richard Ekey
Founder of the Men's Branch of Triumph
Co-Founder Cancer Support Groups
Christ Fellowship Church
Palm Beach Gardens, Florida

Richard didn't pray for physical healing, because at that time he didn't know if remission was God's will. He surrendered and prayed, "Your will be done." Then, not even knowing the final destination, he simply obeyed each command, step by step, and God led him on His way.

Elders, Oil, Healing

Is anyone among you in trouble? Let them pray. Is anyone happy? Let them sing songs of praise. Is anyone among you sick? Let them call the elders of the church to pray over them and anoint them with oil in the name of the Lord. And the prayer offered in faith will make the sick person well; the Lord will raise them up. If they have sinned, they will be forgiven. Therefore confess your sins to each other and pray for each other so that you may be healed. The prayer of a righteous person is powerful and effective.

James 5:13-16

This is a challenging set of verses. As I research the Greek words for **trouble** and **sick**, what amazes me is the extensive range these words cover – the whole gamut, including physical diseases, spiritual sickness, calamity, demonic activity, mental anguish, burnout, sin and separation from God. The translations for **healing**, **well**, and **raise them up** cover an equally broad range.[10]

So, if we've got oil and praying elders, do we have healing? Not so fast. I have seen very Godly, intensely praying people who were not cured in this world. And right next door to them I have seen the ungodly cured without even a prayer.

I have seen Christians anoint an ill person with oil in Jesus' name, pray over them, expect them to be healed, and have no answers if there is no miracle of healing. I have seen both the anointed and the anointer walk away disillusioned, or worse yet, with their faith devastated and their relationship with God shipwrecked.

What is happening here? Why can't we just claim these "promises?"

I want to draw your attention to a tiny word in this passage: **may. So that you _may_ be healed.** I am not a Greek scholar, but I did double check this word in the KJV, NASB, ESV, and AMP. All of them use that word "may." This verse does not say so that you _will_ be healed, but so that you _may_ be healed. I think the question we must ask is, What is _God's_ plan here? What is _His_ will? Remember Jesus, in the Garden of Gethsemane, prayed, **"My Father, if it is possible, may this cup be taken from me. Yet not as I will, but as You will"** (Mt 26:39). God's plan may not include an instantaneous deliverance from pain and trial.

Sometimes, in answer to prayer, God heals instantly in all ways and at all levels. Other times, mental and spiritual healing comes immediately, and physical healing later. Other times, all healing is delayed. Sometimes, God may reveal His will as we pray. Sometimes, He may reveal our responsibility or our next step in the healing process. But other times, He does not reveal His will or His plan in the speedy timing that we may want to know it.

The bottom line is this: God doesn't always offer to lift the pain or trial. But He does always offer us _Himself_. When we seek Him, bowing to His perfect will, He gives us His presence and His comfort. And that is more powerful, more precious, more perfect than any physical healing could ever be.

All healing comes from Jesus. He doesn't _need_ doctors, hospitals, medications, elders, or oil, but He may choose to *work through* them. God's plan for us involves complete restoration, healing, and wholeness: physically, emotionally, mentally, and spiritually (Rev 21:4, 2Cor 5:1-5). Our healing is through Jesus' death (Isa 53:5). He may graciously grant us some healings while we are on this earth. We may wait for other healings until we are in heaven. If God has not yet healed you, it does not necessarily mean that you are not spiritually mature enough, holy enough, or close enough to God. We don't always know what God is up to, and are not to judge others – or ourselves. God is gloriously creative and surprisingly unpredictable, and His timing and His methods of healing each person are often a mystery.

As we seek Jesus, and confess and repent and receive His forgiveness, our spiritual healing can become deeper and more complete. Spiritual healing can be accompanied by emotional and mental healing as we are transformed by the renewing of our minds. Spiritual healing can also be accompanied by physical healing. We don't often know what He is up to. Ask Him, What is *Your* will? What is *Your* timing? What are You working *right now* through this hardship?

My friend Ann comprehends this on a deep level. Her joy in the Lord is so palpable that if you could witness her praising and worshiping in choir, you would never guess the battles she faces on a daily basis.

When I first read in the Bible that I am here for His pleasure, I felt like a puppet on a string. I looked at my fibromyalgia, my diabetes, my herniated discs, my pinched sciatic nerves, my crooked spine, and asked, "What is God up to?" I simply do not yet know God's purpose for all my suffering.

But deep in my heart, I know it's my sinful nature that wants to believe I am a puppet on a string, that wants to live for my pleasure and not for His, that whines and

*demands, "Why me?" Deep in my heart, I desperately want
to be like Jesus. If I were not in so much pain, I don't think
I would have ever learned that I cannot do anything; only
He can. All I can do is be obedient, keep in the Word, sing
His praises, and pray His will be done.*

*And when I reach that place of humbleness, He heals me.
Not always physically, but always spiritually, emotionally,
mentally, deep in my soul. He brings me to understand
that I may not be able to figure out His purposes in all my
suffering, but I can trust His heart. And then I ask, "Why
not me?"*

Ann
Palm Beach Gardens, Florida

Our spiritual state is vastly more important to God
than our physical state. We may become frustrated if
we focus only on the physical. Fix your eyes on what is
unseen (2Cor 4:18): Jesus, His glory, His Kingdom, and
His spiritual work in our hearts. When we fix our eyes
on the unseen, our eyes may be opened to His miracles of
spiritual healing that are occurring right now. But if we
fix our eyes on the unseen and we *still* see no spiritual
miracles occurring, realize that this is not the end of the
story. When we arrive in heaven, we will find out that He
has not been inactive, but has been working behind the
scenes all along.

You met Kimberlymac in Chapter 1, my *Triumph*
Internet Servant Leader with such an open heart to
Christ. I want you to hear her protracted journey of
healing. Watch her tenacity and perseverance. As you
read, notice how her healing did not come fully on the day
of her salvation, but has come in stepwise fashion as she
grows in Him.

*When I was about 8 years old, my great-aunt snapped
and murdered my great-grandparents, beating them to*

death with a rolling pin. I am still saddened by the horror and shame my family endured. Even now I feel sick inside thinking about our fallen world, how the consequences of people's decisions are so far reaching, and how our inherently sinful nature is capable of really horrible things.

I was gripped with a fierce inner fear that I could be the next one to "lose it," and became immobilized by my emotional instability. Somehow, though, I was able to craftily hide my weakness from everyone. Because I bore the pain of it alone, I was haunted by fear and incredible anxiety. I was outwardly disciplined, religious, and strong, yet crippled with fear on the inside.

The heavy burden of mustering up enough emotional strength to hide my weakness was so great I constantly entertained thoughts of suicide. I longed for inner peace.

I met Jesus Christ at 19 years old and gave my life to Him. He became my Savior and my Healer. I expected instantaneous healing of my emotional pain, but the next ten years became internally even more tumultuous as I worked out this great salvation I was given. The anxiety attacks got worse and more frequent, and I handled this by pushing myself more and more, trying harder to do this new Christianity, to live up to the name Christian. I was determined to be the best Christian servant God had ever seen. Outwardly, I did achieve this disciplined excellence, but inwardly I was a huge mess. Every day was a struggle to go on, and I wanted to end it all. I stood at the edge of a ledge, ready to commit suicide.

After my third child, I had a complete physical and emotional breakdown, and it was here, in a heap on the floor, that Jesus met me and I surrendered to Him the complete Lordship of my life. As I began walking this path of Lordship, my true journey of triumph over suffering began. The Potter took me from a ledge, literally and figuratively, broke me, and remade me. I am still emotionally weak, but He is so very strong in me.

I have learned to sit on the Potter's Wheel and be responsive to His touch. I truly like the identity He made for me, from a broken pot to a beautiful daughter of the Living God. I am not yet where I want to be, but I am on the way to a complete triumph over suffering. His perfect love is casting out all my fears. I have peace inside and I am no longer afraid. I am weak; He is strong! I can endure His will for me in Christ Jesus. I no longer fear my emotional weakness, because I know now that His infinite love is in step with His sovereign will for me. Jesus I love You so! AWE!

Kimberlymac
Triumph Servant Leader, Internet
and Author of thebridegroomscafe.com
Charleston, South Carolina

Jehovah Raphah

But he was pierced for our transgressions, he was crushed for our iniquities; the punishment that brought us peace was on him, and by his wounds we are healed. We all, like sheep, have gone astray, each of us has turned to our own way; and the LORD has laid on him the iniquity of us all.

Isaiah 53:5-6

By his wounds we are healed. As we discussed in the previous section, God's plan for us is complete physical, mental, emotional, and spiritual healing – *in His perfect timing*. This healing is by Jesus' wounds, His blood, His death on the cross. I love the Hebrew word for healed, raphah – let's hear how Beth Moore envisions this:

> The word raphah means "to mend (by stitching), repair thoroughly, make whole" (*Strong's*) . . . I picture God focusing steadily on the object of repair. One stitch follows another. It takes time. I picture painful

penetrations of the healing needle. I don't know about you, but I'm quite sure if my healing processes had been painless, I would have relapsed.[11]

God has chosen for one of His Names Jehovah Raphah, The One Who Heals by Stitching. As a physician, this imagery of suturing really captivates me. I realize that even with modern medicine's best technology, repair of a wound leaves a scar. There remains evidence of the original wound, *and also* evidence of the sutures that have sown the wound back together. And this is what really strikes me, the twofold scar: of the initial wound, and of the process of healing.

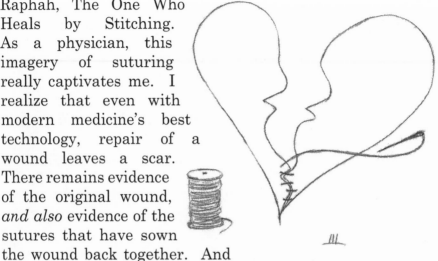

I don't believe God heals in this way because He is *incapable* of stitching us whole without a scar, but because He *wants us to remember*. I think He wants us to remember the pain of the adversity because He has a purpose for us *through* the suffering. A purpose we probably cannot achieve without having endured this trial. A purpose we probably cannot complete without the memory, distinct yet healed, of the pain. And, as Beth Moore implied, if *we* have been the cause of our own tribulations, He may want us to remember this place of brokenness so that we do not need to visit it again.

Even more importantly, I think He wants us to remember the love, gentleness, and patience of the Healer. The meticulousness of His work. His great attention to detail. The gift of His time, as if we were the only ones on the face of the planet in need of His stitching. He wants us to remember that we were helpless and could not heal ourselves. He wants us to remember that He is the Great Physician, and all true deep everlasting healing comes from Him.

He is Jehovah Raphah, the Mender of Hearts, the Reviver of Souls, the Restorer of Minds, the Healer of Bodies. Healing may be a long journey, and may even take our entire lives. Some of our healing may not even be complete until we enter eternity with Him. Yet I believe what He so desperately desires is for us to simply *be* on that journey, seeking deeper revelation of who He is, further transformation of our hearts, and more complete healing in Him.

Adversity Is Satan's Trap

John the Baptist, imprisoned, sent his disciples to Jesus with this question, **"Are you the one who is to come, or should we expect someone else?"** (Lk 7:19).

That appears to be one loaded question! Jesus answered by telling John to assess the signs, to see if Jesus has fulfilled all the predictions of the Messiah. Then Jesus added,

"Blessed is anyone who does not stumble on account of me."

Luke 7:23

What does that mean? Stumble is the word skandalon, which is actually "the trigger of a trap." [12] Specifically this is the type of snare a hunter would use to catch a wild animal. I imagine it this way: A rope is tied to the top of a sapling, bending it down to the ground. At the end of the rope is a concealed loop, waiting to catch an unwary animal's foot. When the inattentive animal steps into the concealed loop, the sapling snaps up, and in a moment the animal is dangling upside-down in the air. What a terrifying word picture!

Jesus is cautioning us about the traps Satan may set when we are in unfavorable circumstances, when we are hit with pain and tribulations, or when life is not turning out as we expected. Let's look at some of these possible traps:

- Anger because life is not going according to our plan.

- Bitterness because fallen people in this fallen world have hurt us.

- Discontentment because we have what we don't want, or jealousy because we can't get what we want. "Having what we don't want and wanting what we don't have."[13]

- Doubting the compassion and power of God because our prayers have not been answered as we expected them to be answered.

- Abandoning trust in God because we feel that He did not adequately protect us from people injuring us, He did not shield us from calamities or natural disasters, He did not shelter us from the consequences of our own sins.

These can be traps too easy to fall into! Now that you can see them, do not step into them! Do not be trapped by the idolatry of your own plan for your own life. Do not be trapped because God appears inactive, seems silent, or looks like He has abandoned you.

God is always at work (Jn 5:17), for our good, whether we can see Him or not. He is not inactive. He is not silent. He has not abandoned us. It may be our own inability to sense His presence that makes Him seem inactive, silent, missing. It may be because of our own blindness that we do not see Him at work. He has a plan for our lives, complete with conquering Satan's traps. Give God room to work, and you may glimpse His awesome plan, you may sense His presence, you may see Him at work in your life, and you may even get a peek of the top of the tapestry.

The Response That Pleases God

If we are to successfully avoid Satan's trap in adversity, I believe that we must know exactly what response pleases God. Philip Yancey writes that our response is the only area that we have control over.[14] I sense that the response that glorifies God is three-fold:

- Face forward
- Learn contentment
- Rejoice in suffering

First Key: Face Forward

"For I know the plans I have for you," declares the LORD, "plans to prosper you and not to harm you, plans to give you hope and a future."

Jeremiah 29:11

The Lord has plans to prosper us, *spiritually* prosper us. To give us hope. To give us a future. Glorious plans for us, both here on earth, and in heaven. His purposes for us take into account all of our pain. Pain the world inflicted. Pain others inflicted. Pain we inflicted on ourselves.

God's glorious plan for us takes all that into account, for He knew it all beforehand. Paul really understands this. He writes to the Philippians, *from prison*:

. . . one thing I do: forgetting what lies behind and reaching forward to what lies ahead, I press on toward the goal for the prize of the upward call of God in Christ Jesus.

Philippians 3:13-14 NASB

Paul handles the agony of the flogging and imprisonment by forgetting what lies behind, and reaching forward to what lies ahead. I think Paul could be focusing on three different things when he refers to the upward call:

- Paul may be focusing on his eternity with Jesus. The NIV translates this **heavenward.** Paul fixes his eyes on his heavenly calling. We must also face forward to our eternity with Christ. We don't belong here; our citizenship is in heaven (Phil 3:20).

- Paul may also be focusing on his relationship with Jesus. Deeper and closer, as Jesus works through adversity in Paul's open heart.

- Paul could also be focusing on the Kingdom work that God has assigned him. He realizes that each time he completes the assigned Kingdom work, God has greater work waiting for him, more challenging work, which can advance the Kingdom even more and bring God even greater glory. Work that he is now ready to do because his faith has been tested and tried and proven genuine, and he has grown deeper in Christ. The upward call of God in Christ Jesus.

You've met Betsy a few times before, a tireless member of my *Triumph* Servant Leadership Team. I have asked her to share with you how God used her darkest trial for His Kingdom purposes.

I had been a Christian most of my life, and at first could not fathom the purpose of my breast cancer. But as God grew me spiritually and strengthened my faith through my suffering, I realized my battle with breast cancer had given me much more empathy for those who were going through health problems of their own.

In a unique set of circumstances, I met a woman who was just diagnosed with breast cancer and was still in shock. She had virtually no family, and I was able to minister to her both physically and spiritually. I was so thankful God was able to use my disease to help even one other person.

Next, I was called to support another woman who was just diagnosed. It looks like God has created a whole ministry for me here! I love seeing how God weaves His tapestry when we all become His hands and feet.

Betsy Burden
Triumph Servant Leader
Christ Fellowship Church and Church in the Gardens
Palm Beach Gardens, Florida

Face forward to the upward call of God. He has such work for us!

So we fix our eyes not on what is seen, but on what is unseen, since what is seen is temporary, but what is unseen is eternal.

2 Corinthians 4:18

What is seen – our woes and our trials – are temporary. What is unseen – God's love for us, our faith and trust in Him, the place He is preparing in heaven for us right now – is eternal. Face forward. Fix your eyes on the unseen:

"What no eye has seen, what no ear has heard, and what no mind has conceived" — the things God

has prepared for those who love him — these are the things God has revealed to us by his Spirit.

1 Corinthians 2:9-10

We are not going to be able to enjoy all these heavenly riches or step into these heavenly responsibilities if we are not ready for them when we arrive there!   Face forward. He has plans for you!

Second Key: Learn Contentment

The second part of glorifying God in our suffering involves learning contentment, or blessedness, the Greek word makarios. **Blessed are those who do not stumble on account of me.**   I want you to hear how my Word Study Book explains this precious word:

> Blessed, possessing the favor of God, that state of being marked by fullness from God . . . one who becomes a partaker of God's nature through faith in Christ. The believer is indwelt by the Spirit because of Christ and as a result should be fully satisfied no matter the circumstances. Makarios differs from the word "happy" in that the person who is happy has . . . favorable circumstances . . . Makarios is the one who is in the world yet independent of the world. His satisfaction comes from God and not from favorable circumstances.[15]

Makarios means that we are fully satisfied, not because of favorable circumstances, not because we are healthy or rich or strong or living the easy life, but we are fully satisfied because Jesus is dwelling in us. We are in this world but not of this world; our contentment comes from God and not from favorable circumstances.

We can be blessed in our tribulations when we can learn not to trust the things of the world nor to look to them for joy. Those who have no hardships may never learn this. Those who have health, money, fame, power, stable relationships can so easily trust in those worldly things and become completely dependent upon them for happiness. Yes, they may have earthly happiness. They may even think that they have discovered true joy. They may be self-sufficient and comfortable in this life, they may enjoy living on earth. They may feel that they are "good people" and think they have no need for a Savior and no need for sanctification.

It appears to me that truly abiding in Christ can start when we realize that we can no longer rely on ourselves, our possessions, our health, our relationships, our jobs or positions. When we realize that we cannot depend on these things for our happiness. When we realize that we cannot trust them for our security. We who are suffering can be blessed because we can have an enormous advantage in this learning process. Since we are in pain, we may have a head start in learning not to expect happiness in the physical. We may have already learned that we cannot trust our possessions or our job. We may have learned that we cannot rely on people for our happiness. We can be that much closer to the important understanding that the only way we can be truly satisfied is to fully surrender to God.

I've invited Ann back again to describe how adversity taught her not to trust in the things of this world for security or happiness. Through this trial, she learned contentment in Christ alone.

In a matter of moments, I was blind. My sister-in-law rushed me to the emergency room, and I learned I had a brain hemorrhage. The doctors told me I would never see again.

At first, I was frightened and angry. But as I lay blind in that hospital bed, God taught me the meaning of true contentment. I learned if I am dependent upon the world for my happiness, I could lose my happiness at any moment. But if I keep my eyes fixed on Jesus, and what is to come in heaven with Him, I will be truly content, no matter what is going on in this world.

My Bible study group visited me in the hospital, laid hands on me and prayed. Several weeks later, God gave me my vision back. I am so grateful, but it doesn't really matter to me, because I learned to find my joy not in my physical health or in the pleasures of this world, but in my relationship with Christ.

Ann

Palm Beach Gardens, Florida

God did heal Ann's blindness, but we know that God does not always promise physical healing here on earth. To me, what is most remarkable about Ann's story is not her physical healing, but her heart transformation: during her blindness, she learned to find her joy in her relationship with Christ. Although she was given physical sight again, she refuses to forget that time of blindness, and *still* finds her joy and contentment in Jesus alone.

So how do we obtain this makarios, this blessedness, being fully satisfied and content no matter the circumstances? As you read the passages below, note the word *learned*. And realize that Paul wrote Philippians *from prison:*

I know what it is to be in need, and I know what it is to have plenty. I have learned the secret of being content in any and every situation, whether well fed or hungry, whether living in plenty or in want. I can do all this through him who gives me strength.

Philippians 4:12-13

Therefore I am well content with weaknesses, with insults, with distresses, with persecutions, with difficulties, for Christ's sake; for when I am weak, then I am strong.

2 Corinthians 12:10 NASB

What was Paul's secret? He learned to be dependent on God. Therefore Paul's happiness, his contentment, did not depend on his circumstances, or on himself, but on God, whose presence and love, faithfulness and power, are unchanging.

How exactly do we *learn* contentment? Realize that Paul wrote this letter to the Philippians near the end of his life, as a very mature Christian. I believe that learning contentment will not happen overnight. It seems to be a process. Sometimes the process may involve loss. For some of us, we may need to lose something in order to learn that we cannot depend on it. Consider Paul's life. He lost prestige, power, and money as he left his life as a Pharisee and became a missionary for Jesus (Phil 3:4-7). There were times he lost his physical health (stonings, beatings, shipwreck, starvation, blindness when he first met Jesus, and eye problems when he was in Galatia (2Cor 11:23-29, Acts 9:1-9, Gal 4:12-15)). We know that he also lost relationships and suffered betrayal (Acts 15:36-39, Phil 2:20-21, 4:15, 2Tim 4:10).

Learning contentment does not necessarily mean that suffering will be removed. It does mean that we move from anger and grief to peace and acceptance. It means that we accept everything in our lives as coming from the loving hand of God; we trust His sovereignty, His goodness, and His eternal plan. We learn, as Paul did, to depend solely on God's grace, not our own strength.

Third Key: Rejoice

We have studied the first two keys to glorifying God in our suffering: facing forward and learning contentment. Let's take a look at the third key, rejoice. Rejoice? In suffering? Are you *sure*?

Yes, *I am sure*. The Scriptures are too replete with this to ignore it. Paul writes **glory in our sufferings** (Rom 5:3) and **rejoice** in suffering (Col 1:24). James writes **Consider it pure joy whenever you face trials** (Jam 1:2). Peter writes **greatly rejoice** (1Pet 1:6), rejoice with **joy inexpressible** (1Pet 1:8 NASB), and **rejoice with exultation** when Christ's glory is revealed through our suffering (1Pet 4:13 NASB). Jesus Himself says **"Rejoice and be glad"** when you are persecuted (Mt 5:12).

Although we live in a fallen world and all creation groans, let's review why we are urged to greatly rejoice with inexpressible joy:

- We know that our eyes may be opened to our sin and we may have an opportunity to be conformed to Jesus' image.

- We recognize that God may be strengthening our faith, and growing us spiritually in ways such as humility, dependence, and forgiveness.

- We have been given the insight that God may be using tests and trials to prove our faith genuine.

- We realize that God may be preparing us for upcoming Kingdom work.

- We grasp that we are destined for hardships – appointed to them – because God may be preparing us for our heavenly rewards and responsibilities.

- We are touched because God may be using us to teach mankind, and also the heavenlies, about Himself.

- We are humbled that as members of the body of Christ, we may be called to suffer for His church.

- We are privileged that we may come to know Jesus more intimately through the fellowship of His sufferings; God may be giving us a piece of His heart.

- We are amazed at how God may be teaching us to worship Him with a pure undefiled love.

- We perceive that God may be using our tribulations to advance His Kingdom.

- We are astounded that our Kingdom work may be of such interest to Satan that he is working to thwart us.

- We are deeply honored because our anguish may indicate that God is counting us worthy of the Kingdom of Heaven.

I pray that you have come far in this course. I pray that you can rejoice in suffering because you have gained some understanding of all these reasons. Now take a deep breath, because we're going deeper. Let's go to John:

As he went along, he saw a man blind from birth. His disciples asked him, "Rabbi, who sinned, this man or his parents, that he was born blind?"

"Neither this man nor his parents sinned," said Jesus, "but this happened so that the works of God might be displayed in him."

John 9:1-3

What if...

- What if our suffering was not for any of these reasons we have been studying throughout this book?

- What if our agony was *solely* to display God's glory?

- And what if displaying God's glory did not look like the blind man's healing, but Paul's thorn that God did not remove?

- And what if, while we are displaying God's glory, we would never understand the reason why until eternity?

Would we still rejoice? Ugh, this is so hard! Yet I truly want to be there. Do you?

I don't believe that suffering is going to lead to the glory of God without an attitude of humility and submission to God's sovereign will. We can glorify God in our tribulations by accepting that life is not all about us, and choosing to allow the Holy Spirit to change us. We are called to trust God, to put our faith in action, to focus on Him and His will, and to choose to be a part of fulfilling His vast eternal plan – whether we can comprehend that plan or not. As we acknowledge Him as Sovereign Lord over all creation, we can allow Him to use us in *any* way He desires for His honor and glory.

We cannot choose whether or not we are afflicted with these sorrows, but we *can* choose how we respond.

- We can focus on "just getting through this valley" or focus on what God has for us *in* the valley.

- We can view our trials with anger and frustration and fight against them, or we can view our trials with acceptance and fight for the Kingdom *through* them.

- We can choose to struggle with fulfilling our own little dreams for our lives, or we can choose to enter the spiritual battle, and be part of fulfilling *God's* vast eternal plan.

- We can choose the response that Job's wife recommends, to **"curse God and die"** (Job 2:9), or we can choose the response Job gave when he found he had lost everything: praise God.[16]

At this, Job got up and tore his robe and shaved his head. Then he fell to the ground in worship and said: "Naked I came from my mother's womb, and naked I will depart. The LORD gave and the LORD has taken away; may the name of the LORD be praised." In all this, Job did not sin by charging God with wrongdoing.

Job 1:20-22

This is the response that glorifies God. Have you achieved this response? Can you praise Him even in unrelenting pain? Will you worship Him with the most pure form of worship – worship in suffering? **"The Lord gave and the LORD has taken away; may the name of the LORD be praised."**

Chapter 11
Hearing the Voice of God

ave you ever tried to understand people who are speaking a different language, a language that you're just starting to learn? You may want to stop everything else that you are doing to focus completely on their words. You probably cannot multitask while you are working to comprehend what they are saying to you.

If you desire to understand them better, you can spend more time studying their language. You may also recognize that you will still only superficially understand what they are saying if you don't study their culture. Also, if you really want to grasp the deeper meaning of their words, you may work to come to know them more on a personal level.

Draw the parallel. If we have spent little time working to learn God's language, and even less time working to understand His character and His ways, we may not often hear Him. If we are trying to hear His voice while simultaneously juggling everything else in our lives, we may not often comprehend what He is saying.

God Uses Spiritual Language
As He Speaks to Us Through His Word

How do we learn God's language, His character, and His ways? The Bible is the Word of God, and for many of us it is the primary way He speaks to us. There seems to be no substitute for spending time reading, studying, meditating on, and memorizing Scripture.

God is Spirit, and it is His Spirit that will communicate with our spirit (Rom 8:16). God's language is a spiritual language, and developing a spirit that is sensitive to His Spirit will probably require much time and practice, as well as intense focus. This can happen during our prayer time, for prayer is "moving closer to God."[1] When we are praying, alone with Him, secluded, away from the busyness of the world, this can be the time that He teaches our spirit to hear His Spirit. Recall how often Jesus escaped alone to pray (Lk 5:16). Recall how Jesus threw the noisy mourners out of the house before raising the girl to life (Mt 9:23-24). I think that if Jesus needed quiet to focus on communicating with His Father, surely I must!

Through Scripture study and prayer, we can come to know Him deeper. We can grow to know His character, His ways, His thoughts, His heart. The more we invite Him to train our spirits to hear His Spirit, the more clearly we may be able to hear His voice. Then we may begin to hear Him not only when we are reading our Bible or praying, but throughout the day as well.

Developing An Open Heart

Training our spirit to be sensitive to His Spirit involves developing an open heart. I believe there are four keys to an open heart:

- Our time and undivided attention
- Our obedience
- Our surrender
- Our transformation

First Key: Our Time and Undivided Attention

Be sure all three legs of your spiritual stool are firm: Bible study, prayer, and your church family. One of Satan's most powerful weapons seems to be busyness. Don't let busyness be your trap. Be sure you give God enough time to speak.

Second Key: Our Obedience

In First Samuel, God has instructed King Saul to completely annihilate the Amalekites and all their livestock. Saul leads the Israelites to victory, and kills all the Amalekites – except their king. He destroys all their livestock – except the very best oxen and sheep, claiming that he would sacrifice them to the Lord. Samuel reprimands Saul,

"Does the Lord delight in burnt offerings and sacrifices as much as in obeying the voice of the Lord? To obey is better than sacrifice . . . for

rebellion is like the sin of divination, and arrogance like the evil of idolatry. Because you have rejected the word of the LORD, he has rejected you as king."

1 Samuel 15:22-23

Soon Saul recognized that the Spirit of the Lord had departed from him (1Sam 16:14) and, because he did not obey God,

"God has turned away from me. He no longer answers me."

1 Samuel 28:15

If God has spoken to us and we have *not* been obedient, we may be quenching His Spirit (1Th 5:19). We may have erected a barrier to hearing from Him. Obedience seems to remove that barrier. Listen to how my friend Caleb describes this with powerful simplicity.

About a year ago I made a decision to do everything *God told me to do. I didn't used to hear His voice much before that, but now I hear Him all the time.*

Caleb, at age 10
Living with his missionary parents in Haiti

Hearing and obedience fosters even more hearing. Yes, I have learned a lot from this 10 year-old fellow.

"He who has My commandments and keeps them is the one who loves Me; and he who loves Me will be loved by My Father, and I will love him and will disclose Myself to him."

John 14:21 NASB

Are you keeping His commandments? Are you doing *everything* God told you to do? Think about how you are living your life. Does it match up with the Word of

God? Are you telling "little white lies?" Are you holding onto unforgiveness? Are you living with someone you're not married to? Are you cheating on your spouse with an emotional relationship at work, at church, or on the internet? Are you getting paid "under the table?" Are you clocking in your hours dishonestly? Are you stealing by manipulating the system? What are you filling your mind with – things of the world, or things of God? Are you so busy with your own life that you don't have time to take care of your spouse? Are you refusing to honor your parents or your in-laws? Are you engaged in porn or other filth? Are you gossiping? Criticizing? Are you too busy for your kids because of your work, your activities, your serving or volunteer work? Are you depending on the church to raise your children in the Lord?   What sins of yours may be blocking out His voice?

God does not give advice and suggestions; He is our Lord and Master; He gives *commands*, commands to be carried out immediately. God commands us to be on a pathway to purity, possessing our vessels in sanctification and honor (1Th 4:4 NASB). Simply put, it is our sins that separate us from God.

I will go away and return to My place, until they acknowledge their guilt and seek My face; in their affliction they will earnestly seek Me.
Hosea 5:15 NASB

God withdraws from us *until* we repent and seek Him. And God withdraws from us *so that* we will repent and seek Him. I have invited my friend Carol to describe a time in her life when a veil blocked her connection with God.

My father was a viciously abusive alcoholic. I grew up hating him especially because of the way he beat my mother, and my hatred did not abate when he abandoned my family when I was in fifth grade.

I came to know Jesus when I was a teenager, but my relationship with God didn't really take off until I started going to prayer meetings and Bible studies and applying His Word to my life.

When I was about thirty years old, I realized that suddenly a black sheet had gone down separating me from God. My prayers were not getting through; I could not communicate with Him. God revealed to me an area of my life that I was not living in obedience; it was time to get it right with my dad.

I had not had any contact with my dad for many years, and I finally found he was in prison. After much praying and repenting and humbling myself before God, I wrote to my dad, "I love you, not because you earned it, but because Jesus deposited His love in my heart for you. I love you, Dad, and Jesus does too."

My father later told me that the night before my letter arrived, he had been on his knees in his prison cell begging God that someone in his family would genuinely care for him. He said he received my letter the very next day.

My father turned to Christ in prison, and even led Bible studies in prison. After he got out, he came to my home, and held me so long I thought he would never let me go. Because I forgave my father, I expected to be misunderstood by my family as being disloyal to my mother after all he did to her, but I have obeyed God and left the consequences to Him. My father had many grandchildren, but mine are the only ones who had a relationship with him – because I got it right with my dad, and right with God.

Looking back, I see that the moment I chose to forgive my father, the black sheet was lifted. Communication between God and me opened up again, and I knew once more my prayers were entering the very throne room of God.

My father was killed in an automobile accident a number of months later, and I experienced the "peace that passeth all understanding" at his funeral because I had obeyed God.

Carol
San Francisco, California

Notice that it was the pain of God's withdrawal from Carol that drove her to repent of her unforgiveness. Her obedience lifted the veil and restored her deep intimacy with God. In addition, her repentance and obedience healed not only her relationship with her father, but her children's relationship with their grandfather also.

Third Key: Our Surrender

I believe the third key to developing spirits that are sensitive to His Spirit is complete surrender. I mean the kind of surrender that is so desperate to hear from God that we are saying "Yes! Yes!" before we even know what we are saying yes to![2]

Let's be honest. There's really no such thing as "incomplete surrender." You either have or you haven't. "Incomplete surrender" is a fighting stance. It means you really have not surrendered at all. I would like you to hear how Alec's full surrender opened him up to hear from the Lord:

Maybe it's a recommitment of salvation, but whatever it is, I feel closer to God. It happened when I was 13 . . . I felt fear of death . . . death is scary . . . death is final . . . if you are not saved. I felt doubtful, I felt worried, and I decided that I needed to make sure that I really had surrendered everything to Christ. So that night, in the quiet of my bed, I said a prayer in my heart and gave my life to God yet again.

At that moment, I felt him calling, calling. So I opened up to anything He had to say, and He convicted me of not loving and appreciating my grandparents, and of shunning outcast kids in school and at church.

That was a number of years ago. Over the course of time, my walk with Him has grown deeper and closer as I strive to obey Him not only in these areas, but all other parts of my life too.

Alec Li
Jupiter, Florida

Fourth Key: Our Transformation

Paul explains how to develop a spirit sensitive to God's Spirit:

Therefore, I urge you, brothers, in view of God's mercy, to offer your bodies as living sacrifices, holy and pleasing to God – this is your true and proper worship. Do not conform any longer to the pattern of this world, but be transformed by the renewing of your mind. *Then* you will be able to test and approve what God's will is – His good, pleasing and perfect will.

Romans 12:1-2, emphasis added

First, offer our bodies as living sacrifices. That is complete surrender. Next, do not conform to this world, but allow Him to transform us to be useful vessels for Him. *Then* we will be able to test and approve His will; *then* we can hear His voice and His calling on our lives.

When we are transformed, we can come to know God's character, His ways, His thoughts, and His heart more and more. When we are transformed, His thoughts can become our thoughts, His ways our ways. We can come to know Him more intimately, so that when He speaks, His call may become more clear to us.

The Greek
word for transform
is metamorphoo.
We've taken that word
right into the English:
metamorphosis,
the change from
caterpillar to
butterfly. Clearly
transformation
indicates
radical change
– a transition
into something completely
unrecognizable!

Just how are we transformed?
Be transformed by the renewing of your mind. The
Greek word renew has some
interesting root words. I would summarize my Word
Study Dictionary by saying that renewing is the process
of making something clearly different and better. It is a
process that must be repeated again and again at more
and more intense levels.[2] Renewing occurs in our minds.
The Holy Spirit can accomplish this renewing process
when we refuse to allow our minds to be conformed to the
world and we instead immerse our minds in the things
of God: Scripture, church, worship, prayer. This invites
Him to convict us of sin and metamorphose us, again and
again, until He has shaped us into vessels useful to Him.

But I Still Do Not Hear Him!

So we are pursuing a pathway of purity, possessing
our vessels in sanctification and honor. We are obedient,

surrendered, and metamorphosed, and we have removed ourselves from worldliness and immersed in Scripture, church, worship, prayer. We have conquered busyness in our lives, we have removed ourselves from the crushing noises of the world, and we are listening. And we hear . . . nothing. No booming voice coming from the heavens. No bush outside our home has caught on fire. No angel has appeared in his dazzling glory. Now what?

Realize that God may already be speaking to us, but we do not recognize it as His voice. As we learn to recognize His voice, as our spirits become more sensitive to His Spirit, we can hear Him more and more.

What will His voice sound like? Usually, God's voice is not audible. Often, He speaks not exactly in words or sentences, but in impressions on our heart. Sometimes He gives us a little glimpse of His plan; other times, His message to us can be more like an explosion, as He blows open our minds with sudden understanding, speaking in just a moment of impressions what would have taken hours to speak in words. Sometimes He tells us *what* to do – like repair a broken relationship – but leaves the *how* up to us to figure out. Often, His calling is vague at first, like an object seen way off in the distance. Over time, it can take definite shape when we obey the piece that we understand and He brings His plan into focus a bit more. As you listen for His voice, remember that God is incomprehensible, unpredictable, unlimited, and infinitely creative; I think He delights in communicating with us in completely unexpected ways.

God May Speak To Us Through Prayer and Scripture

As much as we desire the drama of the burning bush, God seems to most commonly speak to us through

Scripture, church, worship, prayer. When you are reading your Bible and a verse leaps out at you, that may be God speaking to you. When you are listening to the pastor's message and you feel it is just for you, that may be God speaking to you. God may be revealing more of Himself, or answering a question, or directing you on His path. He may be convicting you of sin – and it is probably God you are arguing with if you find yourself justifying, excusing, or defending your sin.

You may be in your prayer time, or worshiping in church, or even going about your everyday life, when suddenly a verse you have memorized drops into your consciousness. It may be God speaking to you.

Be careful here: As we listen to Satan tempt Jesus in the wilderness, we learn that Satan has also memorized Scripture (Mt 4:1-11). So how do we know if it is Satan, or God, dropping a Scripture verse into our minds? It may be hard to figure out; spending much time with God can enable us to recognize His voice with more certainty. Also realize that Satan will often quote Scripture out of context, or twist it around to justify our sin. Remember, as we train with constant practice, and God's thoughts become our thoughts, we may be able to more easily differentiate between God's voice and Satan's voice.

God May Speak To Us Through Other Christians

God may speak to us through other Christians in various ways when we are seeking advice – and when we are not seeking advice.

Suggestions in Seeking Advice

When you have a weighty decision to make, prayerfully seek out trusted Christians for advice. Be sure these Christians you seek out are *deeply surrendered* Christians with a *growing* relationship with Jesus, for Paul cautions in Second Timothy:

For the time will come when people will not put up with sound doctrine. Instead, to suit their own desires, they will gather around them a great number of teachers to say what their itching ears want to hear. They will turn their ears away from the truth and turn aside to myths.

2 Timothy 4:3-4

Don't merely seek advice from someone who will tickle your ears and tell you what you want to hear (NASB).

Suggestions for Handling "Instructions from God" That Come From Other Christians

Perhaps you are feeling God calling you to a certain ministry. One of your Christian friends, who doesn't even know about this potential calling, happens to mention that God has gifted you in that area. It may be God, speaking to you. Be sure, however, that you seek His definite answer in prayer.

Sometimes, when God has given you a calling, Satan may try to use unwitting people, Christians or non-Christians, to thwart it. God is allowing Satan this leeway as a test of your obedience. Let's read an Old Testament example. In First Kings, the Lord has given a mission to one of His prophets, referred to only as **a man of God** in this passage. God sent him from Judah to Bethel to prophesy to wicked King Jeroboam. The man of God goes to Bethel and prophesies as instructed by the Lord, and then prepares to leave.

> **The king said to the man of God, "Come home with me for a meal, and I will give you a gift."**
> **But the man of God answered the king, "Even if you were to give me half your possessions, I would not go with you, nor would I eat bread or drink water here. For I was commanded by the word of the LORD: 'You must not eat bread or drink water or return by the way you came.'" So he took another road and did not return by the way he had come to Bethel.**
>
> 1 Kings 13:7-10

Notice that the man of God believed that he has clearly heard from the Lord. He knew his mission and was walking in it. Now watch how he became derailed:

> **Now there was a certain old prophet living in Bethel, whose sons came and told him all that the man of God had done there that day. They also told their father what he had said to the king.**
>
> 1 Kings 13:11

Note that the old prophet knew what the Lord had commanded the man of God: that he must not eat or drink and must return by a different route. Then the prophet sought out the man of God, and,

> **... the prophet said to him, "Come home with me and eat."**
> **The man of God said, "I cannot turn back and go with you, nor can I eat bread or drink water with you in this place. I have been told by the word of the LORD: 'You must not eat bread or drink water there or return by the way you came.'"**
> **The old prophet answered, "I too am a prophet, as you are. And an angel said to me by the word of**

the Lord: 'Bring him back with you to your house so that he may eat bread and drink water.' " (But he was lying to him.) So the man of God returned with him and ate and drank in his house.

While they were sitting at the table, the word of the Lord came to the old prophet who had brought him back. He cried out to the man of God who had come from Judah, "This is what the Lord says: 'You have defied the word of the Lord and have not kept the command the Lord your God gave you. You came back and ate bread and drank water in the place where he told you not to eat or drink. Therefore your body will not be buried in the tomb of your father.' "

When the man of God had finished eating and drinking, the prophet who had brought him back saddled his donkey for him. As he went on his way, a lion met him on the road and killed him, and his body was thrown down on the road, with both the donkey and the lion standing beside it. Some people who passed by saw the body thrown down there, with the lion standing beside the body, and they went and reported it in the city where the old prophet lived.

1 Kings 13:15-25

Shocking! The old prophet had declared he too was a prophet of God and had a word from the Lord. Yet Scripture says he was lying. The passage does not say that the man of God returned to God in prayer to see if His plan had changed. He just obeyed the old prophet instead of obeying the last command the Lord had given him. The man of God was killed by the lion because he **defied the word of the Lord** and **did not keep the command the Lord gave him.** How can we know whom to trust?

I believe that this challenging passage emphasizes our responsibility to listen to God's voice, and that it underscores how seriously God takes our disobedience. I think it teaches us to trust only God, to return to Him again and again in prayer if we are uncertain. It seems to teach us that God is not going to tell *someone else* to tell us what to do. Will God speak through other Christians to *confirm* our calling? He certainly may. To *encourage* us? He certainly may. To *tell us what to do*? Probably not often.

So will God send a lion to devour us if we become confused and believe another Christian who is actually lying to us? I don't want to read too much into this passage, but I am certainly struck by the fact that it is a *lion* that kills the man of God. **Your enemy the devil prowls around like a roaring lion looking for someone to devour** (1Pet 5:8). Perhaps God will allow Satan to sift us like wheat when we are disobedient.

Suggestions for Handling Unsolicited Convicting Comments That Come From Other Christians

God may also speak to us through other Christians – or even non-Christians – at unexpected moments, when we have not actually sought their advice. Listen closely: they may be telling you something critical, something that will rock your world, something that will *not* tickle your ears. If their words convict you of sin, it may be the Holy Spirit speaking through them.

You met Rhonda back in Chapter 3, when this humble dual-doctorate mother of tennis champions described her first deep surrender to the Lord. Now a grandmother, Rhonda will share her story to illustrate a Godly way to handle unsolicited convicting comments from other Christians. Listen closely:

I had long been a Christian and did not even know I was off track, until the day one of my Christian girlfriends asked me, "What do you want to do with the rest of your life?" I immediately answered that I wanted to be a tennis grandmother to my five grandchildren, raise them up to be state-ranked tennis players just like my own children were, to re-live the best years of my life. I actually thought that was very admirable; but, thankfully, my girlfriend asked that same question several times. When I went home I could think of little else for weeks. Through my girlfriend's persistent questioning, God had grabbed my attention and He and I had many long talks . . . good talks. I began to see that I was putting an earthly activity above a spiritual relationship. I began to feel strongly that I needed to learn more of God's Word so that I could share it freely. I no longer wanted to be cautious about speaking of my love for the Lord and my total dependence on Him.

I immersed myself in His Word and have been transformed. My emphasis has switched from teaching my grandchildren tennis to teaching them the Bible and watching Biblical movies with them. Instead of praying daily for tennis victories, I pray for my family to have a close and loving relationship with Christ our Savior. Instead of talking about earthly things, I am sharing the Word of God. The best part of my surrender to Christ is that my oldest daughter and her daughter are coming very close to our Lord.

Rhonda
West Palm Beach, Florida

Rhonda did not run from the convicting words of her friend, but took them to God in prayer. The Spirit led her out of her worldliness and into a new depth of relationship with Him.

God May Speak To Us Through His Peace

Sometimes, when we are slipping into disobedience, we may have a gentle nagging that churns up our heart, or an unsettled feeling that torments our soul. If we have developed a very sensitive spirit, we may even feel physically nauseous, or possibly overwhelmed with a sense of dread or sheer terror. That may be His Spirit, drawing us back on His path. If we ignore His warning, if we quench His Spirit's call, we may successfully suppress these feelings of unrest – but then we may find that we hear Him less and less, and eventually not at all.

In contrast, when we are struggling with a decision and choose to do it His way, we may be flooded with His peace, the peace that surpasses all comprehension (Phil 4:7 NASB). That may be God saying to us, "Yes, you *are* on My path."

Be careful here: Sometimes, following God's plan will at first mean great terror, not great peace. For example, you may be planning to apologize to someone, to repair the relationship, and you may be terrified, yet you know God is telling you to go. Sometimes the peace does not come until *after* you have done as He has commanded you.

God May Speak To Us Through Circumstances

God can also speaks to us by creating opportunities that He does not want us to miss.

Be wise in the way you act toward outsiders; make the most of every opportunity.

Colossians 4:5

When I ushered Alec into the car to take him with me on an excursion to a nursing home, I didn't know he wasn't too delighted to be going. Watch, though, how he made the most of the opportunity.

When I was a freshman in high school, I went to a nursing home with my mom. I didn't know why we were going. My mom was joining some friends from church who went there regularly to bring the love of Christ to the nursing home; I went because my mom said I had to. On the drive, my mom suggested that we witness to the people, and I agreed. What other reason could there be to go?

When we arrived, my mom started talking to an elderly woman about Christ, and I joined her in the conversation. Another woman leaned over and asked me what we were talking about. I looked into her eyes and realized that at her age, she had only a short time before she would stand before God. So I went over to her and shared the gospel message. She said she had grown up in a church-going family, and as I talked to her she came to realize that she had never made a true heart commitment to give her life to Christ. I offered her the opportunity to surrender her life right then and there – and she did!

My mom and I later learned that the group from church who went to the nursing home regularly had been barred from speaking about Jesus to that very woman. Her family had strictly forbidden them. I didn't know that talking to her about Jesus was forbidden, so I got the chance! Thank You, Lord, again and again and again!

Alec Li
Jupiter, Florida

God is sovereign; there are no coincidences with God. "There are God-incidences, but no co-incidences."

God Reveals Our Calling

Now how exactly will we know our mission, our purposes in life, our calling here on earth? We do not really *discover* our calling, but God *reveals* it to us. He may reveal our calling as we grow to know Him more and become immersed in Scripture, church, worship, prayer.

When we are in the valley, when we are suffering, it can be a critical time to listen and learn. God has meaning and purpose through our suffering – not despite our suffering, but *through* our suffering. He may be taking us through this time of adversity to equip us and prepare us to fulfill the purpose He has for us; the suffering may be a necessary part of the equipping.

God may reveal His purpose to you by burdening your heart. When you are broken hearted over the devastation caused by drugs in your city, that could be God calling you. When your righteous anger burns like a fire inside you over the abandoned street children in Bolivia or the sex slave trafficking in Asia, that may be God laying a call on your heart.

Your calling may be related to your own suffering. If you have cancer and are suddenly struck with the horrific truth that the unsaved who are dying with cancer have so little time left to choose Christ, that may be God giving you a ministry. If you raised your kids as a single parent and are weeping for the plight of single parents today, God may be calling you. If you have had an abortion and are terrified for pregnant teens because you know firsthand the emotional and spiritual devastation of abortion, God may be assigning you ministry work here. The world is full of suffering lost people. We will probably have difficulty reaching the lost for Christ if we cannot relate to them. We may struggle relating to them in their suffering if we have not experienced suffering ourselves.

You've met my friend Kim B. a few times. In Chapter 9, she described how she had been incapacitated with vertigo for over a year. I have asked her back to explain how an earlier hardship propelled her into ministry to those who are suffering.

I was widowed at nineteen. God has burdened me with a desire to help others who are hurting. I don't want the experience of my pain and suffering to be wasted. I've learned that when people realize you have been there and you can relate, they change completely and are willing to talk to you on a whole new level.

Kim B.
West Palm Beach, Florida

You may feel God's calling as a real physical ache in your heart or as a burning inside, such as the disciples felt on the road to Emmaus, their **hearts burning within** them as Jesus opened the Scriptures to them (Lk 24:32).

Or you may suddenly have a passion for a particular ministry work, and a huge sense of urgency about completing the mission. You may then realize that God is suddenly giving you spiritual gifts related to this ministry and connecting you with just the right people necessary to bring it to fruition.

If, when the Holy Spirit is calling us to a mission or convicting us of sin, we ignore Him, we may have quenched the fire of His voice.

Do not quench the Spirit.

1 Thessalonians 5:19 NASB

God may not call forever. We may miss the purpose He has planned for us. After we have repeatedly quenched the Holy Spirit, there may come a time when we are no longer able to hear Him.

Is It God's Voice, Satan's Voice, Or Our Own Voice?

We can't always know. Here are a few points that may help.

- Satan often speaks in vague generalities, "You are a bad mother," whereas God usually speaks in specifics, "You lied to your child."

- Recognize that we cannot just follow our hearts. **The heart is deceitful above all things, and desperately wicked** (Jer 17:9 NKJV). What we must follow is Scripture. Always be obedient to God, to Scripture. Always check to be sure that what you are hearing is in line with Scripture.

- For important decisions, keep going back to Him for clarification. He knows how much you want to walk in His will. As you go back to Him in prayer, He may give you confirmation and further direction.

- Seek wise counsel: Godly Christians who are abiding deeply in Him. As Proverbs teaches,

Plans fail for lack of counsel, but with many advisers they succeed.

Proverbs 15:22

- Be certain that you have His peace. If you are uncertain, or churning around about a decision, don't make a move until He has given you His peace about it. The advice I have been given is, "When in doubt, don't."

Can we think we hear His voice, and yet be wrong? Certainly. Even Paul did (Acts 16:6-10). However,

- if we are seeking Him with all our heart,
- if we refuse to be conformed to the world,
- if we are immersing ourselves in Scripture, church, worship, prayer,
- if we are obeying as best we can,
- if we are constantly inviting Him to transform us,
- if we are coming to deeper and deeper surrenders . . .

. . . then I believe that we can trust Him to correct us when we are on the wrong path. And, as we submit to His training to become more sensitive to His Spirit, we may come to recognize His voice more and more.

His Sheep Hear His Voice

"My sheep listen to my voice, and I know them, and they follow me."

John 10:27 NASB

God expects His sheep to listen to His voice. He knows us, and I think that He expects us to come to know Him and to learn to hear and understand His call. I believe that He expects us to follow Him, to obey Him, and to respond to His call. He has a calling on our lives that He desperately wants to reveal to us, and so fiercely desires us to follow.

I challenge you to implement this guide to hearing God's voice, and ask God for an understanding deep in your heart of your calling. Pray on your knees, and if you feel called, spend time fasting, begging Him to reveal His mission. He has a calling on your life, and part of your equipping may have been *through* your suffering. His calling is a unique calling, specifically for you, because you were designed, shaped, and equipped to fulfill that calling. He is only waiting for you to surrender and respond to Him.

Chapter 12
Seize What Jesus Seized You For

W hat is your life? You are a mist that appears for a little while and then vanishes.

James 4:14

When our lives are over, will it matter how much money we had amassed? How enormous our house was? How much time we spent at work? How many awards we received? How much recognition we got for our work? If anyone will remember us at all?

Three things will last forever — faith, hope, and love — and the greatest of these is love.

1 Corinthians 13:13 NLT

When we are ushered into Heaven, clothed in Jesus' righteousness because we have no righteousness of our own, and we come face to face with our Creator, the only thing that matters will be: Do you know Jesus intimately? Did you give Him pleasure by your relationship with Him? Did you do His Kingdom work as He planned it for you? Did you bring glory to Him during your years on this earth? Did you fulfill His purposes for you in this life?

First Corinthians tells us our work will be tested by fire — did you build with straw, or with gold? (1Cor 3:10-15).

Suffering Has Lost Its Sting

We have covered a lot of ground together. We started with acknowledging the reality of our pain and associated emotions, learning that the more truth and honesty reign in our heart, the less confused our emotions may be. We spent an eye-opening time recognizing that our tribulations may find meaning and purpose when we surrender them into the Lord's hands. We have seen that an intimate relationship with Jesus can develop as a result of *His* unfailing love and *our* willingness to surrender.

We now realize that evil exists because God gave us free will and we chose rebellion. We bowed our hearts to His sovereignty, admitting that His ways are higher than our ways. We also realized that His ways often seem completely incomprehensible because we mostly only see the bottom of the tapestry. He allowed us a glimpse of the top of the tapestry as we explored how He gives meaning to our suffering. He showed us the great purposes our own afflictions may have: to grow our spirits, to develop our intimacy with Him, to advance His Kingdom, and above all else, to give Him glory.

We have learned that His purpose is not to provide for *our* comfort — and it's not to provide for *His* comfort, either, for He weeps when we weep. When we pound down heaven's gate and demand, "Why?" His only explanation is His infinite love plus His absolute sovereignty. We rest, recognizing that we may never understand His plan, but we can surely trust His heart, we can truly believe that He is always working for our good. We can declare with certainty that triumphing over suffering means that suffering has no power over us. Suffering has lost its sting.

We Are God's Poem

How do we respond to infinite love? Love that left heaven to die in our place, to die by crucifixion so that we could spend eternity with Him? There is nothing God needs, but I believe there is *something* we can offer Him. Something He gave to us and no longer has, because He surrendered the rights to it. Something only we can give, because He gave us free will, to either give it or withhold it. That something is *our life.*

For we are God's handiwork, created in Christ Jesus to do good works, which God prepared in advance for us to do.

Ephesians 2:10

This verse tells us that we were redeemed, brought into God's Kingdom of Light, for the *purpose* of doing good works. The word good here is agathos – we studied agathos in Chapter 5: useful and profitable. We learned in Romans 8:28 that God is always working for our good, to give us useful and profitable blessings – but in this verse from Ephesians, look who is working for whose good now! The tables are turned – astonishing! Jesus redeemed us, chose us, and called us, to work not for our own good, but for *God's* good, to be useful and profitable for Him!

We are God's handiwork. Other translations say His workmanship, His masterpiece. The Greek is poeima, "a work, a workpiece, a workmanship . . . He who does the making is performer, doer, poet."[1] I love that. God is the Poet, and we are His poem. Precious . . . God prepared good works **in advance** for us. The parts of our lives that we love, and those that we resent, He intertwined together to enable us to fulfill His purposes. We are His poem, and when the last verse is completed, and we stand before Him, will He read His poem with great joy?

If We Do Not Fulfill Our God-Given Purposes

What will happen if we do not fulfill our God-given purposes? We don't always know the answer to that question. Let's look at some Biblical examples.

Remember John Mark, who abandoned Paul and Barnabas on their first missionary journey (Acts 13:13, 15:36-40). John Mark missed the joy of partnering with God and allowing God to work through him. The Bible records no replacement for John Mark; any thoughts beyond this are merely speculation.

Yet the Bible also explains that if someone missed their assignment, there are times that God may raise up someone else to do the Kingdom work. Recall Epaphroditis, risking his life to **complete what was deficient** in another Christian's service (Phil 2:27, 30). Pastor Todd Mullins explains that if our purpose is part of God's overarching plan for His Kingdom, the work will not go undone, God will raise up someone else – even if that means raising up rocks to do it (Lk 19:40). His **words will not return to Him empty** (Isa 55:11). His **eyes range throughout the earth to strengthen those whose hearts are fully committed to Him** (2Chr 16:9). He will give those fully committed hearts the extraordinary privilege of experiencing the Holy Spirit working through them.

My friend Patricia has a very close walk with the Lord. This amazing evangelist hears from Him very clearly and obeys Him with great joy. She has asked me if she could share a heart-breaking time in her life where she feels that she missed God's call.

The woman was deeply troubled. The Holy Spirit prompted me to call her; I did not know why. But I was busy, so I put it off . . . and in a number of months I learned that she had committed suicide.

God is all in all, He is sovereign, and He certainly does not need me. I don't know what happened between her and God during those few months from when I ignored His call to when she committed suicide. But what I do know is that when God calls you, it is for immediate action.

When the Spirit prompts you, do not procrastinate. When God says, "You're up," do it – NOW. You never know what Kingdom purpose He has planned for you.

Patricia
Philadelphia, Pennsylvania

We will take one more example, from the Old Testament. In the Book of Numbers, God had brought the Israelites to the Promised Land and instructed them to take possession of it. Moses sent spies into the Promised Land, and they brought back a report of a land flowing with milk and honey, but occupied by powerful giants. The Israelites panicked and refused to go in. So the Lord said,

". . . not one of them will ever see the land I promised on oath to their ancestors. No one who has treated me with contempt will ever see it . . . In this wilderness your bodies will fall – every one of you . . . who has grumbled against me . . . As for your children . . . I will bring *them* in to enjoy the land you have rejected."

Numbers 14:23,29,31, emphasis added

The Israelites mourned bitterly, and then concocted a new game plan.

Early the next morning they set out for the highest point in the hill country, saying, "Now we are ready to go up to the land the LORD promised. Surely we have sinned!"

But Moses said, "Why are you disobeying the LORD's command? This will not succeed! Do not go up, because the LORD is not with you. You will be defeated by your enemies, for the Amalekites and Canaanites will face you there. Because you have turned away from the LORD, he will not be with you and you will fall by the sword."

Nevertheless, in their presumption they went up toward the highest point in the hill country, though neither Moses nor the ark of the LORD's covenant moved from the camp. Then the Amalekites and Canaanites who lived in that hill country came down and attacked them and beat them down . . .

Numbers 14:40-45

What will happen if we do not do the work God assigns us? There may come a point when it will be too late. The door may not stay open forever. We might resist God with what we consider "good" excuses, such as family, work, or finances. We may even be brash enough to tell Him that His timing is inconvenient. Yet Ecclesiastes tells us,

Farmers who wait for perfect weather never plant. If they watch every cloud, they never harvest.

Ecclesiastes 11:4 NLT

If we wait for perfect conditions, we may miss His call. We may shrink back in disobedience. And, if we try to make up for our disobedience by doing the work *after it is too late*, God may no longer be working there, and we may fail. We may be attacked and beaten down by the Enemy.

Notice in the passage from Numbers that the generation of Israelites sent into the desert missed the blessing of being used by God. Note also that although it was too late for *this particular* generation of Israelites to do God's will, His plan was still accomplished. His words did not return to Him empty. Since it was His overarching plan for the nation of Israel to take possession of the Promised Land, God raised up someone else to do it: the next generation of Israelites.

We Are Significant

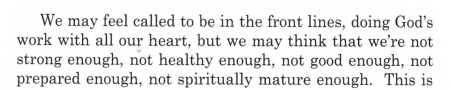

Nothing we are called to do is insignificant. Nothing. Take a look from God's viewpoint. Imagine a 1000-piece puzzle with just one piece missing. When we look at that puzzle, our eyes will probably be drawn to the hole. The puzzle represents the Kingdom of God, and we are the pieces. God requires each of us to be doing His work; His work is not complete until we do our part.

The missing piece itself may feel unimportant. It may feel its job is pretty unimportant. Yet to the Worker of the puzzle, to God, that piece means everything. The puzzle is not complete until all the pieces are in place.

We may feel called to be in the front lines, doing God's work with all our heart, but we may think that we're not strong enough, not healthy enough, not good enough, not prepared enough, not spiritually mature enough. This is

Satan's great lie: that we are insignificant, that anything we do will be meaningless. Think of the feeding of the five thousand (Jn 6). Can you imagine how that day would have looked if the young boy did not come forward before the multitude with his five barley loaves and two fish? If he thought his contribution was insignificant? Jesus can multiply what little we have to offer – infinitely. We need only give Him *everything*, to hold nothing back.

"From everyone who has been given much, much will be demanded; and from the one who has been entrusted with much, much more will be asked."
Luke 12:48

We are the ones to whom much has been given. Jesus has given us salvation and His most precious Holy Spirit, and he expects – no, He *demands* – that we give Him our everything: our hands and feet, our mouth and mind, our time, our every breath, our heart and soul, our whole life. He demands that we be **hot** Christians, declaring in Revelation that He will vomit lukewarm Christians out of His mouth (Rev 3:15-16 NKJV).

God's Call Is Daily

How will we know God's calling? Realize that God has purposes for us everyday, all day. If we are waiting for one huge calling, we may miss the many daily callings He has for us.

God may call us to significant work that takes but a moment and merely requires us to be available and willing to allow Him to rearrange our schedule. I have asked my friend Tina to describe a time when God called her to be available.

I was working in my office, which closed at noon, scrambling to catch up on unfinished work. The door of the office was supposed to be locked, but somehow a fellow walked in whom I had not seen for many years. He was looking for my boss, who was out to lunch. As I talked to him, he broke down, trembling, telling me about his young son who had just been diagnosed with cancer. He said he was having one of the worst days of his life.

Although I needed to get my work done, I dropped everything to speak to the fellow. Miraculously, the office phone didn't ring, our cell phones didn't go off, and no one came to the door as we talked. I realized that although he had grown up in a Christian family and had gone to a Christian school, he had never turned his life over to Christ's control. He was so terrified for his son, and I recognized how desperately they both needed Jesus. I told him, "Unless you have Jesus, you cannot share Jesus." He came to Christ right there, and gave his life, his son, his family, his everything to God's control. His trembling stopped and the fear fled from his eyes as the peace of Christ settled his spirit. He did not know what the outcome would be for his son, but he did know that God was in control, and that he could trust Him. I told him a huge celebration party was taking place in heaven at this moment because he was just now born again of God's Spirit.

Tina
Wilmington, Delaware

God's Call Is Upward

God may call us to a work that is completed quickly, and He may also call us to a work that will take weeks or months or even years. He rarely gives only one job to last a lifetime, for as we grow in Him, He can direct us into His **upward call** (Phil 3:14 NASB). Usually, our calling is not nearly as detailed as we humans would like it to be. If He gave us that much detail, we might either run away in fear, or run ahead and try to accomplish it in our own strength. God wants us to be dependent upon Him, needing to be in close contact with Him, so He can lead us moment by moment.

In 2004, when God first called me to write Triumph Over Suffering, *I thought it was going to be a little one-hour talk. That was terrifying enough for someone who had no speaking ability and would quake in her boots whenever she had to speak in public. If He had revealed to me at that time that His plan was for* Triumph Over Suffering *to be a full book, I may have run away in terror!*

Celeste Li
Jupiter, Florida

God's Call Is To Be His Ambassadors

How God calls us, and what exactly He calls each of us to do, will be as different as our fingerprints. Yet there are a few universal truths about our callings.

- Fulfilling our calling will bring Him glory, for that is why He created us (Rev 4:11).

- God will reveal to us where He is working and invite us to join Him. The word calling means "an invitation."[2] We are not to initiate our own plans

and then ask Him to bless them; we are to work
where He reveals that He is working.

- Most often, we must seek God passionately,
  intimately, deeply, and continually before He fills
  us with His purposes.

- At the core of each of our purposes will be God's
  heart: the reconciliation of all men. Our purposes
  will reflect that what Second Corinthians describes:

**And he died for all, that those who live should no
longer live for themselves but for him who died for
them and was raised again ... Therefore, if anyone is
in Christ, he is a new creation; the old has gone, the
new is here! All this is from God, who reconciled us
to himself through Christ and gave us the ministry
of reconciliation: that God was reconciling the
world to himself in Christ, not counting people's
sins against them. And he has committed to us the
message of reconciliation. We are therefore Christ's
ambassadors, as though God were making his appeal
through us.**

2 Corinthians 5:15, 17-20

That is breathtaking. We are here as His ambassadors.
He is making His appeal through us. On the surface, our
callings may be vastly different, but God's ultimate design
in each of our purposes is to reconcile mankind to Himself.
Jesus told His disciples,

"As the Father has sent me, I am sending you."
John 20:21

What did the Father send Jesus to do? To reconcile the
world to Himself. **"Whoever believes in me will do the
works I have been doing"** (Jn 14:12). We are sent forth
to do the same.

We are God's workmanship, His masterpiece, His poem, and our trials and sorrows have an indispensable role in our calling as His ambassadors, for our purposes are through our suffering. Not despite our suffering, but *through* our suffering.

My friend Anita is a steadfast evangelist who ministers tirelessly in the prisons. You will see clearly from her testimony that her calling is *through* her suffering.

Omniscient God foreknew me and knew everything I would go through to be used by Him for His purposes. When I was 16, I lost twin girls, and was not allowed back in school, so I turned to drugs, shoplifting, and prostitution. I was shot in the head; I was diagnosed with HIV; and I did time in prison.

After decades of this lifestyle, I was knocking on death's door. I prayed on my knees, "Lord, I say with Paul, I am the chief sinner (1Tim 1:15). I am weak, but You are strong (1Cor 4:10)." I submitted my life to God, and He delivered me. Omnipotent God miraculously lifted me from the crack house to the church house.

Since 1999 I have been filled with the Holy Spirit, sanctified, and clean and sober. God says in His Word that He would use the base things of the world to confound the wise (1Cor 1:27), and He does just that in me. Because I have given my life to Him, God is now using all my years of suffering for His glory. I work as a volunteer easing the minds of those with chronic illnesses. I also go into the same prison where I was once locked up, bringing Christ's message of hope to those imprisoned, letting them know that God will deliver them from slavery to their sins and addictions if they surrender to Him.

Anita
Boynton Beach, Florida

What a magnificent example of God **transforming the Valley of Trouble into a gateway of hope** (Hos 2:15 NLT).

God's Call Is To Comfort Others With His Comfort

All our trials and woes can be given meaning and thoroughly put to work in our calling.

Praise be to the God and Father of our Lord Jesus Christ, the Father of compassion and the God of all comfort, who comforts us in all our troubles, so that we can comfort those in any trouble with the comfort we ourselves receive from God. For just as we share abundantly in the sufferings of Christ, so also our comfort abounds through Christ.
2 Corinthians 1:3-5

We live in a world full of troubles and anguish. How can we reach those who are hurting if we cannot relate to them? The deep heart anguish is what enables my friend Margaret to relate to those in pain.

My precious son committed suicide at age 39. God has used my pain as He educated me in His "University of Life" so He may use me to comfort others in like situations and proclaim Him to be totally faithful. All I have seen of the Lord causes me to trust Him for all I cannot see.
Margaret
Philadelphia, Pennsylvania

Just what does it mean to **share abundantly in the sufferings of Christ**? To share abundantly means "to superabound (in quantity or quality), be in excess, be superfluous,"[3] "exceeding a number or measure which marks fullness."[4] Yes, I agree Christ's sufferings were in excess. For many of us, our sufferings exceed fullness, too.

When the sufferings of Christ flow over into our lives, we can relate to those who are afflicted. When we connect with them by allowing Jesus' love and comfort to flow through us, it can open the door for us, as His ambassadors, to bring His love and message of reconciliation. Watch my friend Joanne in action as Christ's comfort flows through her to others.

I have breast cancer. Each month, when I go into the clinic for treatment, I speak to the women also being treated for breast cancer. It is only because I have what they have that they allow me to talk to them. It is only because I can identify with them and relate to them that they trust me. It is only because they know I walk in their moccasins that they will listen to me as I speak about Christ. There is no question God sends us through His schools of suffering for His divine purposes.

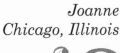

Joanne
Chicago, Illinois

God's Call May Be Through Your Suffering –
Seize It!

I press on to take hold of that for which Christ Jesus took hold of me.

Philippians 3:12

Jesus *takes hold* of us so that we can *take hold* of our purposes. The Greek is katalambano, and I don't think translating it *take hold* seems to do this word justice. Listen to some selections from my Word Study Dictionary:

> To lay hold of, to seize, with eagerness, suddenness . . . to obtain the prize with the idea of eager and strenuous exertion.[5]

Let's translate it *seize*. Jesus seized us and rescued us from Satan for purposes that God in His goodness designed for us. Press on to seize that for which Christ Jesus seized you!

God created us exactly as He desired, He carved and shaped us through our sufferings, He healed our brokenness, and He made us a new creation. He filled us with His Spirit and endowed us with intense passions, which we are not to quench. Harness those passions, and seek God's heart. He wants our fully committed hearts, hearts that have learned through our intimate relationship with Him what pleases Him and desire so desperately to do just that.

Triumphing over suffering means that you recognize that you, in your anguish, are **but a potsherd among the potsherds on the ground** (Isa 45:9). Potsherds do not appear to have much value – but do not forget that the King of all Kings came to earth from the everlasting and *died* for us potsherds.

When you surrender completely to the Master Potter in your suffering, He can take you, His potsherd, gently in His competent hands. He can wash away the filth of sin. He can make you whole in Him as He heals your heart. He can mold you and shape you in order to fully equip you, and He can fill you with His Spirit so His glory will pour forth from you. Finally, He can strategically position you, and invite you to partner with Him as He works through you to fulfill His purposes – the purposes that He specifically designed for you. Seize what He has seized you for. He is waiting!

I will be praying for you
as you go forth
in triumph over suffering.

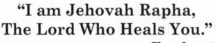

"I am Jehovah Rapha,
The Lord Who Heals You."
Exodus 15:26

Appendix 1
Glossary of Greek and Hebrew Words

This glossary includes the Hebrew and Greek words used throughout the *Triumph Over Suffering* book and *Workbook*. Hebrew is written with characters, and the Greek alphabet does not completely correspond to our English alphabet, so the Hebrew and Greek are transliterated into English. The references for these words are in the Endnotes. (WB) means that the word appears only in the *Triumph Over Suffering Workbook*. All words are Greek unless otherwise indicated.

Adonai – (Hebrew) Name of God. Sovereign Lord and Master, Matchless Controller. One who possesses supreme authority, unlimited power

agape – God's free, unconditional love, no strings attached; Jesus' completely selfless love demonstrated in His death; God's commitment to do whatever it takes to meet all our needs, particularly our spiritual needs; God giving us what He knows is best for us, not necessarily what we desire or deserve. Our agape for God means our unconditional obedience and surrender.

agathos – good; useful and profitable; blessings that are what we need, not necessarily what we want; blessings that conform us to the image of Christ

anav (WB) – (Hebrew) afflicted; literally to be bowed down; humble, poor in spirit

charis – grace; free, unearned, undeserved gift given without expectation of return

doxa – the obvious presence of God; His power, majesty, purity, sovereignty, unchanging character, faithfulness, infinite love

dynamis – power in action; dynamite

eirene – God's peace; literally no barrier between God and us.

El Elyon (WB) – (Hebrew) name of God meaning God Most High; this name describes Him as the Sovereign Ruler in control of all the universe

El Shaddai (WB) – (Hebrew) name of God meaning Almighty and Sufficient One; this name describes His power and might and bountifulness; He pours forth His blessings upon us; all that we have, all that we are, and all we need come from Him.

elpis – translated "hope;" courage to trust while we wait on God's timing for His promised outcome; hope with the complete confidence of the end result; expecting, trusting, knowing that God will make it happen according to His plan. Elpis is a sure thing, a certainty, but a certainty that has not yet happened

Gethsemane – (Aramaic) where Jesus spent the Agony in the Garden; literally it means olive press

hagios – holy; set apart from a common to a sacred use

histemi – to stand firm; to hold a crucial position in battle

katalambano – to seize with great eagerness and strenuous exertion

kataritzo (WB) – to restore, to put in appropriate condition; to make me the person He wants me to be

koinonia – fellowship; a passionate connection because two people can relate or have shared intense experiences

makarios – fully satisfied, not because of favorable circumstances, but because Jesus is dwelling in us.

meno – to abide, to remain, to continue; to stay, to dwell, to tarry; figuratively, to remain united in heart, mind and will

merimna – worry; anxiety

metamorphoo – transformation; a radical change such as a caterpillar to a butterfly

pale – struggle; a hand to hand fight full of trickery, cunning, and strategy

pistis – faith; we believe so deeply we live like we believe it; living our lives in trust of our beliefs

poeima – a distinctly created work of art; masterpiece; our English word "poem" comes from this word

Qanna (WB) – (Hebrew) name of God meaning Jealous; this name means that He demands our exclusive devotion – for our good, not for His

raphah – (Hebrew) to heal; to make whole; literally to mend by stitching. One of the names of God, Jehovah Rapha, The Lord Who Heals

skandalon – a trap; a snare to catch a wild animal; to stumble

sophronismos – rescued from the sins of our mind and emotions and therefore having sound judgment and self discipline

sterizo (WB) – to turn resolutely in a certain direction.

sthenoo (WB) – to strengthen spiritually

thelema (WB) – will; pleasure; carries the connotation of God's pleasure and delight.

themilioo (WB) – to lay the foundation

thlipsis – suffering so great it is as if you are being squeezed in an olive press; tribulation

yatsar – (Hebrew) to form, plan, fashion as a skillful craftsman

Appendix 2
Resources

This appendix is offered as a resource to you. While I am not in a position to endorse or vouch for these resources, I do believe you may find them helpful.

Bibles

Life Application Study Bible, New King James Version. Wheaton, IL: Tyndale House Publishers, 1996.
New Believer's Bible, New Living Translation. Carol Stream, IL: Tyndale House Publishers, 2007.
Maxwell, John C. *The Maxwell Leadership Bible: Lessons in Leadership from the Word of God.* Nashville, TN: Thomas Nelson, Inc., 2007.
Tada, Joni Eareckson, Dravecky, Dave. *NIV Encouragement Bible.* Grand Rapids, MI: Zondervan, 2001.

Cancer Support

Cancer Support Groups of Christ Fellowship
CancerSupportCF@gmail.com
(561) 799-7603 x 2186
LotsAHelpingHands.com/c/602209

Chronic Illness

Rest Ministries and Hopekeepers founded by Lisa Copen. *Restministries.com*
Copen, Lisa. *Learning To Cope With Chronic Illness.* San Diego, CA: Rest Ministries Publishers, 2003.
Copen, Lisa. *When Chronic Illness Enters Your Life.* San Diego, CA: Rest Ministries Publishers, 2002.

Chronic Pain

Tomiak, Tracy, *Thriving, Not Just Surviving: Living Abundantly With Pain.* Calgary, Alberta, Canada: Agape Publications, 2004.
Painconnection.com

Devotionals

Chambers, Oswald. *My Utmost for His Highest.* Grand Rapids, MI: Discovery House Publishers, 1992.
Hurnard, Hannah. *Hinds' Feet on High Places.* Shippensburg, PA: Destiny Image Publishers, Inc., 2005.
KimberlyMac. *Thebridegroomscafe.com*
Roberts, Frances. *Come Away My Beloved.* Ulrichsville, OH: Barbour Publishing, 2002.
Sorenson, Susan and Geist, Laura. *Praying Through Cancer: Set Your Heart Free From Fear. A 90 Day Devotional for Women.* Nashville, TN: W Publishing Group, A Division of Thomas Nelson, Inc, 2006.
Young, Sarah. *Jesus Calling: Enjoying Peace in His Presence.* Nashville, TN: Thomas Nelson, Inc, 2004.

Evangelism

Fay, William. *Share Jesus Without Fear.* Nashville, TN: Broadman & Holman Publishers, 1984.
Knechtle, Cliffe. *Give Me an Answer That Satisfies my Heart and my Mind.* Downers Grove, IL: Varsity Press, 1986.
Mittelberg, Mark. *The Questions Christians Hope No One Will Ask (with answers).* Wheaton, IL: Tyndale House Publishers, 2010.

Family Issues

SAFE-T Counseling Center. Executive Director Nancy Kurth Bustani, M.S. Biblically-based counseling and educational classes related to family issues such as healthy boundaries, parenting, and emotional growth. Also sexual abuse recovery classes related to childhood sexual abuse. (561) 622-5959.
Safetcounselingcenter.com

Foundations of Faith

Strobel, Lee. *The Case for Christ: A Journalist's Personal Investigation of the Evidence for Jesus.* Grand Rapids, MI: Zondervan, 1998.
Warren, Rick. *The Purpose Driven Life.* Grand Rapids, MI: Zondervan, 2002.

Forgiveness

Cassatly, Stephanie. *Call of the Sirens.* Michigan State University Press: *Fourth Genre: Explorations in Nonfiction,* Volume 9, Number 2, Fall 2007, pp. 43-50.
Jackie Kendall, *Free Yourself to Love,* New York, NY: FaithWords, 2009.

Kubetin, Cynthia and Mallory, James. *Shelter From the Storm: Hope for Survivors of Sexual Abuse.* Titusville, FL: Robert S. McGee Publishing, 1995.

Greek and Hebrew Word Study Tools

Baker, Warren and Carpenter, Eugene. *The Complete Word Study Dictionary Old Testament.* Chattanooga, TN: AMG Publishers, 2003.

Strong, James. *The New Strong's Exhaustive Concordance of the Bible, Concise Dictionary of the Words in the Hebrew Bible, and in the Greek Testament.* Nashville, TN: Thomas Nelson Publishers, 1995.

Zodhiates, Spiros. *The Complete Word Study Dictionary.* Chattanooga, TN: AMG Publishers, 1992.

Grief: Loss of a Loved One

GriefShare Seminars and Support Groups, griefshare.org
 Sarah Byrd, National GriefShare Consultant
 Dondi and Sarah Byrd, GriefShare Facilitators at Christ Fellowship Church, *gochristfellowship.com*

Lutzer, Erwin. *One Minute After You Die.* Chicago, IL: Moody Publishers, 1987.

Wright, H. Norman. *Experiencing Grief.* Nashville, TN: B&H Publishing Group, 2004

Loss of Spouse
 Lewis, C.S., *A Grief Observed.* San Francisco, CA: HarperCollins Publishers, 2001.

Loss of Children
 Heavilin, Marilyn Willett. *Roses in December: Finding Strength Within Grief.* Eugene, OR: Harvest House Publishers, 1987.

Loss of Infant Children
 Guthrie, Nancy. *Holding Onto Hope: A Pathway Through Suffering to the Heart of God.* Wheaton, IL: Tyndale House Publishers, 2002.

Multiple Losses
 Sittser, Jerry. *A Grace Disguised: How the Soul Grows Through Loss.* Grand Rapids, MI: Zondervan, 1995.

Suicide
 Hsu, Albert. *Grieving Suicide: A Loved One's Search for Comfort, Answers, and Hope.* Downers Grove, IL: InterVarsity Press, 2002.

Growing in Christ

Christ Fellowship Church
    Campuses in Florida: Palm Beach Gardens, Royal Palm Beach, Stuart, West Palm Beach, and Boynton Beach; also Espanol, and also Online
    Gochristfellowship.com
Blackaby, Henry and King, Claude. *Experiencing God.* Nashville, TN: Broadman & Holman Publishers, 1994.
Green, Melody and Hazard, David. *No Compromise: The Life Story of Keith Green.* Eugene, OR: Harvest House Publishers, 2000.
Moore, Beth. *Jesus, 90 Days With the One and Only.* Nashville, TN: B&H Publishing Group, 2007.
Towns, Elmer. *Fasting for Spiritual Breakthrough: A Guide To 9 Biblical Fasts.* Ventura, CA: Regal Books of Gospel Light, 1996.
Warren, Kay. *Dangerous Surrender: What Happens When You Say Yes To God.* Grand Rapids, MI: Zondervan, 2007.

Healing from Sexual Abuse

Allender, Dan. *The Wounded Heart: Hope for Adult Victims of Childhood Sexual Abuse.* Colorado Springs, CO: NavPress, 1990.
Clapper, Colleen. *The Raindrops On My Windshield Sound Like Popcorn.* Enumclaw, WA: Winepress Publishing, 2009.
Kubetin, Cynthia and Mallory, James. *Shelter From the Storm: Hope for Survivors of Sexual Abuse.* Titusville, FL: Robert S. McGee Publishing, 1995.
RBC Ministries. When Trust Is Lost. Booklet produced by Discovery Series and available at *rbc.org* and *Discoveryseries.org*
SAFE-T Counseling Center. Executive Director Nancy Kurth Bustani, M.S. SAFE-T provides sexual abuse recovery classes related to childhood sexual abuse. (561) 622-5959.
    Safetcounselingcenter.com
Watson, Glenda. *Restoring Dignity.* Booklet produced by Restoration Ministries International and available at restorationministries.co.za
Wounded Heart Ministries, Director Dan Allender, Ph.D. (206) 855-8460.

Health and Wellness

Pfeiffer, Margaret. *Smart 4 Your Heart: Four Simple Ways to Easily Manage Your Cholesterol.* London: King Publishing, 2009.
Rubin, Jordan. *The Great Physician's Rx for Health and Wellness: Seven Keys to Unlock Your Health Potential.* Nashville, TN: Thomas Nelson, 2005.

Thomas, Denise. *Honoring God's Temple: Changing from the Inside Out Personally, Practically, and Finally.* Bloomington, IN: XLibris, 2008.

Intimacy With Jesus

Arthur, Kay. *Lord, I Want to Know You.* Colorado Springs, CO: Waterbrook Press, 2000.

Frost, Jack. *Experiencing the Father's Embrace.* Shippensburg, PA: Destiny Image Publishers, Inc., 2002.

McClung, Floyd. *The Father Heart of God.* Eugene, OR: Harvest House Publishers, 1971.

Murray, Andrew. *The Secret of God's Presence.* New Kensington, PA: Whitaker House, 1982.

Tozer, A.W. *The Knowledge of the Holy.* New York, NY: HarperCollins Publishers Inc., 1961.

Whitten, Clark. *Pure Grace: The Life Changing Power of Uncontaminated Grace.* Shippensburg, PA: Destiny Image Publishers, Inc, 2012.

Witt, Lance. *Replenish: Leading From a Healthy Soul.* Grand Rapids, MI: Baker Publishing Group, 2011.

Young, Sarah. *Jesus Calling: Enjoying Peace in His Presence.* Nashville, TN: Thomas Nelson, Inc, 2004.

Prayer

Arthur, Kay. *Lord Teach Me To Pray in 28 Days.* Eugene, OR: Harvest House Publishers, 1982.

Chambers, Oswald. *Prayer: A Holy Occupation.* Grand Rapids, MI: Discovery House Publishers, 1992.

Maxwell, John. *Partners in Prayer: Support and Strengthen Your Pastor and Church Leaders.* Nashville, TN: Thomas Nelson, Inc., 1996.

Omartian, Stormie. *The Power of a Praying Wife.* Eugene, OR: Harvest House Publishers, 1997.

Scripture Memorization

Navigator's Scripture Memory Course, Topical Memory System. Colorado Springs, CO: Navpress, 2006.

Sexual Addiction

L.I.F.E. Ministry (Living In Freedom Eternally)
Founders: Ron and Joanne Highley
A Biblically based Christian ministry headquartered in New York City that works to help people become free from the bondage of homosexuality and other sexual addictions. *Lifeministry.org*

Spiritual Warfare

Frangipane, Francis. *The Three Battlegrounds*. Cedar Rapids, IA: Arrow Publications, 1989.

Meyer, Joyce. *Battlefield of the Mind: Winning the Battle in Your Mind*. NY, NY: Faithwords, A Division of Hachette Book Group, 1995.

Suffering

Triumphoversuffering.com

Lotz, Anne Graham. *Why? Trusting God When You Don't Understand*. Nashville, TN: W Publishing Group, A Division of Thomas Nelson, Inc, 2004.

Mehl, Ron. *God Works the Night Shift: Acts of Love Your Father Performs Even While You Sleep*. Sisters, OR: Multnomah Books, 1994.

Tada, Joni Eareckson. *When God Weeps: Why Our Sufferings Matter To the Almighty*. Grand Rapids, MI: Zondervan, 1997.

Yancey, Philip. *Where Is God When It Hurts? A Comforting, Healing Guide for Coping With Hard Times*. Grand Rapids, MI: Zondervan, 1990.

Other Media

Copeland, Gloria. *Live Long - Live Strong* CD. Kenneth Copeland Ministries, Fort Worth, TX
(800)-600-7395. *Kcm.org*

Johnson, Nicole. *Stepping Into The Ring: The story of a woman's desperate fight with breast cancer and her deeper enemy – despair. Womenoffaith.com*

Endnotes

I have used the following reference books to bring these Greek and Hebrew words to life. At times I have quoted directly and have used quotations marks; at other times the definitions are a synthesis of what I have gleaned from the following books. I have included the Strong's reference number in parentheses at the end of each reference in order to facilitate research. I have also included the Greek or English words in parentheses for greater clarity.

James Strong, *The New Strong's Exhaustive Concordance of the Bible, Concise Dictionary of the Words in the Hebrew Bible*, Nashville, TN, Thomas Nelson Publishers, 1995.

James Strong, *The New Strong's Exhaustive Concordance of the Bible, Concise Dictionary of the Words in the Greek Testament*, Nashville, TN, Thomas Nelson Publishers, 1995.

Spiros Zodhiates, *The Complete Word Study Dictionary*, Chattanooga, TN, AMG Publishers, 1992.

Warren Baker and Eugene Carpenter, *The Complete Word Study Dictionary Old Testament*, Chattanooga, TN, AMG Publishers, 2003.

Chapter 1 - "In This World You Will Have Trouble"
[1] Elizabeth Kubler-Ross, *On Death and Dying*, New York, NY, Scribner, 1969, p 9. Although the titles of each stage are Kubler-Ross' words, the comments about each are my extrapolation.
[2] Strong, *Greek*, p 60 (no. 3528). (overcome)
[3] Philip Yancey, *Where Is God When It Hurts?*, Grand Rapids, MI, Zondervan, 1990, p 67. Used with permission. The ideas contained in this paragraph and next three were derived from p 67-70 and 255.
[4] Yancey, p 77.
[5] *The ESV Bible* (*The Holy Bible, English Standard Version*), Wheaton, IL, Crossway, a publishing ministry of Good News Publishers, 2001. Used by permission. All rights reserved.
[6] Zodhiates, p 729 (no. 2315). (God-breathed)
[7] Zodhiates, p 729 (no. 2315). (God-breathed)

Chapter 2 - Experiencing and Expressing Emotions
[1] Jackie Kendall, *Free Yourself to Love*, New York, NY, FaithWords, 2009, p 145. The list is found on p 145-146.
[2] Joni Eareckson Tada, *When God Weeps*, Grand Rapids, MI, Zondervan, 1997, p 150-152 discusses some of these thoughts. Used with permission.
[3] Tada, p 152.

[4] I first heard about the "Itty Bitty Should Have Committee" from my parenting instructor Ginny Luther, the founder of Peaceful Parenting. I use the "Committee" with her permission. She said she does not know its origins, but it is commonly used by parenting instructors.

[5] Zodhiates, p 968 (no. 3338). The remainder of the paragraph is my paraphrase. (remorse)

[6] Zodhiates, p 969-970 (no. 3340). The beginning of the paragraph is my paraphrase. (repent)

[7] Strong, *Greek*, p 83 (no. 4710). (earnestness)

[8] Daniel J. Carlat, M.D., *American Family Physician Journal*, Volume 58, no. 7, "The Psychiatric Review of Symptoms: A Screening Tool for Family Physicians," November 1, 1998, p 1617-1624. The list I presented here draws from this article.

[9] Steven Shearer, PH.D., and Lauren Gordon, M.D., *American Family Physician Journal*, Volume 73, no.6, "The Patient with Excessive Worry," March 15, 2006, p 1049-1057.

[10] Zodhiates, p 960-961 (nos. 3307, 3308, and 3309). (worry)

[11] Zodhiates, p 519 (no. 1515). (shalom is OT equivalent of eirene)

[12] Strong, *Hebrew*, p 143 (no. 7999). (root of shalom to be safe)

[13] Zodhiates, p 66-67 (no. 26). (agape)

[14] Zodhiates, p 1372 (no. 5046). The rest of this paragraph is drawn from this reference. (perfect)

[15] Zodhiates, p 401 (no. 1167). (fear)

[16] Mirriam-Webster's Collegiate Dictionary, 11th Edition, USA, Mirriam-Webster Inc, 2003, p 389. (dynamite)

[17] Zodhiates, p 1363 (nos. 4995, 4998). This is my extrapolation based on this reference and the Amplified Bible's translation. (sophronismos = sound mind)

Chapter 3 - Surrender

[1] Zodhiates, p 70-71 (no. 40). (hagios = holy)

[2] Zodhiates, p 139-140 (no. 299). (blameless)

[3] Zodhiates, p 1404 (no. 5206). (adopted)

[4] Zodhiates, p 931 (no. 3084) and Baker p 24 (no. 1350). (redeem)

[5] I think this idea comes from one of Max Lucado's children's books, but I cannot locate the reference at this time.

[6] Zodhiates, p 1351-1352 (no. 4972). The remainder of that section is my extrapolation. (seal)

[7] Zodhiates, p 1469 (no. 5485). Again, the remainder of that section is my extrapolation. (charis = grace)

[8] Dr, John Maxwell taught on this concept at one of his messages at Christ Fellowship Church. Dr. Maxwell explains that since God knows in advance everything that will ever happen, we can never disappoint Him!

[9] Yancey, p 82. Tada discusses these concepts also on p 35-40.

[10] The first time I really thought about this was when I heard it discussed in *Fireproof*. This movie about a troubled marriage

healed in Christ is a must-see. 2008 American Christian drama film released by Samuel Goldwyn Films and Affirm Films, directed by Alex Kendrick, who co-wrote and co-produced with Stephen Kendrick.

[11] Cliffe Knechtle, *Give Me an Answer That Satisfies my Heart and my Mind*, Downers Grove, IL, Intervarsity Press, 1986, p 36. Used with permission. Although except where quoted, the wording is my own, the general ideas in this paragraph and the following two paragraphs are derived from Chapter Two of *Give Me an Answer*, "Does God Really Send People To Hell?" p 35-47.

[12] Knechtle, p 38.

[13] Knechtle, p 42.

[14] Strong, *Greek*, p 71 and 69 (nos. 4102 and 3982). (pistis = faith)

[15] Kay Warren, *Dangerous Surrender*, Grand Rapids, MI, Zondervan, 2007, p 35. Kay Warren says it this way, "My challenge to you is to say, 'I don't know exactly what the question is, God, but my answer is yes!' "

Chapter 4 - God Is Sovereign

[1] Although except where quoted, the wording is my own, many of the thoughts and concepts in this chapter come from the following two books:

Joni Eareckson Tada, *When God Weeps*, particularly Chapter 5 "All Trials Great and Small" and Chapter 6 "Heaven's Dirty Laundry?" Grand Rapids, MI, Zondervan, 1997. Used with permission.

Philip Yancey, *Where Is God When It Hurts?* particularly Chapter 6 "What Is God Trying To Tell Us?" and Chapter 7 "'Why Are We Here?" Grand Rapids, MI, Zondervan, 1990. Used with permission.

Both of these authors handle the topic of God's sovereignty with great reverence for God and tenderness for His people.

[2] Yancey, p 79.

[3] Athough the wording in this next section is my own, the concepts came from Tada's *When God Weeps,* pages 74-76.

[4] Strong, *Hebrew*, p 3 (no. 136) and p 2 (no. 113). (Adonai)

[5] Tada asks a set of similar questions on p 84-87. The paragraph following is derived from Tada p 78-80. Yancey gives a similar discussion of Job on p 104-106.

[6] The concepts in this next section "To Decree" come from Tada p 72-76, and p 81-85, where she discusses these verses. The wording is my own except where quoted.

[7] Zodhiates, p 1223-1224 (no. 4309). (decree)

[8] I think this wording may have come from Tada or Yancey, but I cannot locate the exact reference.

[9] Tada, p 73.

[10] Tada, p 83-84.

[11] Tada, p 85-88. The concepts in this paragraph are derived from p 85-86 and 222; except where quoted, the wording is my own.

[12] Baker, p 465 (no. 3335). (ordain = yatsar)

Chapter 5 - Suffering Can Work To Conform Us To the Image of Christ

[1] I asked Alec's physical therapist if I could quote him. He agreed, but said that he wasn't the originator of the explanation and he didn't know who initially said it. Sounds somewhat like Philip Yancey to me.

[2] Zodhiates, p 62-63 (no. 18). The remainder of the paragraph and the next paragraph are my extrapolations. (agathos)

[3] Zodhiates, p 476 (no. 1382). (dokime and derivatives)

[4] Zodhiates, p 475 (no. 1381). (dokime and derivatives)

[5] Strong, *Greek*, p 24 (no. 1384). (dokime and derivatives)

[6] Zodhiates, p 475 (no. 1381). (dokime and derivatives)

[7] Zodhiates, p 476 (no. 1384). (dokime and derivatives)

[8] Zodhiates, p 476 (no. 1383). (dokime and derivatives)

[9] Zodhiates, p 1425 (no. 5281). (hupomone = perseverance)

[10] Zodhiates, p 1425 (no. 5281). (hupomone = perseverance)

[11] Strong, *Greek*, p 94 (no. 5281). The next paragraph is my extrapolation of from these sources. (hupomone = perseverance)

[12] Zodhiates, p 570-572 (no. 1680). This paragraph is my paraphrase of these pages. (elpis)

[13] Zodhiates, p 1135 (no. 3986). (temptation or trial)

[14] From Joyce Meyer's message to Christ Fellowship in 2013.

[15] Baker, p 383 (no. 2789). (potsherd)

Chapter 6 - Suffering Can Open Our Eyes to Our Sin

[1] Tada, p 253.

[2] Zodhiates, p 721 (no. 2307). (will)

[3] Zodhiates, p 478-481 (no. 1391). The next paragraph is my extrapolation from here. (doxa)

[4] Zodhiates, p 1103-1104 (no. 3860). (give over)

[5] Strong, *Greek*, p 2 (no. 96). (depraved)

[6] Tada, p 253.

[7] Although the wording is my own, the ideas in this section come from Yancey, p 79-80.

[8] Tada, p 215.

[9] Zodhiates, p 753 (no. 2390). (healed)

Chapter 7 - Suffering Can Teach Us Humility, Dependence, and Forgiveness

[1] Zodhiates, p 1413 (no. 5229). (exalting)

[2] Strong, *Greek*, p 93 (no. 5229). (exalting)

[3] Baker, p 11 (no. 79). (wrestle)

[4] Zodhiates, p 299-300 (no. 863). (forgive)

Chapter 8 - Spiritual Warfare: Suffering To Advance the Kingdom

[1] Tada, p 22. This paragraph parallels Tada's writings on p 22.

[2] Zodhiates, p 476.

[3] Tada laid out some of these verses together on p 57-58. The summary at the end is my own.

[4] Zodhiates, p 1265 (no. 4506).   (deliver)

[5] Zodhiates, p 1091 (no. 3823).   (pale = struggle)

[6] Tada. Although the wording is my own, the concepts in this paragraph come from p 107-108.

[7] Strong, *Greek*, p 65 (no. 3794).   (stronghold)

[8] Zodhiates, p 1083 (no 3794).   (stronghold)

[9] Francis Frangipane, *The Three Battlegrounds*, Cedar Rapids, IA, Arrow Publications, 1989, p. 12. Used with permission. This paragraph and the next one are derived from Chapter 1, "Satan's Domain: The Realm of Darkness," p 12. The wording is my own except what is in quotes.

[10] Frangipane, p 12.

[11] Strong, *Greek*, p 20 (no. 1127).   (stay awake)

[12] Frangipane, p ii, iii.

[13] Zodhiates, p 785-787 (no. 2476).   (stand firm = histemi)

[14]The ideas in this paragraph probably come from Frangipane, but I am unable to locate the exact reference.

Chapter 9 - Suffering Can Lead To Intimacy With Christ

[1] Zodhiates, p 736 (no. 2347).   (thlipsis)

[2] I cannot find the reference for this, or where I first heard about the connection between these words, but it probably came from one of the books in the Endnotes or Resources.

[3] Zodhiates, p 361 (no. 1068).   (Gethsemane)

[4] Zodhiates, p 873 (nos. 2842).   (koinonia)

Chapter 10 - How Will You Respond To Your Suffering?

[1] Although except where quoted, the wording is my own, some of the thoughts and concepts in this chapter come from the following two books:

Philip Yancey, *Where Is God When It Hurts?* particularly Chapter 8 "Arms Too Short To Box With God," Grand Rapids, MI, Zondervan, 1990. This book really helped me to grasp the response of facing forward that God desires when we are in a trial. Used with permission.

Kay Arthur, *Lord Teach Me to Pray in 28 Days*, particularly pages 86-106 (Days 16 - 20), Eugene, OR, 1982. This workbook sent me delving into my Bible to understand what it means to pray the will of God. I highly recommend this book for anyone who desires to learn deeper prayer.

[2] Kay Arthur, *Lord Teach Me to Pray in 28 Days*, Eugene, OR, Harvest House Publishers, 1982, p 90-98. This section and the next two grew from what I learned working through these pages in this book.

[3] Strong, *Hebrew*, p 144 (no. 8034).   (name)

[4] Baker, p 1157 (no. 8034). The remainder of the paragraph is my extrapolation from these definitions. (name)

[5] Strong, *Greek*, p 56 (no. 3306). (meno = remain)

[6] Zodhiates, p 960 (no. 3306). (meno = remain)

[7] Arthur, p 95.

[8] Arthur, p 22-24 and 74-75. This section on the Our Father grew from what I learned working through these pages in her workbook, *Lord Teach Me to Pray in 28 Days*

[9] Arthur, p 75.

[10] Zodhiates, p 809, 273-274, 1353-1356, 817, 291-294 (nos. 2553, 770, 4982, 2577, 846). (trouble, sick, healing, well, raise him up)

[11] Beth Moore, *Jesus the One and Only*, Nashville, TN, LifeWay Press, 2000, p 52. The following two paragraphs leap from her description of Jehovah Raphah.

[12] Zodhiates, p 1292 (no. 4625). The remainder of that paragraph is my extrapolation based on the definition in Zodhiates and the commentary in Strong's *Greek* p 81 that says the word is probably derived from a word meaning "bent sapling." Although the wording is my own except where quoted, the thoughts from the two paragraphs that follow are derived from Beth Moore's teaching on this passage in *Jesus the One and Only* on p 87-90. (skandalon = trap)

[13] This quote probably comes from Yancey or Tada, but I cannot locate the exact reference at this time.

[14] Yancey, p 108.

[15] Zodhiates, p 937 (no. 3107). The following two paragraphs are my extrapolation. (makarios = blessed)

[16] Warren, Kay, *Dangerous Surrender*, Grand Rapids, MI, Zondervan, 2007, p 47.

Chapter 11 - Hearing the Voice of God

[1] Pastor Todd Mullins, Christ Fellowship Church, see Chapter 1.

[2] Warren, p 35. Kay Warren says it this way, "My challenge to you is to say, 'I don't know exactly what the question is, God, but my answer is yes!' " We discussed this in Chapter 3.

[3] Zodhiates, p 151 (no. 341). (renew)

Chapter 12 - Seize What Jesus Seized You For

[1] Zodhiates, p 1190-1191 (no. 4161). (poem)

[2] Strong, *Greek*, p 50 (no. 2821). (calling)

[3] Strong, *Greek*, p 70 (no. 4052). (share abundantly)

[4] Zodhiates, p 1150 (no. 4052). (share abundantly)

[5] Zodhiates, p 834 (no. 2638). (katalambano = seize)

With Heartfelt Gratitude I Thank...

My Lord and Redeemer Jesus Christ, who covers me with His blood and clothes me in His righteousness: Apart from You I can do nothing.

My Precious Family, who continue to stick patiently by me, never leaving my side:

My Dear Husband John, who supports me and perseveres with me: Thank you for leading and guiding me, praying for me and protecting me. You have given new meaning to the word love.

My Faithful Son Alec: You have once more endured tirelessly behind the scenes to bring these works to fruition. God has blessed you with many talents and giftings, and He has so worked through you to design this book to be a house of beauty to hold His precious Scriptures. Thank you for your patience, patience, and more patience.

My Cherished Daughter Jenna, who is part of this book in so many arenas: As my writing and language editor as well as my spiritual editor, I cannot thank you enough for your courage to edit me. I am also grateful for the creative spirit God place in you; when my words could not adequately express my thoughts, you spoke it in pictures. And now, I can only stand by and watch with awe as the Lord anoints you for *Triunfo Sobre el Sufrimiento*.

My Devoted Parents: You have impressed upon me God's commandments since I was small, talking about them when we sat at home and when we walked along the road, and you continue to model constant growth in Him to this day.

Pastor Tom and Donna Mullins, and Pastors Todd and Julie Mullins: You pursue Jesus with a fervor that is contagious to us all. Thank you for allowing God to use you as His instruments in founding Christ Fellowship Church – my church home and the place where I first encountered the Lord Jesus Christ. Donna, because of your totally committed heart, I have trusted you as my mentor and advisor and I follow you as you follow Christ.

Pastors Don Bray and Tim Popadic: You have so encouraged, advised, and supported both my husband and me. Thank you for teaching me the meaning of the word grace.

My Triumph Servant Leaders: Bobbie Higby, Betsy Burden, Kellie Sheirs, Linda Bloom, Margaret Zempleni-Long, Joan Hoffpauir, Jan

Symonette, Libby Hammond, Kimberly McCarthy, Teresa Nelson, Patricia Kaigler, Chelsea Kelter, Julie Stine, Bonnie Sapp, Patti Foster, Karen Bauroth, and all who have served as *Triumph* Servant Leaders over the years, including those I may not even know: Thank you for answering the Lord's call to be His choice servants, serving on *His* terms, not your own, and serving without any expectation of reward.

Richard Ekey, indefatigable warrior of *Triumph Over Suffering*: Without your dogged persistence and dauntless single-mindedness, this book would remain a three-ring binder of handouts in a classroom of a dozen people. Thank you for launching the *Triumph* Men's Branch, and for championing the cause to bring *TOS* to wherever God calls.

My Triumph Prayer Team: Donna Briley, Libby Hammond, Betty Johnson, Kellie Sheirs, Nancy Smith, and Debi Zimmerman, and all who have served on my *Triumph* Prayer Team over the years, as well as all my unknown prayer warriors: We surely don't know how to pray as we ought, but we bravely place our prayers into the Holy Spirit's hands, trusting Him to align them with the Father's will. Thank you, for being *my* Aaron and Hur, and for praying for each person who has opened this book.

My Spiritual Editor, Mentor, and Beloved Friend Cathy Moesel: You have embodied perseverance and infinite patience. Thank you for your willingness to speak truth into my life.

My Pray Warrior and Treasured Friend Donna Briley: I am forever grateful for your prayers for me and my family – prayers from before we ever met! Thank you for praying me through the difficult times as the Lord brought beauty from my ashes.

My Sweet Friend Roxanne Nettles, who has known me from before I knew the Lord and has watched me grow up in Him: Thank you for keeping me covered in prayer, and for once again stepping in at the eleventh hour.

My Faithful Prayer Partner Betty Johnson: Thank you not only for your meticulous editing, but also for always being available to encourage me and pray with me.

My Talented Videographer Sandra Loonan: You were determined to bring the *Triumph Over Suffering DVD Series* to completion despite the intense warfare. Your perseverance is particularly stunning to me because you were so young in the Lord when you produced them. I love watching how God continues to use those DVD's over so many years to touch lives and transform hearts.

My Precious One, Kimmy Wood, the youngest member of my *Triumph* Team: As God's eyes ranged to and fro across the earth, your fully committed heart caught His attention. I believe that is why He tapped you for this job. Thank you for your great love of His Word that drove your willingness to answer His call to help.

To all who have loved me, prayed for me, supported me, and encouraged me throughout the numerous editions of *TOS* over these past many years, especially Pastor Rick Miller, Pastor David Helbig, Sarah Byrd, Mona Egea, Nina Mitzelfeld, the Meulenbergs, my Huddle Groups and Bible Study groups, and all the "graduates" of *Why Me?* and *Triumph Over Suffering*: The Lord has worked through all of you in surprising and powerful ways, and I stand amazed and grateful.

And to all who have shared your hearts and lives by contributing your testimonies of living triumphantly in suffering: I pray God will use your bravery and openness to touch the hurting with His piercing love.

Index: Detailed Table of Contents

Part I: Infinite Love
Experience the Love of God

Part II: Absolute Sovereignty
Understand Why We Suffer

Part III: Intimacy With Christ
Seize Your Purpose Through Your Suffering

Contributors

About the Author

Celeste Li, M.D., is the author of *Triumph Over Suffering*. Raised in a Catholic family and with twelve years of Catholic education, she lived for decades with much head knowledge of Christianity but without a true heart commitment. Her superficial happiness and comfort hid her physical, emotional, and spiritual turmoil, and she did not understand why deep inner peace always eluded her.

In 2003 when Celeste came to truly know Jesus and surrender her life to Him, Jesus turned her life upside-down so it would be right-side up. He showed her what it meant to live out that head knowledge as His follower, disciple, soldier, and bond-servant. She lives now in triumph over suffering as she walks in His peace through her adversity.

Celeste is pressing on to seize what Christ Jesus seized her for. Recognizing that people cannot believe in Him whom they have not heard, she is called to bring the gospel message to a hurting world in desperate need of a Savior.

An active member of Christ Fellowship Church since 2003, Celeste is currently serving in Christ Fellowship's Ministry for the Suffering. She also serves with her husband in Christ Fellowship's Parenting Ministry. Yet she still realizes that her most important God-given calling at this time is to her husband and children. Married in 1989, she is devoted to her husband John, as his partner and bold counterpart. (And, as he lovingly points out, he is equally devoted to her!) Together John and Celeste are fully committed to raising their teenagers, Alec and Jenna, as Christians on fire for the Lord Jesus and following closely in His footsteps.

Celeste graduated from Jefferson Medical College in Philadelphia in 1985. Although her specialty initially was Family Medicine, in 1992 she left private practice and entered public health, dedicating her medical work to the care of patients with HIV and AIDS.

Celeste's greatest desire is to bring God glory by knowing Jesus intimately and bringing His message of love and salvation to those who are suffering.

"He must increase, but I must decrease."

John 3:30 NASB

Companion Materials
For Triumph Over Suffering

Triumph Over Suffering Workbook

For those who want to explore more intensely, don't miss the accompanying *Triumph Over Suffering Workbook*. The full-color *Workbook* complements this book by providing thought-provoking questions and additional Scripture studies that parallel each chapter. On each page you will find diagrams, pictures, and charts to help cement the concepts into your mind.

Triumph Over Suffering DVD Series

Celeste Li created this 12 chapter set to complement the *TOS* book, *Workbook*, and class. The DVD's are not designed to be a stand-alone series, but to provide deeper teachings for each chapter in the *TOS* book. Leadership DVD also available.

Triumph Over Suffering Classes

For dates and locations visit triumphoversuffering.com.

Triumph Over Suffering Audiobook

Triumph Over Suffering is available as an unabridged audiobook.

Triumph Leader's Guide

This *Guide* is designed for spiritual development and leadership training for God's servant leaders. Written specially for leaders of *Triumph* classes, it provides the layout of the course, as well as recommendations for handling common challenges the leader may face. It also includes discussion questions for each week, and a weekly prayer guide for the prayer team.

Companion Materials Available Through

- The Source, Christ Fellowship Bookstore
  (561) 799-7600 x7620
- CJL@triumphoversuffering.com
- Amazon.com
- Audiobook soon to be available at your favorite website

Made in the USA
Lexington, KY
06 October 2013